Hedged Out

Hedged Out

INEQUALITY AND INSECURITY
ON WALL STREET

Megan Tobias Neely

 UNIVERSITY OF CALIFORNIA PRESS

University of California Press
Oakland, California

© 2022 by Megan Tobias Neely

Library of Congress Cataloging-in-Publication Data

Names: Neely, Megan Tobias, author.
Title: Hedged out : inequality and insecurity on Wall Street /
    Megan Tobias Neely.
Description: Oakland, California : University of California Press,
    [2022] | Includes bibliographical references and index.
Identifiers: LCCN 2021013951 (print) | LCCN 2021013952 (ebook) |
    ISBN 9780520307704 (cloth) | ISBN 9780520307711 (paperback) |
    ISBN 9780520973800 (ebook)
Subjects: LCSH: Investment advisors—United States—Social
    conditions. | Securities industry—Social aspects—United States. |
    Hedge funds—United States. | Equality—Economic aspects—United
    States.
Classification: LCC HG4928.5 .N44 2022 (print) | LCC HG4928.5
    (ebook) | DDC 332.6/20973—dc23
LC record available at https://lccn.loc.gov/2021013951
LC ebook record available at https://lccn.loc.gov/2021013952

Manufactured in the United States of America

30   29   28   27   26   25   24   23   22
10   9   8   7   6   5   4   3   2   1

Contents

List of Tables and Figure

TABLES

FIGURE

Acknowledgments

This book was made possible by the inspiration, encouragement, and kindness of so many people, those who generously shared insights from their own lives, graciously opened up their networks and even homes to me, intellectually engaged the work, and supported my development as a scholar.

Thank you to Christine Williams, whose intellectual curiosity, thoughtful guidance, endless enthusiasm, and keen insights made this project possible. Your steadfast commitment to feminist scholarship and mentorship inspires me to strive to think bolder and broader (and to write with panache). You are the most flamboyant and generous champion for your students. Thank you for emboldening us to have an impact through our research, careers, and lives—and for showing us how it's done.

I am thankful for the wisdom and encouragement provided by Sharmila Rudrappa, Ken-Hou Lin, Jennifer Glass, and James Galbraith who also served on my dissertation committee at the University of Texas at Austin. Your brilliant ideas and critical engagement of the project helped deepen my understanding of the impacts for inequality and society's well-being. Thank you to so many faculty members of the UT Sociology Department who created an enriching learning environment that I have benefited from: Ari Adut, Javier

Auyero, Simone Browne, Ben Carrington, Mounira Charrad, Sheldon Ekland-Olson, Daniel Fridman, Gloria González-López, Pamela Paxon, Mary Rose, Harel Shapira, Tetyana Pudrovska, Debra Umberson, and Michael Young.

I want to thank the feminist community at Stanford University's Clayman Institute for Gender Research and Women's Leadership Innovation Lab, whose members served as an endless source of inspiration and support. You all make the work of turning feminist theory into praxis tremendously rewarding and enjoyable. Thank you to our fearless leader, Shelley Correll, and to these brilliant and fun women: Lori Nishiura Mackenzie, Caroline Simard, Shannon Gilmartin, Alison Dahl-Crossley, Wendy Skidmore, Aliya Hamid Rao, Michela Musto, Melissa Abad, Marcie Bianco, Sandra Brenner, Marianne Cooper, Gabriela Gall, Erika Gallego Contreras, Karen How, Sara Jordan-Bloch, Sofia Kennedy, Natalie Mason, Shivani Mehta, Cynthia Newberry, Jennifer Portillo, Kristine Pederson, JoAnne Wehner, and Alison Wynn. To Aliya and Michela, I have savored our friendships and wine-fueled conversations on the Caltrain and throughout San Francisco.

The Clayman provided a time, space, and community that fostered my development in so many ways, including generously hosting a book conference that was fundamental to the ideas presented here. It was truly a pleasure and an honor to have Cecilia Ridgeway, Shamus Khan, David Pedulla, Shelley, Alison, and Michela share their brilliance and guidance. Thank you for challenging me to be more expansive in scope and precise in analysis. I relished our conversation that day and it fueled me throughout the revisions.

Thank you to Kimberly Kay Hoang and Adia Harvey Wingfield who provided encouraging and rigorous reviews on the full manuscript that served as a source of motivation and direction. Kimberly provided insights at many stages along the way, and I am grateful for the conversations we had that pushed me to refine the central concept.

I owe gratitude to both of you for the considerable care you took to help further develop and enhance the book.

I want to thank the many people who generously read and thoughtfully commented on parts of this material: Mary Blair-Loy, Bruno Cousin, Ashley Mears, Gregory Jackson, Katharina Hecht, Katja Hujo, Annette Lareau, Karyn Lacy, Rachel Sherman, Sarah Stanton, Jaclyn Wong, Maggie Carter, Forest Stuart and the Qualitative Methods Workshop at Stanford's Sociology Department, and my colleagues in the Organization Theory Seminar at Copenhagen Business School's Department of Organization. I am grateful to many scholars whose conversations and insights have provided great motivation for this research: Elizabeth Armstrong, Emily Barman, Richard Benton, Hugo Ceron-Anaya, Raewyn Connell, Sam Friedman, Luna Glucksberg, David Grusky, Karen Ho, Patrick Inglis, Daniel Laurison, Ruth Milkman, Jeremy Schulz, Liza Steele, and Tom VanHeuvelen.

Thanks to many of the people mentioned above, material from this manuscript appears in *Socio-Economic Review* as "Fit to Be King: How Patrimonialism on Wall Street Leads to Inequality" and in *Qualitative Sociology* as "The Portfolio Ideal Worker: Insecurity and Inequality in the New Economy." Thank you to the editors and anonymous reviewers for your constructive critiques.

I want to thank my writing groups, whose brilliance has improved countless drafts throughout the writing process. To my flamboyance of feminists, Kate Averett, Caitlyn Collins, Kristine Kilanski, and Katherine Sobering, who have helped to mold this work from the very beginning and answered endless "stupid" and substantial questions along the way (and now across four time zones spanning nine hours). Most importantly, your unwavering support, enthusiasm, and care has provided much-needed nourishment. And to Sharla Alegria, Melissa Abad, Pallavi Banerjee, Adilia James, Katherine Lin, and Ethel Mickey, thank you for critically engaging my work and providing an endless source of feminist fun, community, and inspiration.

The support of my colleagues in graduate school at the University of Texas at Austin made this project so rewarding and enjoyable. Thank you to Javier Auyero and the Urban Ethnography Lab's vibrant community of fellows who commented on drafts or otherwise inspired me, including but not limited to Nino Bariola, Jacinto Cuvi, Jorge Derpic, Erika Grajeda, Hyun Jeong Ha, Maricarmen Hernández, Kathy Hill, Katherine Jensen, Cory McZeal, Pamela Neumann, Marcos Pérez, Robert Ressler, Jen Scott, Emily Spangenberg, Esther Sullivan, Kara Takasaki, Maggie Tate, Christine Wheatley, Maro Youssef, and Amina Zarrugh. The Ethnography Lab also provided generous funding to support this research. Many other friends and colleagues shaped this work in meaningful ways: Anima Adjepong, Letisha Brown, Shantel Buggs, Caitlin Carroll, Beth Cozzolino, Daniel Jaster, Alejandro Marquez, Michelle Mott, Robyn Rap, Katie Rogers, Samantha Simon, Allyson Stokes, Brandon Andrew Robinson, and Ori Swed. Thank you to my dear friends Vivian Shaw, Katherine Sobering, and Amanda Stevenson: I am so lucky to have friends like you.

I owe gratitude to my wonderful colleagues in the Department of Organization at Copenhagen Business School who have generously welcomed me into this enriching community. Thank you to Signe Vikkelsø, Lise Justesen, Marianne Aarø-Hansen, Jane Bjørn Vedel, Pedro Monteiro, Leonard Seabrooke, Eva BoxenBaum, Renate Meyer, Silviya Svejenova Velikova, Nanna Mik-Meyer, Sara Louise Muhr, Christoph Houman Ellersgaard, Anton Grau Larsen, Lasse Folke Henriksen, Susana Borras, Miriam Feuls, Christian De Cock, Jesper Strandgaard, José Ossandón, Christian Borch, Eleni Tsingou, Ursula Plesner, and Aixa Aleman-Diaz, among many others.

In particular, I want to express my gratitude and appreciation to the people who participated in this study and made it so rewarding. Thank you for generously sharing your time, experiences, and ideas to support this work. I also want to acknowledge my team and mentors from back when I worked in financial services. To the future founders of "Kittens and Sprinkles LLC," thank you for fostering a supportive environment of mutual respect and hard work while also having a sense of fun and humor.

Thank you to my editor Naomi Schneider for your enthusiasm, insights, and guidance over the past several years and the excellent team at the University of California Press. I appreciated the encouragement of Kim Robinson, who generously shared her ideas on the project. It has been a pleasure to work with Summer Farah, Teresa Iafolla, Dawn Hall, Francisco Reinking, and the rest of the marketing and production team who have put such time and care into this manuscript. Thank you to Letta Page for your careful and lively copyediting—and your keen sociological comments, too.

I am forever grateful for the love and encouragement provided by my family (who also generously read and reread many drafts). I owe a big thank you to Greg and Chris, who supported, encouraged, and housed me in New York. Without your love and good humor, this research would have not been possible. Thank you to my parents, Jamie and Cajer, who share an infectious concern for society and commitment to the well-being of their community, which they put into practice every single day. Mom, you taught me the insatiable curiosity of a journalist and the power of telling people's stories. Dad, my favorite community banker, thank you for showing me how finance affects people's lives in meaningful ways. And to Brooke, my sister, fellow sociologist, and earliest mentor, thank you for inspiring me to pursue a rewarding career and showing me all that I can be and do in the world. Thanks to Bowie and to Huckleberry, who devotedly sat at my feet for hours on end and whose memory will always be a blessing, and to Lou, whose vibrant kicks gave the impetus for the final push. And lastly, I am grateful for Rob, who always expresses joy and love in suffering me and my work gladly.

Preface

Just as the boom accelerated the rate of growth, so the crash enormously advanced the rate of discovery. Within a few days, something close to a universal trust turned into something akin to universal suspicion. Audits were ordered. Strained or preoccupied behavior was noticed. Most important, the collapse in stock values made irredeemable the position of the employee who had embezzled to play the market. He now confessed.

JOHN KENNETH GALBRAITH (1955), *The Great Crash of* 1929

Fast forward to nearly eighty years later and not much had changed. In 2007, the stock markets boomed, housing prices soared, and my gray pinstripe suit jacket was one size too big. Donning simple makeup and practical loafers, I had made every effort to blend in with the men in suits. Surely, this would be the key to success on Wall Street, I thought. A recruiter invited me to interview for an analyst job in the Seattle office of a "financial boutique," where I would do background research to inform the investment team's decisions. I was a recent graduate with a bachelor's in history.

I remember the day of my interview well. Cocking my head backward, I gazed up at the fifty-six floor tower. Built in the 1990s, the tower swayed like a ship, the better to withstand coastal storms and earthquakes. In its grand lobby, a security officer issued my visitor's badge, escorted me to an elevator, and pressed number 56. My stomach jumped as the elevator shot upward, its doors opening on the top floor. There, I had sweeping views of the city. Gazing at the Space Needle, Puget Sound, and the Olympic and Cascade mountain ranges, punctuated by Mount Rainier's 14,000-foot peak, I felt like I'd arrived at the top of the world.

Amid elegantly minimalist black leather chairs (à la Mies van der Rohe), Chihuly glass sculptures, and lush leafy plants, the well-coiffed receptionist (a white twenty-something) welcomed me with a perfunctory smile. As she walked me to the interview room, I briefly noticed a poster reading "Respectfully Question Authority." The image was an abstract human head (and the brain inside it)—just one of a series of artful posters lining the hallway to communicate the firm's values: antihierarchy, antibureaucracy, and independent thinking. The receptionist left me in the glass-bubble meeting room, which extended beyond the building's walls to jut out into the Seattle sky, then disappeared down the hallway. Moments later, the recruiter opened the door for the first in a day-long parade of interviews. An Asian American man with a fit build, dimpled smile, and tailored outfit, he introduced himself as Darren.[1] Shaking my hand firmly, he settled into a seat across from me.

Darren looked me straight in the eye and asked plainly, "Do you know what a hedge fund does?"

A knot formed in my stomach. I hesitated. "No." I didn't want to lie.

"That's great!" Darren responded earnestly, with an encouraging smile. The firm, he said, preferred to train people into "our own way of thinking about investments." Especially for research support positions, the firm regularly recruited people like me—fresh out of college, with degrees in the humanities and social sciences—over those with degrees in finance or business. "We want our employees to be critical thinkers, not rule followers," explained Darren.

And so, my three-year stint as an analyst at one of the world's largest hedge funds began.

. • .

When I joined the firm in late 2007, American inequality, the gap between the haves and the have-nots, was as stark as it was before the Great Depression. The annual holiday party took place two weeks after I started my job, and it was a doozy. The hedge fund's 250 employees were in a celebratory mood because a large asset manager had paid over $1.5 billion to acquire the firm. My colleagues were giddy at the thought of their extra-large bonuses. I attended the extravagant soiree in a $30 dress, bought on credit at Target and paired with the white feather boa and masquerade mask guests were issued at the door. I wouldn't get my first paycheck (for my $40,000/year starting salary) for weeks yet, and I was barely making rent with savings from my summer gig as a nanny. Over what would be a long night, my new colleagues, decked out in their designer duds, would swirl about the chic industrial warehouse, drinking Veuve Clicquot champagne and eighteen-year-old, sherry-cask Macallan Scotch whisky from bars carved out of huge blocks of ice. Tradition held that the last one into work the next morning had to buy everyone breakfast, so the investment analysts took cabs back to the office and slept on the floor by their desks. I will never forget the sounds of colleagues vomiting in the bathroom the next morning. Later, it would seem like an early omen of the purge to come. When the financial crisis hit in 2008, a third of the employees at that party were laid off unceremoniously.

Later, I would learn that hedge funds capture the upper echelons of a society in which elite, white masculinity has been redefined as the capacity to manage risk and insecurity. Facing an unpredictable and risky stock market, hedge fund workers (predominately white men) protect their interests by working around the clock and building tight-knit networks with people who are like them, who can help them get ahead. By restricting access to outsiders, hedge fund insiders can demand the high pay that widens economic inequality.

All of this I learned from my later research, for which those early years working in the industry laid the groundwork. The next few years not only taught me what a hedge fund does, it granted me entrée into an elite social world inaccessible to most people, and certainly new to me given my middle-class upbringing. There on the fifty-sixth floor, I experienced firsthand the day-to-day work of the reigning "haves." I learned the industry jargon: how to hedge an investment, short-sell a stock, and generate "absolute returns" (pulling a profit even when the market drops). And because my time at the hedge fund coincided with the biggest stock market crash of my lifetime (and likely my parents' and grandparents' lifetimes, too), it sparked an ongoing interest in how the financial sector creates instability and inequality.

Only a month after the raucous holiday party, in early 2008, the tenor at the office took a 180°. Insiders knew a crisis neared and that the firm would lose a critical amount of money, but no one knew how much or how to prevent it. Two major hedge funds that managed several billion in assets, Sailfish Capital and Peloton Partners, imploded in January and February, as their investments in toxic residential mortgages failed. Much like Melvin Capital, which suffered massive losses in the GameStop mania in early 2021, these were well-regarded, high-status firms. Their founders—not coincidentally, all elite white men, one of whom would blame his firm's failure on disloyal investors rather than bad investments—included a protégé of SAC Capital's Steven Cohen (nicknamed the "Michael Jordan" of hedge funds) and alums from Goldman Sachs.[2] Their failures foreshadowed the severity of the looming credit crisis: the hedge funds were the canary in the coal mine, hinting at the economic catastrophe to come. Hundreds of thousands of families began to default on their mortgages, and the housing bubble was about to burst.

After Bear Stearns, Lehman Brothers, and Washington Mutual collapsed one by one, my team was tasked with identifying instability in other financial firms that could put our own business at risk. Our unit was what the industry calls a "fund of funds": a hedge fund that invests in other hedge funds. My team did background research on the firms and executives—mostly white men—in whom the hedge fund had invested. I did everything from monitoring civil litigation and news coverage to verifying personnel employment, reviewing regulatory filings and audited financial statements, and performing competitive intelligence research. Over time, I would learn how to look for "warning signs," indicators that a firm could be in trouble, in operating documents, newsletters, and financial reports.

Meanwhile, the hardship on Main Street proliferated. Each Monday, I received an email alert with a word file composed of all the past week's news coverage and civil filings relevant to the hedge fund industry. My job was to review the several-thousand-page file for information potentially affecting our team's investments. As the year went on, the number of civil filings increased. Eventually, those Monday emails would cite tens of thousands of home foreclosures, each and every week. We were invested in hedge funds that were shorting these home mortgages,[3] meaning that our firm would profit—or, more accurately, lose less money—as everyday people lost their homes. The firm's assets plummeted, but it was nothing like what happened as people lost their homes and their jobs. The firm would recover long before the rest of the economy. And hedge fund managers would, over time, profit from the losses hitting Main Street so hard—much like the stock market rebound during the coronavirus crisis in which Wall Street profited while many workers and entire economic sectors struggled to survive.[4]

To be sure, hedge funds and their investments have an important social value in a capitalist society; by investing money for institutional entities (pensions, universities, foundations, and municipal and federal governments), they create wealth with which to pay retirees, students, public servants, and nonprofit workers. The people I worked with, like most workers across the board, weren't trying to harm anyone and likely wouldn't have thought of their trading in those terms. But as I read the filings each week in 2008, I grappled with the nagging question of whether it was right for Wall Street to profit when families lost their homes. How did my coworkers make sense of their risky investments and opulent salaries as thousands upon thousands of their fellow citizens were rendered homeless?

By the time I left to pursue a doctorate in 2010, the firm had stabilized and started to rebound. The industry, as a whole, came out of the crisis better than ever. Still, the culture of the firm and industry had changed. The crisis loomed in people's memories, even as they returned to business as usual. When I returned to study the industry in 2013, the people I spoke with said the crisis marked the end of hedonistic parties and traders buying Ducati motorcycles on bonus day. And as the industry changed, new puzzles emerged. Why did firms call themselves meritocratic when hierarchical networks provided access to opportunities, especially capital? Rather than examining how people employed at hedge funds justified their work, I wanted to know how they organized their work, how this organization restricted access to the industry, and how foreclosing access allowed their incomes to soar.

The crisis scarred the industry's reputation. The Occupy Wall Street movement drew attention to the machinations of the 1 percent and to the suffering affecting so many in the 99 percent. Media representations and national headlines put financial industry executives and traders on the front pages. At the same time, when the 2013 movie *The Wolf of Wall Street* became a box-office hit by depicting broker dealers as high rollers and greedy fraudsters, I wondered whether popular depictions of the highly unethical, illegal behavior was distracting us. Why weren't we looking at the perfectly legal, quotidian behaviors and banal job functions that create tremendous social problems, such as economic instability and socioeconomic inequality?

In *Hedged Out*, I get past the sensationalist portrayals to investigate how the social world of the hedge fund industry contributes to the making of a tumultuous stock market and highly stratified labor force. Drawing on six years spent with hedge fund workers at industry events and interviews with dozens of insiders in New York, Texas, and California, I show how the workaholic lives of hedge fund workers are a response to a universal perception of uncertainty and insecurity. Despite the rhetoric of meritocracy, these tendencies stem from systemic devotions to elitism, whiteness, and masculinity. *Hedged Out* is about creating and defending enormous wealth, justifying practices, and working the system while trying to keep others from doing the same—it's about the networks of trust that shore up security for elites in insecure times.

Introduction

Hedging In and Out

Perhaps J. P. Morgan did as a child have very severe feelings of inadequacy; perhaps his father did believe that he would not amount to anything; perhaps this did affect in him an inordinate drive for power for power's sake. But all this would be quite irrelevant had he been living in a peasant village in India in 1890. If we would understand the very rich, we must first understand the economic and political structure of the nation in which they become the very rich.

C. WRIGHT MILLS (1956), *The Power Elite*

A greedy fraudster or a visionary entrepreneur. These two tropes dominate media portrayals of hedge fund managers. I would venture a guess that these caricatures frame your own idea of a hedge fund manager, too. But behind the tales of designer suits, helicopter commutes, and illicit pursuits is the less sensational story of Craig,[1] who met me for coffee one morning at a busy Starbucks near New York City's Grand Central Station. Every day, he commuted into the city by train from the New Jersey suburb where he lived with his wife and two children. On that day, Craig had primped because he met me only a few hours before a job interview—a sign of the ease with which he job hunted. A forty-something white[2] man, Craig wore a pressed gray suit and had freshly trimmed his gray-speckled beard, a contrast with his usual wardrobe (sneakers and a t-shirt) as a trader at a midsize hedge fund with a nerdy startup culture and $2 billion in assets under management. When the markets went in his favor, Craig could earn several million dollars a year, easy.

While Craig's trades in the stock market and the resulting riches might appear to be the result of well-earned, individual success, Craig's high earnings capture a broader social problem facing the United States. Income inequality has skyrocketed. In the forty years since the Carter administration removed a cap on interest rates charged by banks, signaling a new era of financial deregulation, the richest 1 percent have doubled their share of the nation's earnings.[3] Wall Street became riskier, more complex, and obscenely lucrative.[4]

Today, the hedge fund industry drives the divide between the richest and the rest. In the United States, where the median household income is roughly $51,000, hedge fund portfolio managers, on average, bring home $1.4 million each year.[5] Even entry-level analysts collect nearly $680,000.[6] These salaries have launched many hedge fund workers into the top 1 percent of households (which, on average, bring in $845,000 per year).[7] Which is to say, where most research on inequality focuses on the poor and working class, this book sheds light on the growth and persistence of inequality by studying the prosperous—the "haves" rather than the "have-nots"—especially the elite white men who garner most of this industry's astronomical payouts.

As in other high-paying economic sectors (for instance, technology and law), women of all racial groups and racial minority men are drastically underrepresented in the hedge fund industry. Firms run entirely by white men manage 97 percent of all hedge fund investments.[8] Across an industry employing some 55,000 Americans, women are outnumbered more than four to one (holding approximately 19 percent of all positions); in senior positions, that rises to about nine to one. These numbers are in keeping with the demographics of the 1 percent: women, who account for about half of the nation's labor force, comprise only about 16 percent of the 1 percent, and some 90 percent of the heads of families in the top 10 percent of earners are white.[9] *Why* people of color and white women are underrepresented both among top earners and on Wall Street begs examination. What are the deep mechanisms of inequality that prevent all but white men from equal access to an industry that controls so much wealth?

Put differently, the forces preventing women and racial minority men from becoming top earners are well documented,[10] but that's different from understanding *why* elite white men garner such high compensation at hedge funds (more so than in other eras and contexts where white men control the upper echelons). Glimpses into the social worlds of these power holders can help us see how race, gender, and social class, as systems of inequality, work together to create and insulate outsized salaries, bonuses, and other compensation—in and beyond hedge funds.

As hedge funds amass riches, most American workers accrue debts. The United States has an uneven, hourglass economy: a few in the upper class, most in the lower, and a squeezed and shrinking middle class between them.[11] Since the 1970s, working-class wages have declined 5 percent (adjusted for inflation), middle-class wages have stalled, and top earners' income has skyrocketed. These trends are the product of a whole host of government policies: tax cuts for the wealthy, deregulation of financial services, scaled-back protections for workers, and welfare "reform" for the poor.[12] The resulting inequality is a pressing social problem, threatening everything from personal well-being to education rates, social unrest, and even our democracy.[13] Using hedge funds as a case study, I explain how this vast inequality was created and what can be done to change it.

This is an insular industry, and few scholars have had the access needed to investigate its inner workings.[14] After working at that Seattle hedge fund, I returned to the industry as a sociologist. Drawing from my six years of interviews, observations, and analysis, I present an insider's look at the industry to explain why it has generated extreme wealth, why mostly white men like Craig benefit, and how it can be reformed to create a more equal society.

What Is a Hedge Fund?

By now, I suspect, you might be wondering, *what is a hedge fund?* A hedge fund is a private financial firm that pools large sums of money from wealthy people and large institutions to invest in the stock market. The high volumes mean hedge fund investments can bring enormous profits, but only to those who qualify to invest in the first place. The US Securities and Exchange Commission (SEC) requires that each hedge fund investor have a minimum net worth of $1 million (excluding a primary residence) and a minimum annual income of $200,000. Less than 13 percent of Americans qualify on their own, and yet the industry invests money for a wide segment of society. Pensions, governments, universities, and other nonprofit endowments comprise nearly 60 percent of hedge funds' client investments.[15] Hedge fund investments affect states, businesses, and workers worldwide.

Hedge funds use a variety of investment strategies, from algorithmic trading to leveraging debt to event-driven investing in response to corporate and geopolitical events.[16] The inner workings are purposefully opaque—in the name of protecting proprietary trade secrets—and often convoluted. That means hedge funds are difficult to understand and scrutinize, which makes them risky but can also confer advantage (the opacity can be a source of competitor confusion, boosting profits). This is just one of several ways that hedge funds differ from investment banks. Hedge funds, with their exclusive clientele, can charge higher fees and thus generate higher profits while employing fewer people to share in the pot. Further, because the fees charged by hedge funds are taxed as capital gains, rather than income, their tax bills are comparatively low.[17] This allows for extremely high earnings, especially for those at the top.

The industry invests money for a wide segment of US society and for people and governments around the globe. As I mentioned, institutions comprise the majority of their investors who foot the bill for the high fees.[18] In fact, Harvard University's endowment fund is involved in such risky investments—about one-third in hedge funds— that the *Wall Street Journal* labeled the Ivy "a hedge fund that has a university."[19] The investments made by hedge funds influence the salaries and pensions of most people who work for colleges and universities, public schools, city services, government agencies, and large nonprofits. Even though you may not yet fully understand hedge funds, it is likely that their work affects your life in some way.

With respect to the money flowing out, hedge funds generally invest in land, real estate, stocks, bonds, debt, currencies, and derivatives.[20] The astronomical size of these investments means that their impact is felt far and wide. Hedge funds have collapsed currencies and sparked recessions around the globe, spurred the privatization of US schools, slashed and burned newspapers, and suppressed workers' bargaining power, contributing to the stagnation of middle- and working-class wages.[21] Thus, it is not only the high compensation meted out to hedge fund workers that widens inequality but also the investments themselves. Again, the work of financial investors affects, well, everyone else.

In 2020, the global hedge fund industry managed $3.7 trillion in assets—an all-time high—through over 16,000 firms employing 390,000 people, including outsourced labor (the average hedge fund employs only twenty people).[22] US-based hedge funds alone manage assets totaling 12 percent of the country's GDP. For reference, in its 1950s heyday, General Motors' revenues accounted for roughly 3 percent of US GDP, with $806 million (which would be nearly $8 billion in today's dollars) in net profits shared among nearly 600,000 workers.[23]

Slimmer staffing helps to explain the high incomes, at least at the upper levels of hedge fund hierarchies. In 2010, just after the Great Recession, the world's largest hedge fund, Bridgewater Associates, posted annual investment returns of $15 billion—more than the *combined* profits of Google, eBay, Yahoo, and Amazon. Yet, Bridgewater had 1,200 employees; in 2010, Amazon had 100,000. Additionally, those lower in the hedge funds' hierarchies earn salaries near the national median (base salaries for administrative and recruiting roles fall around $50,000—similar to what I earned), but members of the investment team *start* at upwards of half a million in total compensation. Senior managers and other leaders can command base salaries of a million dollars annually, plus a cash and stock bonus that may double or triple their take-home pay. Bridgewater's founder, Ray Dalio, earned *$3.1 billion* in 2010. Personally.[24]

These extremely high profits are possible because many hedge funds can bypass regulatory scrutiny, avoid taxes, and even undermine governments. Only hedge funds that manage over $100 million in assets, for instance, must register with the SEC. And the hedge funds that do register encounter less regulatory oversight than investment banks because the SEC considers their high-net-worth-investors to be less risky, more sophisticated, and in need of less legal protection than the average consumer. The lax scrutiny allows hedge funds to pursue risky investments and take big swings. To exploit loopholes in transnational regulatory and tax structures allowing for lesser oversight and greater profits still, most US-based hedge funds use a blended "offshore/onshore" investment structure.[25] In this way, hedge funds behave like the private wealth managers studied by sociologist Brooke Harrington: they undermine state authority in ways that give elites special privileges that ensure inequality persists from one generation to the next.[26] Operating with relative autonomy, mobility, and secrecy, hedge funds are unfettered by any given sovereignty. Their accumulation of wealth can go relatively unchecked.

Hedge funds have profited beyond other financial firms in recent decades because they encounter fewer regulations, charge higher fees, pay lower taxes, and employ fewer people. They are relatively small and nimble, with big pools of cash to insulate risk and big pools of profit to show for their efforts. The firm's few employees share in these benefits because their bonuses come from the fund's profits as well as their own personally held fund equity, but the bulk of the take goes to those at the top—the elite group of predominantly white men known almost innocuously as hedge fund managers.

A New Gilded Age?

Today's extreme inequality can be a bit harder to spot than in previous eras, if only because of the day-to-day work of elites. These high earners act and look very different from the robber barons of our imagination. Craig didn't don the trappings of a millionaire: he's got a no-frills mentality, straightforward demeanor, and only arrived at our first meeting in a bespoke suit because he had a job interview later that day. And if you passed him on the street, you'd never think he belonged among the hedonists on, for instance, the high-finance television drama *Billions*. These aren't the Gilded Age elites who lived lavishly off of their inherited wealth, as the economist Thorstein Veblen wrote of the leisure class in 1899, and conveyed their class status through conspicuous consumption in a leisurely lifestyle. Hedge fund workers are all but defined by an absolute preoccupation with the work of accumulation.

This gives us a clue as to how and why the financial sector has become a primary driver of inequality over the past forty years. Economist Thomas Piketty's 2013 book *Capital in the Twenty-First Century* was tremendously popular and raised awareness about the proliferation of profits going to the top 1 percent. Piketty's research made it plain that, unlike twentieth-century top earners who relied on passive forms of income to preserve existing wealth, today's elites actively work for their earrings. The working rich, not the leisure class, are the economic and politically powerful elite of the twenty-first century.[27]

In many ways, the ranks of the working rich are more open than the leisure class of the past. The civil rights movement, women's rights movements, and others have helped to diversify the membership of elite institutions. Still, inequality has increased. This is because, as sociologist Shamus Khan has established, new entrants can climb up the rungs, where the old elite held more firmly fixed class positions. It's just that not everyone has equal access to the next rung on the class ladder. The cumulative advantages of an elite upbringing—such as private tutoring, family libraries, music lessons, extracurricular coaching, and elite connections—ease advancement.[28] Meanwhile, new entrants to elite occupations encounter what the sociologists Sam Friedman and Daniel Laurison call a "class ceiling," preventing the working and middle class from achieving upward mobility.[29] As a result, the new elite do not necessarily make it to the seats of power.

The hedge fund workers I interviewed predominantly framed their upbringings as solidly middle class, though in reality, they were nearly all from upper-middle-class/affluent families and were very well educated (our friend Craig held a PhD in biology). Their embrace of a rags-to-riches discourse of bootstrapping and meritocracy, which US society views as more admirable than coming from a well-to-do family, fit well with other elites' tendencies.[30] Expressions of extravagance and entitlement are no longer elite status markers, sociologist Rachel Sherman shows, but symbols of the ease of privilege and reminders, by comparison, of the morality of productivity.[31] My interviewees commonly presented themselves as outsiders and underdogs; a little probing revealed that their parents included the dean of a business school, the chief executive officer of a Fortune

500 company, and the chief financial officer at an investment bank. Concealing those indicators of generational privilege reinforced the assumption of their own individual merit—the idea that they alone were responsible for (and, perhaps, deserving of) their professional and financial success.[32]

The tendency to present oneself as "self-made" stems, in part, from a heightened perception of insecurity on Wall Street.[33] When the stock market fails, traders suggest it takes fortitude, resilience, and commitment to bounce back. Craig planned ahead for periods of unemployment, like the one he was facing when we met (his recently restructured firm had given him a nudge to move on before he was let go). Craig's experiences reflect a more widespread culture of risk and insecurity in the United States,[34] which sociologist Marianne Cooper argues instills a sense of emotional vulnerability even among the affluent. Managing that unease motivates people like Craig to work harder and, thus, fuels inequality. The intensification and fetishization of work are a product of job precarity even among the country's top earners.[35]

Exacerbating this tendency, as their jobs become less predictable, people feel compelled to protect their monopoly on resources and opportunities by working harder—or at least building strong reputations as tireless workers. The escalating incomes driving economic inequality aren't, as dominant explanations would have it, the result of technological advancements increasing efficiency and allowing higher profits to flow upward.[36] Scholars aiming to debunk this explanation point out, for instance, that the top earners in financial services out-earn their peers in sectors like technology and medicine, which have seen similar advancements.[37]

Wall Street differs from those other industries because it has been purposefully deregulated; neoliberalism, in other words, has paved the way for the explosive growth of the hedge fund industry. Since the 1970s, neoliberal policy, based in the belief that markets should be allowed to function with minimal government intervention, has scaled back worker protections and financial regulations. As a result, the financial sector's share of US corporate profits tripled in half a century, even as its share of US employment remained nearly stagnant (rising only 3 points, from about 4 percent in 1950 to just over 7 percent in 2001).[38] In the past, if the manufacturing sector saw robust, steady growth, we could expect fairly strong wages for even low-level workers coupled with an expansion of their ranks (regardless of many technological advancements, though not all). That's not true for the financial sector, which shares its profits with a vanishingly small number of people. Additionally, financial actors, with their elite networks and resources, are uniquely able to influence politics to favor deregulation, leverage bargaining power within the industry, and stimulate market demand for their products, like convincing friends in high places to invest in their hedge funds.[39]

Economists broadly attribute earnings to human capital, specifically how workers themselves factor into the supply side of the classic supply-and-demand equation for wages.[40] Wall Street, following suit, rationalizes high incomes by pointing to the supposedly unique skill sets and talents of hotshot traders. A quick glance at Forbes' annual list of top incomes, however, reveals the massive flaw in this logic. The *lowest* annual income reported among the twenty-five highest-paid hedge fund managers was $225 million in 2018, a notoriously bad year for the financial industry. The top four took home over $1 billion each, with James Simons of Renaissance Technologies claiming $1.7 billion that year alone.[41] No amount of human capital can explain these earnings. These admittedly extreme cases show that the money being made in hedge funds defies any rational calculation of supply and demand. Moreover, because men out-earn women who have comparable levels of human capital and work in similar financial-sector jobs,[42] it is plain that human capital cannot, in and of itself, account for these astronomical, unequal earnings.

Finally, hedge funds invest in ways that put downward pressure on the wages of average workers. Since hedge funds invest in huge quantities of corporate stocks, their investments drive executives to downsize their firms' payrolls, increasing stock values and, thus, dividends to shareholders.[43] Rather than cutting costs, these management practices serve to redistribute earnings from working-class people to executives and financiers. This is a key piece in a broader shift in US corporate governance that has left workers across economic sectors with less negotiating power, fewer protections, and ever-more instability.[44]

The Spirit of Finance Capitalism

Hedged Out sheds light on a widespread transformation in the organization of work that has enriched the C-suite and Wall Street. The everyday work of financial elites fosters solidarity as well as fragmentation, and these processes maintain and reproduce inequality. In examining a less visible sphere of economic elites, I find an interconnected—and politically mobilized—financial elite. Like the "power elite" theorized by foundational scholar C. Wright Mills—the government, military, and corporate leaders—the financial elite have intertwining interests that contrast with recent characterizations of a fragmented, dog-eat-dog world of corporate power brokers.[45] At hedge funds, factions and boundaries delineate who is included and excluded, tightly binding the ties among the select few: the financial elites.

A key to this solidarity lies in a system of patronage that organizes the industry. "Patronage" refers to using one's own power to support, endow, or privilege a given person—you can think of it as an investment in human capital. Patrimonialism, theorized by German social theorist Max Weber, describes a system of patronage in which the leader's authority rests on trust, loyalty, and tradition shored up by transactional processes. Crucially, Weber identified patrimonialism as a gendered and racialized system, grounded in paternal rule and tribal ties.[46]

Indeed, though economic sociology has often omitted this fact, gender and race were both central to capitalism's origins.[47] Julia Adams's work on the emergence of the early modern capitalist state in the Golden Dutch Age is a notable exception to that tendency, revealing that Dutch capitalism arose through literal patrimonialism. State builders and merchant capitalists were family patriarchs whose exchanges provided the basis for capital accumulation. In this transitionary period, Adams shows, paternal authority fostered a twin flourishing of bureaucracy and patrimonialism within an emerging capitalist economy.[48]

At hedge funds, patronage is how a select group of white men groom and transfer capital to other elite white men.[49] Industry insiders often cite the example of Julian Robertson of Tiger Management. Nicknamed the "Wizard of Wall Street," he converted his financial success in the 1980s into initial funding for an empire of more than 120 hedge funds managing more than $250 billion in assets today. That the industry calls such early funding "seeding" or "seed capital" connotes fecundity and familial reproduction in the transfer of wealth—the initiation of a family line. Insiders refer to Robertson's constellation of firms as the "Tiger Cubs" and "Grand Cubs." With each generation, the Tigers in this shared lineage, with overlapping investment strategies and returns, become wealthier and wealthier, proudly policing the boundaries of those who belong and those who do not.[50]

But patronage on Wall Street contradicts a central tenet of Weber's theory. The famed German scholar predicted that as states modernized, rational bureaucracy would *replace* patrimonialism, rather than flourish alongside it as Adams found even in the early Dutch capitalist state. And so, patronage in the financial industry presents a puzzle: it evokes the leisurely "old money" of the Gilded Age while simultaneously embodying contemporary finance capitalism.

Overall, Weber was right: bureaucracy did become the norm. In 1941, as the United States was poised to join World War II (two years into the fighting), American philosopher James Burnham controversially predicted the death of capitalism. Where Karl Marx thought socialism would prevail, Burnham instead anticipated a new era of bureaucracy in which executives, bureaucrats, technicians, and soldiers ruled together as a managerial class. Indeed, within just a few years of Burnham's declaration, a new strain of midcentury literature would capture an emerging suburban life tethered to corporations through their managers. Journalist William Whyte's bestselling *The Organization Man*, C. Wright Mills's *White Collar*, and business professor Alfred Dupont Chandler's *The Visible Hand* seemed to confirm Weber's—and perhaps Burham's—forecasts: bureaucratic corporations and their managers had taken over the United States.

The days of the "organization man," characteristic of managerial capitalism, were, however, numbered. By the century's end, corporations had transformed yet again. So, too, had the US economy. No longer did executives understand corporations as organizations that owed certain responsibilities to the workers who developed their products and profits. Commitment to workers proved a short-lived trend (one hard fought for by workers and unions), eroding just as women and racial minority men began to enter those workers' ranks in greater numbers. Thanks to investor demands—and concerted efforts to hamstring most labor unions[51]—both public and private firms have restructured, downsized, digitized, and outsourced labor, removing many of those managers. For many workers, working conditions have deteriorated and employment has become insecure, which has created more uneven working conditions and growing inequality. The result is what's called the *new economy*[52]

With this transition, the corporation's primary function has become distributing value to shareholders (in the form of stock dividends) rather than developing a product for consumers. Advocates of the "lean and mean" firm, stripped of middle managers and bureaucratic red tape, believe it empowers workers to better innovate, adapt, and communicate.[53] Meanwhile, feminist scholars such as Rosabeth Moss Kanter, Kathy Ferguson, and Joan Acker have long theorized how organizational bureaucracy works as a tool of men's domination. More horizontal organizational structures and egalitarian decision-making, they argue, can more evenly distribute power among members (even if it does not fully alleviate gender inequality).[54] But the parallel capitalist trend to flatten companies, which importantly did *not* democratize decision-making or power, happened at the same time that women made inroads into mid-level management.[55] Not coincidentally, the very jobs that are downsized and eliminated in the name of removing bureaucracy and flattening hierarchy are jobs gender-typed as women's work: human resources, personnel management, and administrative roles.[56]

Wall Street has pioneered this system of profit seeking without power sharing. And with it, patronage has persisted, not disappeared or relegated to the Global South and sidelined to criminal activities as some have suggested.[57] Financial expansion and the inequality it creates instead lend credence to the existence of patrimonialism within capitalism. Piketty, evidencing the system's persistence, cites the intense concentration of privately owned capital.[58] Privatizing public wealth and deregulating financial markets has led autonomous and highly profitable firms, like hedge funds, to proliferate.[59]

These private enterprises amass wealth within a corner of capitalism made possible by rational bureaucracy. The loopholes and legal exceptions privileging hedge funds with lower capital gains taxes, fewer regulatory restrictions, and access to offshore bank accounts are not afforded to many other financial institutions.[60] Contract law, property rights, and trusts enable elites to turn an asset, such as a company stock, into enduring financial advantage.[61] Like the family offices studied by anthropologist Luna Glucksberg, this amassing of rights and wealth within private enterprise allows elites to enact patronage in the shadow of the finance system's bureaucracy.[62] In other words, contrary to the neoliberal tenets of promoting unfettered competition and reducing government interventions, the state grants protections that allow firms to monopolize assets in ways that minimize the competition.

On Wall Street, the retreat from bureaucracy stems from intertwining market and social forces. Bureaucracy, associated with middle management and administration (devalued, feminine-typed jobs), is treated as tedious, stifling, and old-fashioned, compared to masculine-typed ways of doing business: working to cost-cut, outsource, downsize, streamline, and deregulate. Because the average hedge fund only lasts five years, workers understand their job precarity and plan to switch firms every few years.[63] They endeavor to manage this uncertainty by building and leveraging social capital. That means their social networks guide investment decisions and drive market trends, accelerating the rapid stock market jumps and drops that create instability.[64] In response, hedge fund managers strive to build lean and nimble firms, adaptable to the unstable terrain (a trend that's occurring in politics and technology, too). White men's social capital secures their claim to corner offices, further solidifying the power of their capital relative to others. That is, the relationships that allow white men to forge ties with each other to manage insecurity and secure class advantage aren't as readily available to women or racial minority men.[65]

How did bureaucracy become the force of inefficiency and patrimonialism the salvation? I find that financial deregulation and the market instability it creates[66] appear to foster patrimonialism. That's because, as sociologist Charles Tilly notes, uncertainty leads people to rely more on trust and reputation in decisions regarding with whom they should do business. We "close" our networks, turning to traditional forms of social organization like familal, religious, and ethnic communities tightly infused with patrimonialism.[67] Indeed, in insecure contexts, family-run firms more effectively handle relations with workers.[68] Among elites staving off potential instability, patrimonialism closes networks in ways that concentrate rather than distribute resources. Therefore, insecurity breeds insularity and widens inequality.

All this helps to explain the dominance of elite white men, in the financial sector and beyond. Trust is the thread weaving the fabric together. A central bond in patronage, trust involves a willingness to admit vulnerability within the safety of the patronage network.[69] When facing uncertainty and ambiguity, scholars Cecilia Ridgeway and Shelley Correll demonstrate, people turn to the most available frames to make sense of the situation: social statuses including gender, race, and class, which are tied, via deeply ingrained beliefs, to certain innate qualities, characteristics, and propensities.[70] Because these provide a shorthand for which people we see as "like us," sociologist Lauren Rivera argues, people are most likely to give opportunities to "people like us." Social statuses—the obvious and taken-for-granted ways that people make divisions and boundaries around who to include or exclude— become proxies for who is trustworthy or who is passionate or who "fits" in.[71] These interactions become patterned, forming the building blocks of white supremacy and gender inequality as social institutions.[72]

In a deeply stratified and finance-driven society, elites build trust networks that provide access to credit, while the middle and working classes take on debt to subsidize stagnant wages. Racism and sexism in lending, such as home loans and consumer credit, is the predictable organizational outcome of parsimonious distributions of trust and loyalty.[73] The poor are routinely denied such access to credit, having been stereotyped as "untrustworthy" by elite lenders making decisions in a context of implicit us-versus-them tribalism. This, too, helps to explain why finance has widened economic inequality over the past forty years.[74]

White men's privilege is not only self-sustaining but also accelerating over time as its beneficiaries concentrate power and resources. This system of patronage may characterize elites beyond Wall Street, including those helming large and powerful organizations such as Apple, Exxon, UnitedHealthcare, Harvard University, and the Oval Office. But within the financial sector and amid hedge funds' unimaginable profits, patrimonialism has undeniably hedged out women and racial minority men.

Hedging the Risks and Rewards

Another common explanation for the outsized earnings on Wall Street is that high risk justifies high rewards. In her ethnography *Liquidated*, anthropologist Karen Ho interviews investment bankers who, time and again, make sense of their compensation as relative to the risks they take in the stock market.[75] They do not, however, note that their bonuses often endure even when risky bets fail to pay off.

When it comes to performance-based bonuses, Wall Street elites again insist they operate within a meritocracy, that the market doesn't care about social statuses but smart decisions. Yet sociologist Louise Roth has found that even women who graduated from elite business schools are paid less than men to do the same jobs in finance.[76] Since, as I mentioned earlier, we all use social statuses as heuristics—mental shortcuts that equate race, class, gender, and other statuses with specific qualities—those include perceptions of who has merit and can justifiably take risks (even when they don't pay off, the risks are seen as well-reasoned bad investments, not evidence of bad investors).[77] That is to say, meritocracy actually increases the potential for bias, because evaluators believe they are making objective decisions even though the whole idea of merit is actually anchored in their own biases. Their merit-based discretion leads to even greater disparities in pay and promotions.[78]

Investment bankers' jobs, relative to hedge fund managers', are stable, institutionalized, and lower paid. By investigating hedge funds, one of the most risky, unstable, and high-paying arenas in finance, I reveal how elite, white masculinity has been redefined as the capacity to manage risk and insecurity. I show how white men fiercely defend their monopoly over high-risk, high-reward positions through everyday actions within an ostensibly meritocratic system.

Hedge fund workers, we've seen, justify their outsized incomes as warranted by the risks they take. Yet they explicitly market their products to clients as minimally risky. Surprisingly, that mismatch stems from the fact that the hedge fund industry's founding "father" was a Marxist sociologist.[79] After earning a PhD at Columbia University in the 1930s, Australian Alfred Winslow Jones channeled his academic training into mastering financial markets. Driven by a sense of skepticism that investors could accurately predict the future, he focused instead on the techniques these financial workers used to mitigate the risk of unexpected market swings. Using the statistical skills he learned as a sociologist, his observations of what he called "technicians'" investment practices, and his knowledge of corporate law, Jones developed a measure for stock market risk that allowed him to *hedge* the risk of betting on the stock market. He took 20 percent of profits as his compensation, charging no fees at all if his investment lost money.[80]

Today, a major topic of industry debate focuses on the paradox that hedge fund managers must be simultaneously risk-averse—to profit during market downturns—and risk-takers—to outperform during market upturns. Hedge funds generate high returns by using strategies developed by Jones, such as betting against the asset ("short-selling") and borrowing to increase exposure and risk ("leveraging") when investing in stocks, bonds, commodities, and derivatives. Hedge fund strategies are designed to manage risk and allow the firm to perform during bear and bull markets alike, because their returns aren't correlated with the performance of stocks and bonds.[81]

Pundits, for their part, lambast the industry (or at least bad apples within it) for making excessively risky trades.[82] This focus on bad actors, however, tends to overlook the systemic risks hedge funds pose to the stock market and society as a whole. While hedge fund managers strive to create stable, long-term, and protected wealth for their investors, it is not their job to evaluate potential economic and societal risks. Thus, the industry has been linked to increased systemic risk and volatility, such as the implosion of the mortgage bubble in 2008, which eroded the wealth of US families.[83]

Even more profound than the recurring crises are the implications of purposeful financial risk-taking for mushrooming inequality. A "hedge," as in "to hedge your bets," refers to an investment designed to minimize risk and increase profit during market downturns—a context characterized by acute risk and vulnerability. It's meant to close off risk like a hedge closes off private property. And that means there's another side to the hedge—the vast area of those being kept out. Amid elite boundary-making, explicitly tied to and reinforced by the bonds of masculinity and whiteness, I argue that everyone else is effectively *hedged out*. Building on Michèle Lamont's insights into how the upper middle class maintains its social boundaries through definitions of culture, I introduce the concept of "hedged out" to explore the fervent boundary-making around gender, race, and social class that allows insiders to hoard resources and opportunities, sharing them almost exclusively with similar others.[84]

Hedging, and hedging out, create and sustain a system of inequality in three important ways. First, the hedge forms a protective boundary. The founders of hedge funds—and perhaps private equity, venture capital, and information technology firms—establish organizations with few layers of bureaucracy that protect the executive's autonomy and privileges. With less regulation, transparency, and bureaucracy than their counterparts at investment banks, hedge fund workers wall themselves off from institutional oversight and shield themselves from losses associated with market turbulence. That they hedge out "others" reflects a logic of social, professional, and economic risk management in an industry characterized by the extreme salience of risk in every decision, big or small.

Second, hedging captures a gendered, racialized, and classed system. Gender-essentialist beliefs are rampant on Wall Street, where client investors hew to the idea that men are naturally more emboldened and savvy risk-takers than women.[85] Hedge funds run by women do not, in actuality, differ in performance or risk outcomes, but they remain more likely to fail because women managers have more difficulty raising capital, all because risk-taking is treated as a leadership characteristic all but exclusive to men.[86] To the extent that women *are* more risk averse in the stock market, it is more likely attributable, as economist Julie Nelson has shown, to socialization, which discourages girls from taking as many risks as and later penalizes women for being daring, bold, or aggressive in their careers.[87] Men with less class and racial privilege encounter penalties, pushback, and punishments for such daring as well.[88] Risk aversion makes more sense when we consider context and constraints.

Meanwhile, those who take entrepreneurial risks tend to be white, men, and affluent. Class- and race-privileged men have encountered fewer penalties for risk-taking throughout their lives, and should they find themselves on Wall Street, they will be seen as uniquely able to master risk (both benefiting from and reinforcing the original stereotypes). White, class-advantaged men, then, form the upper echelons of the social hierarchy of the hedge fund industry, where they are seen as particularly valuable workers. Women and Asian American men, for their part, are regarded as risk-hesitant and thus less valuable, and Black, Brown, and working-class men are typed as "reckless," unsuited to the work of risk management. This blunt social-professional hierarchy determines who is allowed entry to the inner circles and who is hedged out.[89]

Third, this social organization privileges networks of trust and loyalty—social ties that provide certainty in an uncertain world. When facing a high-risk context, people believe trust reduces uncertainty, and so, in financial services, where risk really is high, trust is a powerful currency.[90] We also know that people are more likely to trust people like themselves with respect to race, class, and gender.[91] So, as a form of social exclusion, the practice of hedging out others—those unlike "us" and therefore instinctively untrustworthy—is a useful link between the patrimonialism reminiscent of a bygone era and the modern financial sector emblematic of an advanced industrial economy.

The tools laid out in legal scholar Kimberlé Crenshaw's theory of intersectionality are invaluable as we dig into how whiteness, masculinity, and class privilege—working in concert—empower the lives of elite white men. Crenshaw introduced the concept of intersectionality to show how "race and gender interact to shape the multiple dimensions of Black women's employment experiences."[92] By centering Black women's experiences, she and sociologist Patricia Hill Collins identified a system of power and inequality upheld through the ongoing interactions of race, class, and gender.[93] Crenshaw's and Hill Collins's insights have sparked one of the most important academic movements over the past thirty years, and over time researchers have drawn out even more intersecting systems (including, for example, sexual orientation) of disadvantage. Intersectionality has less often been applied to examine *elite* power and privilege than to its absence, though it is no less useful for my investigation of whiteness, masculinity, and class privilege within the halls of power.[94] Within and beyond finance capitalism, the permutations of privilege that enrich elite white men create vast inequalities.

This book's title, *Hedged Out,* refers to the dominant practices, discourses, and ideologies that have fomented a select group of white men's power in modern-day finance capitalism. In the current era, elite, white masculinity is about being bold, taking risks, amassing fortunes, and mastering uncertainty. It also hedges against some of the ugliest, most overt forms of masculinity, such as open sexism and physical violence, because this brand of masculinity is a classed expression cloaked in good taste, politeness, and deference to a meritocratic sorting of the haves and have-nots. Informed by the lives of hedge fund workers, this book explains how the "working rich" are defined by risk and, in an era of extreme uncertainty, handsomely rewarded for the skill with which others believe they manage that risk.

Hedge Funds: Access and Methods

Feminist scholars have long called attention to the obvious power imbalance between the people who are studied and the researchers with the power to tell their stories. Like high finance, the halls of Western academia have been populated by class-privileged white men, and their scholarship has reflected the lens through which this select group interprets the world.[95] Feminist sociologists, led by the work of Dorothy Smith and Patricia Hill Collins, among others, challenge the theoretical traditions born out of this stratified academy, insisting instead that rigorous scholarship requires foregrounding women's experiences and recognizing them as experts on the forces affecting their own everyday lives.

Ethnographers who study political and economic elites, however, point out that the power dynamics of studying these groups, broadly speaking, are different from those of studying less class-privileged groups. Invoking feminist methodologies, which center the subjects' own knowledge, in this context could have the consequence of naturalizing, if not reifying, elite power, authority, and status.[96] As we've already learned, the elite white men who dominate hedge funds believe their success reflects nothing but hard work, smarts, tenacity, and other individual traits; they are, as their own referent category, unlikely to identify patterned discrimination as a driver in their success, even if asked directly. By participating in the everyday lives of elites, ethnographers gain a deeper understanding of their norms, practices, and beliefs that goes beyond the common assumptions and portrayals.[97] Embedding into subjects' social worlds shows the ethnographer the specific power dynamics therein—and how the interviewees navigate them.

Of course, ethnographic participant-observation hinges on access—the ability to gain trust such that research subjects stop being hyperconscious of the researcher's presence and interpretations. Given that I worked in the hedge fund division at a large asset manager from 2007 to 2010, I started this research with a direct, nuanced understanding of the social world of hedge funds, allowing me to contextualize data from interviews and fieldwork as well as the connections and access to return to the industry for six years (from 2013 to 2019) of research. Using insider access and applying a sociologist's perspective, I am able to present fresh insights on a rapidly changing high-stakes industry pushing inequality to new heights.

Early in my research, in fact, I positioned myself as an industry insider and made efforts to uphold the appearance rules of this social world. Calling to mind the industry jargon I remembered, in 2013, I dug out the wool suits and high heels I'd worn in my days as a hedge fund researcher and analyst. I just hoped to blend in at industry events. At one conference, I stepped into a headshot booth crammed full of boutique makeup and hair products to get a free professional photo. The result looks nothing like "me" today: with straightened hair and a heavily made-up face, I am pictured standing with my arms crossed. It was, per the photographer's instruction, my very best "power pose."

Over the course of my research, I learned that the more I positioned myself as an academic rather than as an insider, the more trust

people expressed and the fewer reservations they had about participating in my study. I switched to introducing myself primarily as a
scholar who studied gender and race in the finance industry, and
people showed more interest in talking with me. This was even true
of white men (who usually expressed concern for gender but not always for racial equity in our interviews).

My recruitment script itself yielded rich data. More often than
not, industry insiders agreed that gender was "a problem" and suggested they wanted to help create change. But they often became de-
fensive about race, arguing that the industry is a meritocracy. At
times, this appeared to be influenced by the fact that I myself am a
white woman; perhaps interviewees felt subtle pressure to embrace
a pro-woman sentiment but less to align with antiracist beliefs. However, this response held even for a few people of color, revealing both
the deep-seated logic of Wall Street meritocracy and, perhaps, the
repercussions people of color might face for acknowledging, calling
attention to, and challenging industry racism. Their responses suggested that gender inequality is less threatening to this cultural investment in meritocracy, as women's lack of representation can be
(wrongly) attributed to the pull of childbearing or the pressures of
work-family balance. The dearth of people of color, however, has the
potential to put this worldview in crisis by pointing out a notable failure of that meritocracy.

The way I obtained access has theoretically important consequences for this study. By achieving outsider rather than relying on insider status, I gained insight into the exclusionary mechanisms at work
in this financial sector. The relationships I established with industry insiders allowed me to both observe and experience firsthand social inequality and boundary-making processes. My own social position allowed me to establish relationships and rapport in varying ways with
various social groups (specifically with women's networks focused on
empowering women and among men who expressed greater aware-

ness of gender inequality and often viewed me as a daughter figure or a sexual object). Cecilia Ridgeway's insights into how status characteristics frame social interactions sheds important light on how my access informed my understanding of the social hierarchies at play.[98] Through my interactions in the work-obsessed, profit-seeking, risk-and-reward context of hedge fund managers, race, gender, sexuality, and social class status became more readily visible and salient to me as the researcher. (I provide more detail on how these experiences shaped my findings in the Methodological Appendix.)

I interviewed forty-eight industry professionals and observed twenty-two industry events and thirteen workplaces in New York, Texas, and California. I recruited a sample that is more gender and racially diverse than the industry as a whole, because I wanted to understand variation in people's experiences and what it reveals about relationships of inequality.[99] A representative sample would have left me with, well, a pool of white men from well-to-do backgrounds, which would not have allowed me to investigate fully why some people thrived and others did not. And though, in most settings, a near 50–50 gender split and roughly one-in-three inclusion of racial and ethnic minorities would never constitute "diversity," it does in the hedge fund world, where people of color were notably underrepresented. At conference panels with upwards of six hundred attendees, I never counted more than a handful of Black attendees (at least as I perceived them). Strikingly, this was amplified by the fact that, in these conference facilities, the lower-wage service workers who made the conferences possible—the hotel workers, bartenders, security guards, and cleaning staff—were almost all people of color. It was readily apparent that a representative sample of hedge fund workers would not allow me to foreground the experiences of those so regularly hedged out.

Notably, I will foreground but not generalize from the experiences of women and non-white men industry insiders as I engage with the ways masculinity and whiteness shape the experiences of elite white men. There are too few of the former to generalize their accounts. Rather, the meaning gleaned from this approach arises from recognizing variations in people's experiences and what these variations convey about structures of power. As exceptional cases in this context, people of color and white women can insightfully characterize the quotidian norms and practices that so predominantly benefit and empower elite white men.[100]

Overview of the Book

The case of the hedge fund industry reveals how the everyday work being done on Wall Street allows for extremely high rewards that worsen economic inequality. By excluding women and racial minority men from power-holding positions, Wall Street elites can strengthen the perception that they alone hold the keys to beating the stock market, and they can demand even higher pay. In other words, my goal in this book is to convince you that race, gender, and social class, as systems of inequality, lie at the heart of a system of white men's privilege that determines who can join the financial elite. This is a social problem hiding in plain sight, because it's so taken-for-granted that white men make up society's "power elite." I help to explain how this unequal system appeared, how elite white men sustain it, and what can be done to change it.

Hedged Out follows the careers of hedge fund workers to account for the billions of dollars flowing to just a few. In chapter 1, I detail why the industry arose and gained prominence in particular historical moments and how it elevated and refined the hegemonic ideal of elite, white masculinity on Wall Street. Next, in chapters 2 and 3, I outline common paths into the industry and job competition in this cutthroat labor market—both processes that appear meritocratic yet rely on the possession of considerable social and cultural capital. In chapter 4, I provide an overview of how managers run these firms and the division of labor. I explore how founders strip away bureaucracy and remove middle managers to create a "flatter" firm. Understood as more flexible and responsive to market demands, this social organization funnels power, status, and wealth to executives and hedges out women and racial minorities. Climbing the rungs of the hedge fund ladder, the next two chapters show, involves extreme highs and lows—volatility and insecurity that hedge fund workers must manage and mitigate just like risk in their asset portfolios. Client investors and colleagues, believing that elite white men—even those who may accrue notable losses in their investments—are best equipped to tame turbulent markets, significantly bolster the chances that the people who make it to the top will turn out to be more elite white men. In chapter 7, I return to the work, asking how hedge fund workers make sense of their work's impact on society and its implications for inequality. In the conclusion, I take you inside a hedge fund launch and the ensuing vicissitudes of entrepreneurship in a notoriously risky industry.

In a field that ultimately comes down to winners and losers, I aim to find out how the winners understand their success, particularly in relation to those who lose (or never even get into the game). Elitism, whiteness, and masculinity largely determine who gets the W in this risky game, though not always in predictable ways. I close the book by arguing that, unchecked, this structurally unequal financial sector will accelerate inequality over time. Systemic change is the only way to slow this concentration of money, status, and power into fewer and fewer hands, and to disrupt the economic dominance of elite white men that so forcefully forecloses upward mobility for everyone else.

1 From Financial Steward to Flash Boy

"I knew they were the cowboys. I knew they were the smart ones," Cynthia said with a knowing smile as she explained what drew her to hedge funds. Cynthia, a white woman in her sixties, donned square-framed eyeglasses that were bejeweled and magnified her eyes, which caught the light as they darted around while she talked. She had graying hair dyed chestnut brown, almost black, and wore heavy makeup with pink blush strokes punctuating her expressive face. In keeping with her appearance, Cynthia spoke expressively and enthusiastically, dramatically gesturing and bending toward me as she told me the secrets of the hedge fund world.

As a woman, Cynthia is a rarity in this world, yet her path through financial services follows the emergence of the industry itself. Of her early years on Wall Street in the 1970s and 1980s, she said, "Being a woman was always an issue." At first, Cynthia applied for a job on the trading floor of the American Stock Exchange (now the New York Stock Exchange), but then a woman in human resources took her to the floor and said, as Cynthia remembered, "I would love to hire you, but I don't think it's safe for you. The boys are going to be pinching your heinie." Recalling the memory, Cynthia laughed in disbelief: "I swear to god this is what she said to me. I thought it was hilarious, because after having been with all girls [at an all-girls college], I'm going, 'Show me the boys. This is fun!'"

And so, this didn't deter Cynthia early on in her career. But, since no one would hire her as a trader, she took a position in the family office of an investment bank. Family offices invest the money of a wealthy family, in this case the founder of the investment bank, and were some of the earlier investors who drove growth in hedge funds.[1] I found that family offices have been a common gateway to hedge funds for women in the industry, in part because the "family" association creates a space in financial services for women as the prudent keepers of the family "purse," so to speak.[2] Cynthia said the man who gave her a chance said to her, "You know what, I'm hiring you because I want to be the one to say that I hired you because I think you have a future." Of that moment in her career, she said, "It was absolutely magical."

Cynthia, however, had wanted to trade stocks and bonds: "I wanted to make a lot of money. That was just the buzzword." And so, Cynthia quickly grew bored in the family office, which she described as "dry." She transferred to the trading room and became the unit's first woman stockbroker. Of the move, she remembered her colleagues saying, "You are crazy. They talk dirty over there."

But the move worked out, although Cynthia "stuck out like a sore thumb." She recalled, "People you would get on the phone and call them and try to pitch your stock and get them to trust you with money, and they would go, 'I have never worked with a girl before.'" Once she gained their confidence, she thought this worked in her favor, because "I would get all their money, because we [women] are very nurturing and we are very long-term [in their investments], so it helped me." If she could convert a client, she believed gender stereotypes worked in her favor.

Cynthia eventually became the first woman vice president at one of the largest firms on the Street. The unit grew to 250 men and seven women. She considered both to be major accomplishments for that time: "It's historical, when you think of it now." When she became a vice president, she thanked all of her clients. It felt especially momentous because her unit was an industry leader: "[In] that division, you were like anointed."

During her lengthy experience in financial services, Cynthia had hedge fund clients and "knew how they operated." This sparked an interest in the industry and inspired her to launch a hedge fund with a close friend in the late 1990s. While she considered this an upward move in terms of status on Wall Street, she took a role as head of client services—a downward move in terms of status and money in asset management. In chapter 2, I examine the importance of social circles in pathways to the industry and how this funnels women out of asset management and into lower-paying and lower-status roles in client services.

A decade after that first hedge fund shut down, I met Cynthia at a coffee shop on the Upper East Side in Manhattan. At that time, she ran her own hedge fund consulting firm out of her home nearby. Cynthia spoke wistfully of starting her own hedge fund as an asset manager but didn't think this would be feasible because of the path her career took to client services.

While this was likely true, the image of a hedge fund manager was also an obstacle for her as a woman. Cynthia explained how hedge fund managers had earned a reputation for being independent, daring, and perhaps even reckless. Hedge funds are known as the antiestablishment segment of finance, where people go to flee bureaucratic banks, corporate politics, and stringent regulations. While Cynthia called hedge fund managers cowboys—a masculine image typically associated with whiteness[3]—others referred to them as mavericks or nonconformists, reflecting the prevailing masculine discourse about hedge fund managers being independent, antiestablishment, and even contrarian. These images are implicitly classed and racialized, too, as working-class and racial minority men are more likely to be perceived as reckless and threatening when they take risks or rebel against the establishment.

Similarly, in news coverage of industry icons, such as the revered Warren Buffett and the villainous Jeffrey Epstein, the media either glamorizes their high-rolling lifestyles and philanthropic pursuits or demonizes them for their ostentation and recklessness. Meanwhile, on the big screen, the impetuous, contrarian Mark Baum in the blockbuster hit *The Big Short* and the opportunistic, schemer Bobby Axelrod in the Showtime drama *Billions* capture the public's imagination of the current reigning archetypes of elite, white masculinity on Wall Street. To situate how these archetypes came to be, I paint a historical backdrop of the changing media icons of Wall Street, the people whose work inspired them, and the corresponding shifting ideologies of elite, white masculinity in finance.

An Elite Ideology of Hedgemonic Masculinity

On Wall Street, a dominant ideology of elite, white masculinity prevails in an institutional context with amplified perceptions of risk and insecurity. By ideology, I refer to a set of ideas, beliefs, and ideals that a provide a lens through which people understand their social worlds. Karl Marx called attention to how the dominant ideology serves to justify the interests of power holders in society. Masculinity refers to the social ideals and expectations for men in a particular context, while whiteness refers to the value placed on or privileges associated with being white.[4] In reference to Raewyn Connell's theory of hegemonic masculinity, I call the reigning dominant ideology of today's elites *hedge*monic masculinity. This ideology values entrepreneurialism, trustworthiness, and financial risk-taking, and associates these attributes with elite white men, serving as a protective hedge that legitimizes their dominant position and outsized earnings.

Hedgemonic masculinity builds on Raewyn Connell's theories about masculinity, power, and domination by revealing the inner workings of elites. Drawing from the philosopher Antonio Gramsci's theory of how capitalist power operates through a hegemonic system of cultural ideology and discourse,[5] Connell's theory of hegemonic masculinity explains the persistence of men's domination by accounting for a social organization that asserts, upholds, and legitimizes the dominant position of certain men in society. She defines hegemonic masculinity as "the configuration of gender practice which embodies the currently accepted answer to the problem of legitimacy of patriarchy, which guarantees (or is taken to guarantee) the dominant position of men and the subordination of women."[6] A central component of Connell's theory lies in how masculinity is not a fixed construct but rather consists of multiple dominant and subordinate masculinities through which contests of power take shape and shift over time. Moreover, hegemonic masculinity is defined in relation to other masculinities and femininities. Thus, hegemonic masculinity casts elite white men as fundamentally different from and superior to women and men marginalized by race, class, sexuality, and nationality.

Moreover, masculinities interact with racial and imperial ideologies as sites of exploitation and contestation within capitalism. In her book *Dealing in Desire*, sociologist Kimberly Hoang identifies how transnational financial deals are a key site in which these power contests play out. She theorizes how sex workers, who cater to transnational businessmen and local entrepreneurs in Southeast Asia, facilitate financial deals that enact competing hierarchies of transnational, racialized masculinities. Amid a context of rapid economic change, Asian ascent, and Western decline, these deals become a site where performances of masculinity—supported by the labor of Vietnamese women—assert and contest Western superiority. Hegemony operates through the intersection of gender and race in economic transactions.[7]

Thus, masculinity, femininity, and whiteness are varied, contextual, and relational rather than fixed constructs. Hegemonic masculinity captures both the cultural ideals for the dominant masculinity in a particular context, like Cynthia's hedge fund cowboys, and how social hierarchies are formed through various masculinities and femininities that interact with sexuality, race, nationality, and social class status.[8] While the content of hegemonic masculinity changes, the form remains. By tracing how these social hierarchies have evolved over time, I provide the context in which hedgemonic masculinity emerged and became the dominant ideology of elite, white masculinity among financial elites that justifies their enormous incomes in a deeply unequal era.

Three Eras of Elite, White Masculinity in Finance

It is no coincidence that the faces of Wall Street in the movies and on television are largely white and men's—both now and in the past. I trace three historical eras in modern finance and the corresponding cultural icons for elite, white masculinity: the earnest community banker of the postwar era, the shrewd investment banker of the 1980s and 1990s, and the eccentric hedge fund manager of the twenty-first century. Classic Hollywood films capture the cultural salience of elite, white masculinity in each era of finance, and vices reflect what is at stake for complying with masculinity. And while these have immediate implications for the people involved, these icons have reverberating consequences for gender, racial, and social class inequalities in society during each era.

I begin in the era following World War II when community banks dominated the financial sector. Then, the ideal for elite, white masculinity was the community banker as financial steward: a figure whose local knowledge guided investments in small business and home ownership. Protagonist George Bailey in the 1946 classic movie *It's a Wonderful Life* captures this era. Alcohol is the vice of the day, reflecting the pressures on the company man.

During the second era, characterized by the rise of investment banking in the 1980s and 1990s, the shrewd investment banker who made corporations "lean and mean" became the archetype of masculinity. In the 1987 Hollywood hit *Wall Street,* the opportunistic stockbroker Bud Fox and his greedy idol Gordon Gekko, a "corporate raider," serve as the icons of this era. Cocaine is the notorious vice of 1980s Wall Street and corresponds to the amped up, bulldozer mentality of finance in that decade.

Finally, the third era features the rise of shadow banks—credit providers less regulated than the banks—which have brought a new archetype of elite, white masculinity. The 2015 blockbuster and Oscar best-picture nominee *The Big Short* depicts the awkward, nonconforming hedge fund managers who made millions exploding—and exploiting—a rigged system during the 2008 financial crisis. The era's vice is best captured by an addiction to work fueled by prescription drugs like Adderall. Electronic trading has transformed financial services, giving trading and investment management a gaming effect.

Thus, while hedgemonic masculinity captures the new dominant ideology of financial elites today, it is not without precedent as elite, white masculinity has long reigned on Wall Street. In each era, a distinct ideology rationalizes the dominant position of elite white men. This provides insight into the evolving contexts that enable these men to dominate economic positions of power over the last eighty years. In each time period, the financial sector has reinforced a system of inequality, and this system has changed over time, as both whiteness and masculinities are shifting and contextual rather than fixed ideological frameworks.

I show how each period reveals what is at stake in society at large. The inequality regime on Wall Street determines who gets access to credit, how Main Street manages businesses, and who reaps rewards

TABLE 1. Three Eras of Elite, White Masculinity in Finance

	Community Banking	Investment Banking	Shadow Banking
Scale	Local	Global	Global
Persona	Financial steward	Master of the Universe	Flash Boy
Movie	*It's a Wonderful Life*	*Wall Street*	*The Big Short*
Time	banker's hours	Trading hours	All hours
Vice	Alcohol	Cocaine	Adderall

from the stock market. The current era provides a clue to understanding the increasing incomes, the cultural infatuation with work, and why white men dominate the "winners" of this period of rising economic inequality. I include this historical context to show how our current era is a new iteration of a system that has long entrenched social and economic inequality by hedging people out.

Community Banking (1945–1979): It's a Wonderful Life

Peter Bailey was not a businessman. That's what killed him. Oh, I don't mean any disrespect to him, God rest his soul. He was a man of high ideals, so called, but ideals without common sense can ruin this town.

MR. POTTER, *It's a Wonderful Life*, 1946

The widespread critical acclaim and popular reception of the 1946 classic movie *It's a Wonderful Life* speaks to its lasting cultural resonance. The protagonist, George Bailey, inherits his father's, Peter Bailey's, building and loan company—a depository financial firm designed to provide residential mortgages and promote home ownership. Feeling overburdened with responsibilities to his family and community, Bailey attempts suicide after the local bank owner, the greedy Henry Potter, absconds with a deposit large enough to bankrupt Bailey's lending company. A guardian angel shows Bailey the potential aftermath of his death: the bank's predatory lending and corruption turns his hometown into a dreary place rampant with poverty and illicit behavior. After realizing his role in providing valuable credit necessary for the community's well-being, Bailey prays to return to life, and his prayers are answered.

It's a Wonderful Life highlights the central figure of the community bank and banker in providing loans to deserving small businesses and prospective homeowners. Community banking reigned during the era of "shared prosperity" following World War II. In this model of banking, community banks, rather than large retail and commercial banks, took deposits and gave loans to local businesses and consumers in exchange for a transaction fee and interest-rate charge. While the leading investment banks of the twentieth century were sizeable, such as J. P. Morgan & Co., there were a greater number of smaller banks than today, because of laws that restricted banks from establishing branches in other states.[9] Since the majority of banks were local, they catered to the local community's needs, as interpreted by bank managers and loan officers, instead of targeting large customer bases as banks do today.

The community banker was the archetype for elite, white masculinity in finance during the postwar era: a financial steward committed to preserving what he believes is the local community's social and economic well-being. As C. Wright Mills detailed in *The Power Elite*, men from the old upper class oversaw the banks, while those with upper-class aspirations worked as high-level "operations" men of the banks.[10] These upper-class men controlled the distribution of credit based on their idea of how to best cultivate economic growth in local neighborhoods and business communities. The ideal for elite, white masculinity in the era upheld upper-class white men's monopoly as credit lenders, casting them as prudent stewards of capital.

The preeminent role of men as gatekeepers in the community banking model is accounted for in Raewyn Connell's classic book

Gender and Power. According to Connell, gender inequality persists through men's dominant position in the labor market, government, and heterosexual nuclear family. Connell identifies the role of creditworthiness in delineating social value in a capitalist economy, which renders women in a subordinate economic position. Then, a married woman could not hold credit without her husband—another form of being hedged out. Lenders discounted the income of a married woman of childbearing age, assuming she would lose this income if and when she became pregnant (this stipulation could be waived with proof of the use of birth control and intention to abort any pregnancies).[11] When a woman got married, divorced, or widowed, she had to close and open new credit accounts, denying her the necessary track record to establish creditworthiness.[12] And for business loans, banks could require women to have a husband, father, or son cosign the loan (many state laws even required it) until the 1988 Women's Business Ownership Act outlawed these practices.[13] Men's command over lending and borrowing contributed to the prevailing gendered division of labor of the time.

While this era of suburban expansion and so-called shared prosperity enabled many white families to live a comfortable, middle-class lifestyle, it came at an emotional and psychological cost. It was in this context that Betty Friedan's book *The Feminine Mystique* became a best seller. Friedan documented the widespread discontent of white, college-educated housewives who felt trapped and stunted by suburban life. White men's dominant position also came at an emotional price, as captured by the era's leading vice of alcohol. In Connell's depiction of an average family during the era, the father "takes, as a right, a couple of nights out for beers with the boys each week."[14] The undertones of the effects of depression and alcohol abuse taint the plot of *It's a Wonderful Life,* too. Martini's bar is a meeting place for the men in town and where George Bailey goes after working "banker's hours" from 9 to 3. Bailey imbibes to lessen the burden he feels as the breadwinner responsible for his family's business. The heteronormative nuclear family placed a heavy psychological burden even on those who reaped the benefits of money, status, and influence.

A credit-fueled suburban lifestyle organized the division of household labor in the postwar era. Lenders privileged heterosexual white families who upheld a gendered breadwinner/homemaker model, in which a father worked for wages outside the home and a mother labored without pay within the home. These households, primarily white middle-class families, became homeowners through loans subsidized by the Federal Housing Authority (FHA) and the Veteran's Association (VA). Consumer debt grew tremendously during this era: in 1958, only twenty-seven banks offered credit cards, but by 1967, 1,500 banks serviced an estimated eleven to thirteen million active accounts.[15]

The benefits, however, were largely restricted to white families, and the tolls were considerably greater on racial and ethnic minority families who were mostly denied living wages, credit, and homeownership. This has been the result of a segregated labor force as well as discriminatory lending and banking practices that hedged communities of color out. Lenders either denied access to consumer credit, home and auto loans, and even deposit and savings accounts to families of color or provided these services with higher fees and interest rates.[16] Into the early 1970s, applications for consumer credit required the applicant to disclose their race and ethnicity. One major consumer finance lender had the following point system: seven points for white borrowers, four points for a "person of Spanish origin," and zero points for Black borrowers. Loan officers more heavily scrutinized applications from racialized minorities and denied credit to applicants in "racially mixed marriages" and from "blacked out" areas—that is, "largely Black, low income neighborhoods in large cities."[17] Because of racism in lending, suburban Black households carried double the debt of their white neighbors.[18] Racism in banking and lending isn't only a historical disadvantage, it also persists to this day in a system of white supremacy that George Lipsitz has called the "possessive investment in whiteness."[19]

Home loans have had the greatest impact on cumulative disadvantage in wealth, because homeownership is a primary way that households accrue wealth. During the postwar era, the FHA and VA insured home loans to make them more affordable for white Americans, yet denied this benefit to people of color and other borrowers in neighborhoods concentrated with racial and ethnic minority households—a practice called "redlining" that enforces residential segregation. And the GI Bill was written in a way that enabled local offices to discriminate against Black and Latinx veterans. Veterans of color held less than 100 of the 67,000 GI-insured mortgages in New York and New Jersey, even though African Americans alone comprised 9 percent of the Army during World War II.[20] Despite efforts to prohibit discriminatory lending—spearheaded by the National Association for the Advancement of Colored People (NAACP)—banks continued to redline racially segregated minority neighborhoods by labeling them "risky investments," even though the wealth of Black homeowners and the value of their homes increased during this period.[21] The lasting ramifications of these policies, magnified by racism in lending today, has created enduring racial wealth disparities. Mortgage lenders continue to designate racialized minority households as "high-risk borrowers" to justify giving them the predatory subprime loans with higher fees and interest rates—one of the underlying causes of the 2008 financial crisis.[22]

Activists called attention to the gendered, racialized, and classed order of the community banking era: the "community" served by this model was reserved for a select few. A policy movement mounted to address inequality in access to credit and pervasive sexism and racism by lenders. The efforts of advocacy groups such as the NAACP, National Organization for Women (NOW), and National Welfare

Rights Organization resulted in three key policy responses in the 1970s. First, the Equal Credit Opportunity Act of 1974 prohibited discrimination based on sex or marital status, and later added race, religion, and national origin in 1977. Second, the Home Mortgage Disclosure Act of 1975 required lenders to disclose mortgage loans by classification and geographic location to prevent redlining. Finally, in 1977, the Community Reinvestment Act required banks to service lower-income borrowers in their community. The goal was to align the interests of the "community banker" with the entire community.

In the community banking era, local bankers issued auto, home, and small business loans to meet the needs of the community; however, unfairly vetting access to credit served as a hedge to uphold a classed, gendered, and racialized order. Members of the upper class deemed some people creditworthy—white men—and other people unworthy of credit—women and racialized minority men. The era's configuration of elite, white masculinity naturalized the financial steward's elevated status and monopoly over lending. While the financial steward model reflected a value to serve the local community's interests, the investment bankers of the 1980s and 1990s understood themselves as acting on behalf of the stock market.

Investment Banking (1980–1999): Wall Street

I am not a destroyer of companies. I am a liberator of them! The point is, ladies and gentlemen, that greed, for lack of a better word, is good. Greed is right, greed works. . . . And greed, you mark my words, will not only save Teldar Paper, but that other malfunctioning corporation called the USA.

GORDON GEKKO, *Wall Street,* 1987

The 1987 Hollywood hit *Wall Street* explores the limitations of greed, ambition, and excess through the story of the opportunistic young stockbroker Bud Fox. Fox is hired and mentored by his hero, the wealthy Gordon Gekko who is a "corporate raider," performing hostile takeovers of companies. He buys a majority of stock in a company to gain voting rights and then puts pressure on executives to sell business units and lay off employees to increase the share price. Gekko trains the impressionable Fox to do insider trading and pillage companies. "Greed is good," Gekko famously proclaims, justifying any measure necessary to make money. When Gekko targets the company where Fox's own father works as an aircraft mechanic and heads the labor union, Fox realizes Gekko's dealings are unethical. But it is too late: the SEC and FBI arrest Fox for insider trading. He then conspires with the authorities to convict Gekko. Fox and Gekko represent the downfall of elite, white masculinity on Wall Street—a consequence of greedy and risky behavior.

Wall Street's newfound fixation with risk-taking didn't emerge in a vacuum but was the product of policy change in Washington, DC. Starting in the late 1970s, a series of policy reforms deregulated the financial sector and opened up global capital markets.[23] In 1980, Jimmy Carter signed the Depository Institutions Deregulation and Monetary Control Act that allowed banks to merge, raised insurance on deposits, and removed the Federal Reserve Board of Governors' authority to set maximum interest rates. This gave way to the expansion of the financial sector and investment banking. After restrictions on interstate branches were scaled back in the 1980s and '90s, community banks dwindled and were replaced by national banks.[24]

Alongside growth and consolidation in the commercial banking sector, investment banking surged with a new ideology of "shareholder value," a model of corporate governance that prioritizes maximizing dividends for shareholders rather than developing the product and workers. Aggressive investment practices such as junk-bond sales, leveraged buyouts, and hostile takeovers became emblematic of the ethically dubious, emerging frontiers of finance. Becoming rich by making scrappy transactions on the crowded floors of the stock market turned traders into legends. As stock markets soared during the "bull markets" of the 1980s and '90s, investment bankers interpreted this growth as proof that their efforts to correct market inefficiencies worked.[25]

During this era, new reigning ideals for elite, white masculinity appeared in the media icons of the macho trader and the savvy investment banker who mastered the stock market by being bold and aggressive.[26] Investment bankers became the "Masters of the Universe," a term coined by Tom Wolfe in his 1987 satiric novel, *Bonfire of the Vanities*. Wolfe used the title to describe young men driven by greed to make millions by investing in junk bonds and leveraged buyouts. The "Masters of the Universe" archetype reinforced masculine cultural ideals that valued greed, ambition, and risk-taking.

The "Masters of the Universe" icon captures the prevailing gender and racial order in financial services that persisted into the 1990s and early 2000s. Aggressive workplaces like the trading floor and investment bank privileged men and penalized women who struggled to uphold norms for masculinity and were held to different standards when they did. Louise Roth identified how women in finance have been expected to both conform to norms for masculinity and follow cultural ideals associated with normative femininity. Meanwhile, sociologist Adia Harvey Wingfield has found that Black men who comply with industry norms for white masculinity risk being perceived as too aggressive, threatening, or unethical, and have to make extra efforts to seem easygoing and approachable to their white colleagues. The era's ideology of masculinity naturalized the successes of white men by casting them as better suited to make cutthroat deals.[27]

Wall Street became notorious for a work hard and play hard lifestyle during this era. Investment bankers spun in a frenzy of trading during the stock exchange hours of 9:30 a.m. to 4:00 p.m. Rather than frequenting Martini's, the symbolic neighborhood bar of the community banking era, investment bankers were depicted as having their martinis with a spoonful of cocaine, as in the movie *The Wolf of Wall Street*. A frenetic cocaine-fueled euphoria captures the vice of the era.

This highly competitive culture was also a breeding ground for other social ills, including rampant sexual harassment. The most infamous case was at Smith Barney, which had a notorious basement party room called the "Boom-Boom Room."[28] A broker named Pamela Martens became the lead whistleblower in the largest class-action lawsuit of its kind against an investment firm. Even though she managed a portfolio with $187 million in assets and over 1,000 clients, Martens was fired in 1995. While she was employed, supervisors routinely addressed her and other women using epithets for female anatomy and requested that women wore short skirts at company events.

Others on the twenty-three-plaintiff case—nearly two thousand women eventually joined the suit—reported experiencing ongoing sexual harassment and assault. In one instance, the firm's top broker sexually assaulted Lisa Mays, a wire operator who entered trade orders, by following her into her office and backing her into a corner one morning. The advances only stopped because another colleague arrived. In cases like this, when a supervisor abuses his power to take advantage of a woman subordinate, it reinforces the social hierarchy at the firm. On Wall Street and beyond, women who transgress traditional gender roles and assume positions previously held by men are more likely to be harassed. This is especially true for women who hold positions of power as well as for gender, sexual, and racialized minorities.[29] Back then and today, the rampant sexual harassment on Wall Street serves as a form of boundary-making, a hedge that maintains the social order.

The investment banking era's implications for social inequality extended beyond the doors of Wall Street's biggest firms. The shift in corporate governance from retaining and reinvesting earnings to downsizing labor, streamlining companies, and boosting share-holder profit made work more precarious and insecure for workers throughout the economy.[30] These measures subsequently increased executive earnings, and the restructurings disproportionately affected more marginalized workers, such as women and racialized minority men.[31] The rise of investment banking had lasting negative impacts for many workers.

In sum, investment bankers acquired the status of "Masters of the Universe" who conquer the stock market by being ambitious, aggressive, and bold. This era of elite, white masculinity featured distinct obstacles for women and racial minority men in financial services. Beyond finance, the rise in investment banking and shareholder value ideology has degraded working conditions throughout the labor market. While this ideology continues to reign on Wall Street, the archetype for elite, white masculinity has changed over the past twenty years because of growth in the hedge fund industry.

Shadow Banking (2000-present): The Big Short

Mark Baum: *It's time to call bullshit.*
Vinny Daniel: *Bullshit on what?*
Mark Baum: *Every fucking thing.*

THE BIG SHORT, 2015

The Oscar nominated, blockbuster hit *The Big Short* captures a new ideology of whiteness and masculinity on Wall Street. The movie—based on Michael Lewis's best-selling book—portrays the true story of hedge fund managers who predicted the housing market bubble and made billions betting against the investment banks invested in failing home loans. The heroes of this story are not the suave, attractive bankers of previous eras; rather, the protagonists are socially awkward, eccentric nonconformists who fight a rigged system. The movie reflects a pervasive industry ideology that casts bureaucracy, specifically big banks and big government, as suspect and inefficient. The film's heroes view investments, rather than regulatory and legal interventions, as the tools for correcting wrongdoing in a capitalist financial system.

One of *The Big Short's* three protagonists, Michael Burry, perhaps best captures this changing archetype. Burry, the founder of Scion Capital, is a medical school graduate who specialized in neurology. Concerned by his unique ability to focus, perhaps obsess, Burry's supervisors during his residency at Stanford Hospital sent him to see a psychiatrist. Burry rejected the bipolar disorder diagnosis and, instead, attributed his distinctive worldview to losing an eye during childhood. Depicted as valuing honesty, Burry met his wife when she replied to his Match.com profile, in which Burry candidly described himself as "a medical student with only one eye, an awkward social manner, and 145 thousand dollars in student loans."[32]

The candid and fastidious Burry represents the end of Tom Wolfe's "Masters of the Universe" and the rise of the meticulous "Flash Boys."[33] Electronic trading has exponentially increased the speed of trade execution and outpaced the trading floor of the 1980s and 1990s in size and number of trades. Before, traders executed trades in person or by phone; today, computer trading programs run electronic trades in a fraction of a second.[34] The Flash Boys refers to the "Flash Crash" of 2010 when a rogue trader, operating out of his parents' London home, drove a thousand-point stock market crash in thirty-six minutes. The crash overwhelmed the circuit breakers designed to halt rapid drops in stock prices, exacerbating the plunge. By the time the market closed, it had incurred $1 trillion in losses, the steepest one-day fall on record. Thus, the term Flash Boys captures lone, tech-savvy operators who can move the market in a matter of seconds.

This archetype of the technologically savvy and mathematically brilliant Flash Boy nerd has a different connotation than the "Greed is good" icons of the previous era. Today's traders are less likely to party with cocaine than they are to fuel their addiction to work with performance-enhancing prescription drugs like Adderall and hobbies like video games—another vice of the era.[35] And the toll of working around the clock, and the resulting collapsed boundaries around work and the rest of life, means that sexual harassment has not gone away with the Boom-Boom Room. Yet, it has taken new forms on Wall Street during the #MeToo era, which I explore in detail in chapter 5.

The icon of the Flash Boy reflects a fundamental change in the organization of Wall Street. At the turn of the twenty-first century, the culminating effects of deregulation, globalization, and financial innovation led to the rise of the shadow banking industry, and with it a new archetype of elite, white masculinity. Shadow banks refer to credit intermediaries that feature less regulation relative to commercial or investment banks. Examples include hedge fund, venture capital, and private equity firms. Shadow banks are the regulatory "black box" of finance. Although regulatory oversight of shadow banking increased after the Dodd-Frank Wall Street Reform and Consumer Protection Act of 2010, hedge funds still incur less oversight than their counterparts at the "too big to fail" investment banks.

Shadow banks have proliferated over the past thirty years at the expense of the traditional banking sector. Shadow banking grew from less than 4 percent of the total US business sector in 1974 to as much as 37 percent in 2013 as their global assets increased from $26 trillion in the early 2000s to $80 trillion in 2014.[36] In the aftermath of the 2008 financial crisis, government regulations and interventions in failing investment banks led investors to transfer funds to this less-regulated sector of financial services. While shadow banking remains small relative to traditional banking, it captures the fastest growing parts of finance. It also presents potentially significant risks to the economy's well-being because of the opacity of shadow banks' investments.

In the shadow banking era, the proliferation of credit intermediaries like hedge funds and the subsequent increase in the amount of debt circulated by financial markets poses greater and less calculatable systemic risks. This has important ramifications for inequality in a context where more households must take out debt to subsidize their lifestyles and whose savings are invested in their homes and stocks, which makes them more vulnerable to financial crashes. The shadow banking era is characterized by heightened instability and inequality because the financial sector extracts resources from the working and middle class especially during times of economic crisis and hardship.[37]

It is no coincidence the households hardest hit during the Great Recession and the more recent coronavirus pandemic are those characterized as single-mother, racialized minority, and low income. The subprime mortgage crisis that precipitated the financial crisis of 2008 endangered the well-being of the middle class because their wealth is largely held in homeownership rather than the stock market. As economist Edward Wolff's research has shown, this disproportionately affected younger, less-educated, single-mother, and racialized minority families. These disparities in credit are indicative of an era in which racism is cloaked in designations of the "high-risk borrower," as Patricia Hill Collins and Eduardo Bonilla-Silva have theorized, and shows how those with privilege extend advantage to one another.[38] Racial inequality is also maintained through white people showing favoritism to one another, whether it be by hiring, lending, or investing in one another.[39]

Growth in shadow banking is perhaps a sign of a retreat from bureaucratic institutions and a shift toward smaller firms funded through trust networks. Networks of trust have returned as the fabric of enterprise in late-stage capitalism. To guard against risk and uncertainty, people place trust in tight-knit forms of social organization.[40] Highly uncertain environments, like financial crashes and crises, lead trust networks to close off and restrict social exchange.[41] In an era of ongoing financial uncertainty, investors may lose trust in large financial institutions and instead build local networks that provide a sense of stability.[42] Thus, recent growth in the shadow banking industry suggests a retreat from bureaucratic institutions as investors lose confidence in the "too big to fail" financial institutions. Shadow banking—and hedge funds in particular—captures a movement toward less regulated firms driven by patrimonial networks of trust.

A new masculinity, hedgemonic masculinity, has emerged among financial elites in the shadow banking era that reflects this reliance on patrimonial networks of trust and the protective hedges they create. Amid contexts of uncertainty, such as periods of economic and social transformation, people rely even more on gender, race, and social class to inform their transactions.[43] Masculinity and whiteness confer status and privileges to white men, especially those who are elite, designating them as more trustworthy, an advantage that helps to explain why gender and racial inequality are so pernicious.[44]

This new era of hedgemonic masculinity reflected in the archetype of the Flash Boys and *The Big Short* nonconformists set the stage for the data I gathered. It is no longer the investment banks, but rather actors at shadow banks, that provide a key to understanding why white men reign among the "winners" of widening income and wealth inequality and why almost everyone else gets hedged out.

Risk and Speculative Money

The sociologist Alfred W. Jones, who founded the world's first hedge fund in 1949, is an example of how hedgemonic masculinity reflects speculative and calculative logics for managing risk in the stock market. Today, Jones's firm, A. W. Jones & Co., would be called an opportunistic long/short equity fund, because it made short-term and long-term investments in the stock market. Jones simultaneously made investments in some stocks that he expected to appreciate over time and in other stocks that he predicted would decrease in value, using techniques that allowed him to profit from both. By reconsidering neoclassical economic theories of the market, Jones developed strategies that allowed him to hedge exposure to potential market losses and profit from the stock market even during market downturns. Hedge funds call these profits "absolute returns," because they aren't tied to the stock market's jumps and falls.[45]

Jones called this strategy a hedge because he combined a risk-averse technique of investing in assets that will slowly appreciate over time with two potentially risky and speculative investment techniques: leverage and short-selling. Short-selling is when an investment manager bets against a security expecting it to fall. For example, in 2014, the global oil markets underwent a major meltdown. In June 2014, oil cost $115 a barrel; by February 2016, oil hit a thirty-year low of $26 a barrel. Imagine that back in early 2014, an investor anticipates the oil crash and prepares to short oil. To do this, first she takes out a loan in the form of a barrel of oil from a bank or other lender.[46] She then sells the oil barrel when she thinks it has reached its peak prices, in this case $115. Then the investor waits for the stock to drop in value. Once the barrel reaches what she thinks is the bottom price—$26 in 2016—she buys the barrel at the lower price and pays her lender back in kind, the barrel of oil. From this exchange, she makes the difference—$89—on each barrel. This is how investors can make considerable profits even when the market falls.

Leverage, Jones's other technique, refers to when an investor borrows capital or uses other financial techniques to increase the scope of the investment.[47] Using the analogy from before, imagine that the price of oil rebounds in the second half of 2017. The investor above anticipates that oil prices will rise, so she invests $100 in oil and then takes out a loan from the bank for $1,000 at an interest rate of 6 percent to maximize her investment. At the end of the year, if oil prices increase by 15 percent, the value of her investment will rise to $1,265, an increase of $165. If she decided to sell the oil stock, she would pay back the bank $1,000 plus $60 in interest. This would leave her with $105 in profits, even though she only invested $100 of her own money. Although leveraging can increase profits, it involves higher levels of risk. If oil prices had dropped by 15 percent, she would have compounded her losses. A hedge fund that is "highly leveraged" has more debt relative to equity, which accelerates its profits or losses and heightens the risk involved.[48]

Jones's history as a sociologist and Marxist captures the contrarian mindset valued in this industry. His primary financial innovations pertained to risk management. To generate consistently high profits, Jones combined less risky investment strategies, such as investing in stocks he anticipated would grow incrementally over time, with potentially higher-risk techniques, such as short-selling and leverage. Central to Jones's investment philosophy is an ability to anticipate stock market shifts by analyzing the social dynamics of markets— how manias and panics among investors shape their activity. He used social theory to understand the changing direction of financial markets and then applied technical and mathematical methods to capitalize on social phenomena.[49]

While hedge fund strategies today are loosely based on Jones's innovations, technological advances have made hedge fund investments more theoretically and mathematically complex. By design, these investments are difficult to understand, regulate, and value. New financial technologies such as electronic trades, automated credit scores, and virtual contracts enabled financial firms to bundle risky assets into complex securities—such as asset-backed securities and collateralized debt obligations—and derivatives of those securities— such as credit default swaps—to sell to investors.[50] This process, called securitization, allows lenders to redistribute assets to other firms like hedge funds and, thus, reduce their liabilities.[51] Securitization has substantially increased the amount of credit circulating and created more complex financial futures and derivatives vehicles. While decreasing the risk involved for each particular exchange, securitization has generated unexpected and unprecedented systemic risks, such as those that sparked the 2008 financial crisis and ensuing global recession.[52]

Jones's inventions, in tandem with the advent of securitization, laid the groundwork for a new era of turning money into money, divorced from physical commodities. These developments have fundamentally transformed the nature of capital. In the nineteenth century, Karl Marx identified how capital is created through the sale of commodities.[53] He denoted the circuit M-C-M' to capture how money (M) is invested to create commodities (C) that are sold to generate more money (M'). This money becomes the capital that allows a capitalist to produce more commodities. Securitization has allowed investors such as hedge funds to transform money through an M-M' continuous circuit. Money (M) can now be invested into abstract financial derivatives (M')—a security that represents a contract for the exchange of underlying assets—that generate more money. The creation of capital is no longer tied to physical commodities in finance capitalism allowing for obtuse products and enormous profits that are divorced from the underlying economy.

Value and Worth in the Financial Era

Alongside transformations in the US financial sector, the meanings associated with elite, white masculinity on Wall Street have shifted. An ideology of hedgemonic masculinity undergirds the entire industry, to the detriment of people of color and white women who aspire to work and advance in this industry. This ideology upholds systems of inequality—white supremacy, gender inequality, and finance capitalism—that create the conditions in which hedge fund managers can charge and justify high fees on investment profits. At hedge funds, beliefs about race, class, and gender garner respect for white men and legitimize their authority, status, and high pay, conferring value and worth to elite white men. This select group is deemed valuable for their perceived technical experience as well as for their social capital.

This new form of whiteness and masculinity is a response to the increasing complexity, uncertainty, and risk posed by modern financial markets. These ideologies implicitly value the independent thinking that enables someone to outsmart a turbulent market. Meanwhile, networks that value trust and loyalty serve as stronger forms of social capital that afford a sense of certainty. Both values—for independent thinking and trusting relationships—are responses to an environment of elevated risk and uncertainty.

The next chapters follow the arc of a hedge fund career: pathway to, getting in, moving up, reaching the top, view from the top, and who wins and who loses. The social fabric of firms that adhere to an ideology of hedgemonic masculinity are organized around trust and loyalty, which helps to explain why a select group of people gain access to this highly lucrative part of finance and others are hedged out. Hedgemonic masculinity naturalizes the desired characteristics associated with elite white men and the relationships that form among them. This legitimizes their control over money, status, and power, creating an environment that allows them to demand high incomes and exert political might.

2 Pathways to the Working Rich

Sitting near the back of the audience in a gilded nineteenth-century hotel ballroom in Midtown Manhattan, I peered through rows of black suits to watch Joseph, a well-known hedge fund personality. He gave a "Fireside Chat"—an interview on sofa chairs in front of an audience at a professional conference. A fifty-something white man, Joseph sported gelled black hair, had a square jaw, and wore a crisp designer suit.

Joseph switched from his professional accent to one straight off the streets of Long Island. He said he grew up "hustling papers around my neighborhood" to help his parents pay the bills. Joseph's origin story reflects a rags-to-riches myth embraced by the hedge fund world. Even from a blue-collar background, just hustle, hard work, perseverance, and a little luck could lead you to riches at a hedge fund.

Joseph said he grew up in a middle-class Italian American neighborhood in an outer borough of New York City. His father, a construction worker, paid for Joseph's tuition to earn a bachelor's degree at New York University—the first college degree in his family. Joseph went on to graduate from Yale Law School.

Then Joseph landed an interview for a job at an elite investment bank. He said, "I wore a 100 percent polyester suit, shirt, and black narrow tie—all polyester to the point of flammability." At the conference, the line read like an overly rehearsed comedy routine. The audience erupted in laughter.

Later, Joseph explained, the job interviewer pulled him aside and told him to buy a designer suit to look like he had already "made it." Joseph recalled, "I was completely mortified, because I thought I looked fantastic." He got the job but was fired eighteen months later. "At the time, I was like a walking junk bond," Joseph quipped to more laughter from the audience.

Joseph spent the $11,000 he received in severance to buy a designer suit. He applied for a sales position at the same firm that had just fired him. The firm hired him again—with a clean record—and earmarked him as an internal transfer. Joseph worked there until he raised enough money to launch his own hedge fund only seven years later. Dressing for the part, Joseph explained, helped him to embody the person he wanted to become. He concluded by saying, "There will be moments of great despair, but it will work out if you are on a path with a purpose."

Although Joseph's path is not the norm in the industry, he captures two prevalent cultural ideals on Wall Street: the scrappy bootstrapper and "fake it till you make it" mentality. Cultural ideals, like the value in dressing the part, expose how hedge fund workers idealize what it takes to advance. In general, elites tend to compare themselves to their peers with even higher incomes, wealth, and status.[1] This motivates them to earn more. If hedge fund workers believe the myth that it takes a $10,000 suit to advance, they will strive to achieve this, even if they never actually buy that suit. As they compete to uphold the ideals for success, the bar rises higher and higher.

The $10,000 suit is the symbolic barrier to entry in this elite industry. Once a person can prove that they can wear the suit, literally and metaphorically speaking, then they can dress down for the part of the Flash Boy. In other words, an entrant must conform before they can nonconform. This ability to transition from the $10,000 suit to the t-shirt and sneakers with ease reflects how elites are cultural omnivores, that is, having versatile tastes such as enjoying both Tchaikovsky and 2 Chainz.[2] This versatility—comfort with so-called highbrow and lowbrow culture—has become a new symbolic boundary that distinguishes the elite.[3]

Joseph described hedge funds as meritocratic. But the dynamics of this cutthroat industry suggest otherwise. Hedge funds are generally small, lucrative, and competitive. Among the forty-eight people I interviewed, most worked at firms with five to twenty-five workers, resembling the average hedge fund. These small firms feature fewer protections for workers than the large banks. And firms survive only five years on average. According to the people I spoke with, this environment promotes meritocracy and free market employment. As one hedge fund manager said, "Everyone is replaceable." Even with insider networks and industry experience, finding a new job takes months and hundreds of applications. Employment is insecure, but the prospects of making money—"real money," as insiders say—are high.

People rarely enter the industry on merit alone. While Joseph echoes the common rags-to-riches myth, few people I interviewed followed the path of a self-starter. In this chapter, I first explore what motivates people to enter the hedge fund industry. Their motives capture the dominant industry beliefs about elite masculinity and whiteness that prioritize the know-how and symbolic value of men from class- and race-privileged backgrounds. I then examine why this particular group of people came to work in the industry and how an elite upbringing and education eased their entrance into the hedge fund elite.

The Allure of Hedge Funds

What leads people to apply for a job at a hedge fund? For the most part, people who embodied the ideal for hedgemonic masculinity—

white men from elite backgrounds—didn't describe a motive for pursuing a hedge fund career. It appeared, to them, a natural fit. Those who did and did not embody the ideal described an image of a hedge fund manager that drew them to the industry: a maverick with a passion for innovative investing and a talent for influencing the direction of world markets. Today's icon is the wealthy intellectual who, free from the chains of financial insecurity, can eschew the establishment and call their own shots. And people of all genders embraced the rhetoric of autonomy, intelligence, and innovation, which uphold an ideology of elite, white masculinity. The hedge fund archetype legitimizes and valorizes less oversight and accountability than other firms—allowing hedge funds to create boundaries around who can access the industry's immense wealth and who is hedged out.

Freedom from the Iron Cage

Industry insiders cited both the money and the industry's reputation—the place for the bold, antibureaucratic contrarians described in chapter 1—as an appeal. This reputation came up when I asked Cynthia how many employees worked at her first hedge fund. She said emphatically, "We had like nothing, like five, but you know like the biggest funds only have, like billion or two billion firms, only have twenty-five people. You do it lean and mean. You outsource everything else." By "billion or two billion firms," she meant the firm's assets under management. Insiders usually characterize a firm by the monetary, rather than employee, size.

"What's the idea behind lean and mean?" I asked.

"Well, because hedge funds, remember they're the cowboys. They just want to trade. They just like to do what they like to do. They don't want the layers and the bureaucracy. That's when all the money comes in and all the people come in. And everybody would multitask. It's just the business structure of a hedge fund," Cynthia said.

She cited a firm that managed $10 billion with only twenty-five employees. "I think that's unbelievable," she said in awe. Then, Cynthia leaned toward me, widened her eyes, and said:

> It's really that simple, but it wasn't like sitting here thinking, "let me see how I can milk people to make two billion dollars in a year." It wasn't that at all. It was like friends and family [who invested the money] . . . it was really the best and brightest, and they just ended being mired down by all the bureaucracy. And not because they wanted to do anything illegal. They just want to be able to do what they wanted to do. So, it freed them to be able to do it.

Eschewing bureaucracy, according to Cynthia, liberates you from work—a notion echoed in the entrepreneurial spirit of the gig economy.[4] But at hedge funds, it's a freedom only granted to wealthy friends and family.

Cynthia reflects a heterodox outlook common in the industry. At a conference, a hedge fund billionaire and industry leader named Sam called himself a "revolutionary" as he sat on stage in a traditional blue oxford shirt with the top button casually unbuttoned. A white man with gray hair, he said, "I'm antiestablishment. I'm a revolutionary. But I grew up in a revolutionary era during Vietnam and when Steve Jobs was the model of a revolutionary." He said he set out to change how business is done: "I started off with audacious goals, and I have audacious dreams." He broke down barriers, he said, between executives and employees to encourage openness and meritocracy. Industry insiders often cited this man's firm as the exemplary hedge fund.

People I interviewed often echoed these ideals when describing their motivations for joining or founding a hedge fund. Ken, a forty-something white hedge fund founder, said, "I'm just not a go-punch-the-clock kind of person." He preferred entrepreneurship over working for a bank. Similarly, Albert felt disillusioned with investment banking, so he started his own hedge fund. A white man in his forties, Albert said, "I promised myself that if I no longer was 'having fun' or I failed to be really engaged then I would stop and go and do something else. And invariably what happens is they have a habit of paying you just enough to keep you going on. But slowly you started to recognize that you were prostituting yourself." Albert thought the high pay fostered a sense of complacency. The term prostituting—a strong word to describe a highly coveted, elite job—has a stigmatized, feminized connotation, implying that his bureaucratic work was emasculating and demeaning. And so, Albert took a risk to "build something that you believe to be good and uncompromising," a hedge fund.

For others, hedge funds provided the chance to make bolder, large-scale investments. Margaret, an Asian American investment analyst in her twenties, framed moving from an investment bank to a hedge fund as a rational career choice. Latent in her account is a story about the prestige, reputation, and sizeable impact of the industry. I asked her how investment banking differs from hedge funds. She replied, "The caliber of people that are hired—and it is very correlated to compensation—by a hedge fund. They look for something different. It's a combination of both very raw ambition but also a certain amount of creativity that comes from loving public markets." Margaret echoes Karen Ho's ethnography of Wall Street in which a culture of smartness entices elite students.[5]

But from Margaret's point of reference as an Ivy League graduate, intelligence does not distinguish the financial elite's inner circle, because Wall Street is brimming with smart people like her. For her, an ambitious and passionate drive to affect world markets set hedge funds apart. Margaret said, "The beautiful thing about being able to invest in the public markets is that everything that happens in the world impacts what you do, and you get to invest in everything that happens in the world . . . those things require you to really be on at all times." The fact that activity in global markets never ends made Margaret feel important. Insiders like Margaret view hedge funds as the ivory tower of finance, because the industry has enough money to "move markets"—change the price of stocks, bonds, and currencies—around the world. While Ho's investment bankers viewed their purpose as making firms more efficient, hedge fund workers saw themselves as the architects of the global economy.

Beyond Security: Financial Freedom

The people I interviewed acknowledged money as a primary reason to work at hedge funds. But their explanations didn't align with typical cultural notions of greed. For Jeffrey, a fifty-something white founder, money represented independence. When I asked him to explain what he said, he responded, "I'm not a spender. I'm not a consumer. And believe me I quit [a top-tier firm] and took four years off to travel. I'm not going to get into the philosophical thing, but to me money is independence. It's not, 'Hey, I can buy a fancy car, or I can get my wife bigger earrings.' That just doesn't interest me." Jeffrey didn't value money for the material goods it brought but for freeing him from an employer. Traveling symbolizes that freedom: the ability to drop everything without financial constraints. Jeffrey distanced himself from the stereotype of the greedy rich who consume designer goods, jewelry, and cars.[6] Instead, Jeffrey valued a lifestyle of leisure and mobility—another form of elite consumer capitalism. The desired status distinction brought by money is experiences rather than goods.

Those from less privileged backgrounds, like Joseph, wanted to achieve upward mobility. Some even wanted to better the elite, which is indicative of the class tensions of eras with acute economic divides. Vincent, a white founder in his fifties, said, "So I'm a poor kid from a tough neighborhood from New York." As he told me this, his working-class New Yorker accent became more pronounced. He continued,

"And I put myself through college and law school, working full-time jobs, packing trucks for UPS and then later on in more professional, I would call it more internship-type roles, in law firms and investment banks."

Vincent said he stood out at his first job out of law school, "Everybody went to Harvard. I went locally to Rutgers. It's a good school, but I certainly stood out." And so, he changed careers to out-earn his former colleagues in an even more lucrative profession: "It was just me being a savvy street kid from New York saying, 'If you can't beat 'em, you join 'em, when they won't let you join 'em, you beat 'em.' And so, I made the switch from law to trading at an investment bank, and just rose."

When we met, Jamie was launching a hedge fund—his family's "lottery ticket." A thirty-something multiracial man, Jamie felt unsatisfied in the corporate rat race. Jamie had it all: a professional job, a suburban home, and a wife and two children. Having grown up in a blue-collar household in which money was a constant source of tension, Jamie didn't want money to limit the opportunities available to his two daughters. Yet, he found that "American Dream" lifestyle unfulfilling.

Jamie was inspired by his mentor, a professor who invested on the side and made enough money to retire at age forty-two yet continued to teach because he loved it. Jamie also dreamed of working for the pure joy of it, rather than for the wages necessary to pay the bills: "Where I'm doing what I'm doing because I just want to, not because I have to get paid." Working for the passion, instead of necessity, conveys an elite status: having an abundance of wealth to afford a leisurely lifestyle but also the strong drive and work ethic to continue to work.

Men of all racial and class backgrounds—but no women—echoed Jamie's desire. They defined "financial freedom" as independence from needing a salaried income.[7] Jerry, a Mexican American man in his twenties, said he founded a hedge fund because he loves investing and wants "complete financial security." When I asked him to define this catchphrase, Jerry said: "total financial independence," as in free of all financial concerns. For most people, security implies a steady paycheck and secure employment. For hedge fund workers, security means having the money to retire but continuing to work for the fulfillment gleaned from the labor. Rather than securing a nest egg as in the traditional notion of retirement, financial freedom means liberation from all financial constraints for life.

The goal of achieving financial freedom is largely unattainable for most people in the United States, even for those who work at a hedge fund. This dream captures freedom from wage labor only made possible by vast amounts of wealth. Scholars call this elite status a "rentier life": one in which you make sufficient money to retire early and live off passive income provided by the interest on your investments. In keeping with a culture that values work, hedge fund workers dream of retirement, but not actually retiring. In other words, to become de-commodified workers—or to free themselves from market dependency—these workers strive to accumulate riches, which coincidentally further tethers them to financial markets and drives their incomes ever higher upward.

Thus, the pursuit of amassing a large fortune serves as a marker of entrepreneurial success and individual autonomy. And the financial freedom discourse imbues the high incomes with an entrepreneurial spirit that deems them justifiable. Reflecting a neoliberal and white masculine ideology, this mindset posits that risk-taking and bootstrapping leads to success, rather than the resources reaped from affluence, racial privilege, and men's networks.

Tracks to the Industry

A key to the elite social organization of this hard-to-access industry lies in the four major paths people take to a hedge fund. All four tracks appeared to be meritocratic, but each required considerable social and cultural capital in the form of elite social networks and an Ivy League or graduate degree to prove the candidate was a "good fit." With only two exceptions, the people I interviewed had prestigious undergraduate degrees. Half had completed postgraduate education. Financial support from family or employers usually enabled them to get a start in this business. Even Joseph had help from his father, a blue-collar worker, who put him through school.

My interviewees usually attributed getting into hedge funds to their dedication and hard work, yet they mentioned a time when friends, family, or previous colleagues opened a door. In a context where elite pedigrees outnumber elite jobs, firms generally prefer to hire someone with a direct social or family tie, which are read as a strong indicator that someone will be a "good fit." Initially, these requirements appear most directly associated with social class; however, a closer examination reveals how complying with hedgemonic masculinity is another criterion that legitimizes and naturalizes access to this high-paying industry.

In the first track, the social circle track, a person finds an opportunity to work at a hedge fund through a personal, often family, connection. Next, in the investment banking track, a person enters financial services through an internship and then training program at a major investment bank. In the third, the trading track, people start out trading on the stock market floor and then develop the expertise and record necessary to get a hedge fund job. In the final, fourth track, the academic track, a person comes from another high-status field like academia or law. The four tracks aren't mutually exclusive, and while each track can open a door, it still took social capital and "fit" to walk through.

The Social Circle Track: It's "Who You Know"

In this "social circle" track, the most common route to the industry, a person from an affluent background gets a hedge fund job through familial, or family-like, elite social ties that reveal the patrimonial structure of the industry. The high stakes lead insiders to restrict access to people perceived as trustworthy, reputable, and loyal, usually people who are "like them" in terms of race, gender, and class.[8] This track favors white people from elite backgrounds who more easily solicited trust in doing business among the affluent.

As Jeffrey said, "People are looking for someone they can trust. Over time I started to understand the validity to that, especially when you are dealing with wealthy families." Jeffrey thought hedge funds valued trust because of the high stakes and uncertainty—even more so than elsewhere on Wall Street: "A person who I can trust is actually going to look out for my best interest, and I think that may be pronounced in the hedge fund industry because the stakes are so high."

For this reason, those who were class-privileged often found jobs through family contacts and friends. Though this was consistent across gender and race, I observed a gendered pattern in how people were funneled into jobs: men were more often recruited for technical investment roles, while women were sorted into relational client-facing roles.[9]

A friend of a friend recruited Andrew, a lawyer by training, to the investment side of the business. A thirty-something white man who wore thick plastic square-rimmed eyeglasses, Andrew left the top button of his shirt unbuttoned under his blazer, and his wavy brown hair reached mid-ear, much longer than the industry norm. He didn't embody the industry's clean-cut look. On his firm's website, he sported stubble and flashed a toothy smile in his headshot. Andrew gave off a relaxed vibe, as though he didn't take himself too seriously.

Andrew's casual demeanor was consistent with how he framed his path to hedge funds. "I lucked into the industry," he said. After finishing law school, he came across a job as a trader. He said, "I was at a wedding, and a woman that I know, her husband was a headhunter who was looking for people at a distressed prop [proprietary trading] desk at [top-tier investment bank name deleted]." Within four years, Andrew transitioned to a job at a hedge fund.

Andrew was lucky. He was at the right place at the right time. But his "luck" is largely only available to people who have class- and race-privileged networks. Andrew, an attorney at the time, was recruited to work in distressed trading, a position requiring investment expertise that is gender-typed masculine. After that first job, Andrew felt "little bit burnt out" and took off for two years. He said, "I tried to write screenplays and did yoga. I tried to follow that creative writing side of me for a couple of years." He eventually found his way back to a hedge fund founded by people he knew personally.

White men often found jobs during informal activities, like skiing and charity poker. Several heterosexual white men said they didn't invite women, deeming it "inappropriate" because of their girlfriends and wives. A forty-something white hedge fund founder, Justin cited a recent ski trip in Colorado: "One guy helped another guy get a job. It was a male-bonding thing, sitting in a hot tub. If a girl is there, it's gonna be weird. . . . It's okay to be there without my wife and kids, but if there's a woman [he trailed off]." Since these events are an important part of doing business and networking, women, and perhaps gay men, may miss out on key opportunities.

The industry's heteronormative social organization funneled women into client roles. Even though Cynthia had decades of investment experience on Wall Street, her friend recruited her for a client services role at his hedge fund. A former trader, Cynthia stood in stark contrast with Andrew, an attorney recruited to distressed trading. In the late 1990s, she said, the opportunity arose at a dinner party when her friend Bert asked her to help him launch a hedge fund: "It's just crazy how much money you are going to be making. Come and be with me."

Cynthia thought a strong reputation and social capital were the keys to working at a hedge fund: "What's so great about it [is] everybody who knew everybody who knew everybody who knew everybody. And everything was based on your reputation." Cynthia's social circles overlapped with the industry and familiarized her with the culture. She said, "On a personal level, I knew a lot of hedge fund managers." She used upper-class descriptors for hedge fund managers: smart, wealthy, and polite: "I looked at them as being really smart, making a lot of money, really wired, and very polite. And you really had to know the people. It was the old-fashioned way of doing business, where your word is your bond. And to me, that is just so important. It is the basis of any relationship." Cynthia's praises reflect the class respectability of elite masculinity that is fitting for an industry that began by managing money for wealthy people—and still does. "Old-fashioned" and "bond" reflect the benevolent, patrimonial leadership based on trust and loyalty.

Cynthia captures a sense of kinship that stems from the industry's origins. Hedge funds often begin as proprietary trading and family office firms that manage either the firm's or wealthy family's money.[10] Hedge funds may appear a relic of the Gilded Age when industrial titans, such as Rockefeller and Carnegie, preserved their fortunes in private foundations. Yet, hedge funds capture how kinship is an entrenched feature of elites to this day. By creating close-knit, patrimonial ties, elites can unfetter themselves from the oversight and restrictions posed by the bureaucracy of twentieth-century managerial capitalism.

Through Cynthia's career, alumni service, and philanthropic pursuits, she had built vast social networks, within and beyond Wall Street. When I met her for coffee, I found Cynthia with an artist friend brainstorming how to network the Manhattan art world. As we talked, she cited crossing paths with big names in Wall Street, Hollywood, and philanthropy. Afterward, Cynthia generously spent another half hour suggesting the most helpful and interesting contacts for me. And when we parted ways, she directed me to the subway by way of Al Roker's house and Madonna's block-long estate, both neighbors of Cynthia's. First, I thought Cynthia was showing off her elite social capital. But then I realized she was modeling a deeply ingrained social practice, part of what French sociologist Pierre Bourdieu called *habitus*.[11] Matching high-status contacts was a finely honed skill she had likely developed in her elite upbringing and throughout her career.

Similarly, Jennifer shows how people more often notice white women for their relationship skills than their other expertise. A forty-something white woman and famous Wall Street CEO's daughter, she got an MBA from the University of Chicago and began her career at a top investment bank. In the late 1990s, a good friend's hedge fund manager husband offered her a client services job. Jennifer said, "He really liked me. We were personal friends. He had seen things that I had written, and we were buddies. And so, he felt that I had the right mix of financial industry experience as well as the personality and skills." He recognized, she said, "my communication, relationship-building skills, which is really what I am strongest at." A hedge fund manager might use their elite social circle to search for someone to fill a client-facing job because the skills valued—likability and communication—are on display in informal social gatherings. And these skills reflect not only gendered but also racialized and classed expectations for women. As sociologist Sharla Alegria finds in technology, white women get channeled into relational jobs in ways that women of color are not.[12]

When we met at a social club in Midtown Manhattan, Matthew stood tall and self-assured with the ease afforded by an elite pedigree—even his nursery school is renowned. A Black man in his early forties, Matthew recalled how, early in his career, walking home from work as an investment banking trader, he bumped into an old friend who was the student president of his boarding school. The friend was with his father, an affluent man, who was launching a hedge fund. Right there on the street, he invited Matthew for a job interview: "And by chance, and this was totally by chance, the dad was like, 'I'd like to interview you. We're starting a hedge fund. Why don't you come in and talk to me?'" And so, Matthew met with the man, who offered him a job that same day as a convertible arbitrage trader.

Unlike the elite white men who often took opportunities like this for granted, Matthew knew he benefited from class privilege: "There's an example [of privilege]. I didn't get that for anything except that I went to a high school with that guy. For me to deny that is ridiculous. But I think that a lot of people who sit in some of these seats, they don't even think about that because it's just a total function of how the world works for them." Most people, he said, who follow this path believe it to be meritocratic and thus feel entitled to it: "It's the concept of how the world should work. 'Hey, I'm a white guy that went to Princeton. Somebody should hand me something. Of course, you are going to say yes to me.' Right? Never a question in your head, but that's not the way the world works for a lot of others."

Although elite schools have become more diverse, Black students more often compose the upwardly mobile, new elite who lack the ease and social ties of their upper-class white peers.[13] But not Matthew. From an elite family, Matthew had the same class advantages and still encountered roadblocks from racism, revealing the salience of race among elites. Most elites, Matthew said, do not recognize the privilege they have, because it appears normal. Knowing how racism shaped his own experiences made Matthew more aware of class and gender privilege. He, like other men of color, said that while he could bond with white men colleagues, the industry's close-knit social ties tended to be racially segregated (as I examine in chapter 5), which limited his access to client investors and job opportunities.[14]

The majority of my interviewees had elite networks either through their families or universities. However, Sasha, a thirty-something Black woman and first-generation immigrant raised in a working-class family, proved an exception to the rule. Sasha said she struggled to build networks because people often didn't respond to her emails after networking events. In contrast to Andrew, for instance, Sasha's self-presentation was immaculate—indicative of the extra labor required of Black women in predominantly white industries.[15] Sasha wore pantyhose, high heels, and a structured dress with her hair pulled back into a sleek bun. Sasha said, "I didn't get here because of my networks. I'm from Jamaica. My parents' networks aren't going to help me here." Instead, she got her MBA at a state school, because "I was cheap," she said. A hedge fund headhunter recruited her to an accountant position in the back office, a less prestigious and lower paying department. Later, she found a higher-paying position in client services. "If I could do it all over, I would have gone to a named school, because people put a lot of weight into school," she reflected. "Not everybody can go and pay $50 thousand a year."

Because trust is especially important for doing business in the hedge fund world, family networks, college friends, and religious communities open, or prevent, access to employment. Those from elite backgrounds perceived these opportunities as natural and inevitable, while those lacking class privilege identified social capital as the primary barrier to getting a break. Moreover, these networks shaped how each person accessed these opportunities, funneling women—even with investing experience—into client services positions and men into investment roles based on perceived "fit." Elite social ties are not only gendered and classed but also racialized, shaping the stability and trajectory of people's careers. In the next section, the investment banking track, the job gives access to high-status networks.

The Investment Banking Track: It's the "Natural Next Step"

On the investment banking track, a college student, usually an Ivy Leaguer, enters financial services through a major investment bank.

First, the person crunches numbers as an investment banking intern—for upwards of five grand a month—during a summer in college. If then hired for a junior analyst program, the person stays on after graduation and works over 120 hours a week to make six figures—and a chance for a future job that could make millions. Next, a hotshot boss at Goldman Sachs spins off their own firm or a recruiter calls about a job at a hedge fund. While this path resembles Matthew's, it is more accessible to those without an elite upbringing, as it provides opportunities to build networks and attract recruiters.

This track led Margaret, an Asian American woman, away from the sciences and into investment banking when she graduated with a bachelor's degree from Princeton University. Wearing a cream turtleneck sweater and simple makeup with her hair pulled back in a low ponytail, Margaret sat across from me in a conference room in her firm's Upper East Side office as she told me about her path to a hedge fund. Of her training, she said, "My educational background had nothing to do with what I am doing now." She explained how her degrees in linguistics and cognitive neuroscience usually led to careers in academia or the CIA—neither of which appealed to her: "So I tried to sort of do a little bit of career exploration and a little bit of soul searching and ended up finding a very good number of very smart people that I respected that were going into this industry." Margaret followed her "smart" peers—and the investment banks' recruiters at Princeton's career fair[16]—and applied to a summer internship at an investment bank. Karen Ho calls the elite university pipeline to investment banks a "human kinship bridge," because it creates an alumni network of fictive "kin" that is racialized, classed, and gendered.[17]

It should come as no surprise then that Margaret was hired and excelled. Industry insiders emphasized that firms prefer employees whose credentials appeal to prospective investors in promotional materials, implying that an Ivy League degree is more valuable than formal training in financial modeling. As an Ivy League graduate,

Margaret was presumed to possess the intelligence and analytical skills to learn on the job, conducting research on mergers and acquisitions. Specialized training in finance isn't an explicit requirement—at least not for those with an elite degree.

During her year as an investment-banking analyst, Margaret worked exceedingly long hours. At times, she slept on a sofa in the lobby, a typical rite of passage for entry-level analysts. This made her current seventy-hour week seem reasonable. Since her degree was unrelated, Margaret learned everything on the job. She recalled, "It's not rocket science, but it is challenging." Investment banking, she explained, is the training program for Wall Street.

While in investment banking, Margaret noticed more women working in entry-level positions, which she attributed to recent diversity initiatives. She emphasized, however, that the firm mostly employed men in her unit and noticeably more so in higher-level positions. Margaret recalled, "It was not until you start talking to very senior people that there became an odd dynamic, a tangible difference in being a woman versus being not." Margaret attributed the fewer numbers of women in upper-level positions to a phenomenon well-established by gender scholars where women in finance and related fields are pushed out, often framed as "opting out," as they move along in their careers.[18] In general, among executives and MBAs, women and men begin their careers on a more equal footing. But over time the turbulence of these careers—especially in financial services—and the demands of parenting play a heavier toll on women's careers than men's, leading women to hold fewer high-ranking positions and to earn less compensation.[19]

Investment banks have a steep pyramid structure with limited opportunities for upward mobility. Three months into her job, Margaret started receiving calls from "every headhunter in all of New York City," competing with one another to hire analysts for other sectors of financial services. Headhunters are a common gateway from investment banking to hedge funds. Margaret said, to advance on Wall Street, "the most obvious options are private equity and hedge funds, in terms of where to funnel your skill-set post-investment banking." Since Margaret found the analysis most appealing, after a year, she responded to the headhunters and took a job at a startup hedge fund.

Overall, the diversity initiatives at investment banks made this a more accessible track for women to enter the hedge fund industry. Yet, some women expressed skepticism about joining a firm that used recruiters—the primary gatekeeper for those without elite social capital. Melissa, a twenty-something white woman, worked in a sales position at an investment bank's hedge fund unit but wanted to work at a small hedge fund. A recruiter contacted her about an attractive position; that is, until she discovered that the manager had a reputation for being difficult and aggressive. Because of this, Melissa didn't trust firms that use recruiters, because it indicated underlying problems, such as a negative culture or bad management, that tarnished the firm's reputation and prevented it from hiring through networks. Finding a job through a social tie, she said, gave her a better sense of the firm's culture.

Indeed, Sasha found her first hedge fund job through a recruiter. During our interview, she called the firm, "a shit show." Later, while having Easter dinner at her house with a friend who also worked at the firm, I learned more. The friend, Asif, who is South Asian American, explained how the two founders, both men, were lifelong best friends but had a falling out and hadn't spoken to each other for years, despite continuing to work together. It had gotten so bad he wanted to leave, but he said, "I've got to pay the mortgage," gesturing to his wife and children.

Sasha then recounted how one man had a substance abuse problem. Sasha said, "He was always drunk."

"No, he was on cocaine," Asif interjected. "That's why he did all those all-nighters."

"One day he walked into the office like this," said Sasha, doing an impression of the man by stumbling over to me and leaning on my shoulder. "It was 2:30 p.m.! It was so sad." She shook her head. Sasha eventually left the firm to work at a startup hedge fund in a man's house—an "uncomfortable" experience because of the close quarters.

Since entry-level investment banking programs are more diverse than hedge funds, this track may be a more common starting point for women and minority men in the hedge fund industry. The women I interviewed never recounted finding jobs at hedge funds through the networks they built in investment banking. Instead, headhunters provided an alternative entry point for those lacking professional or personal connections to the industry. While these gatekeepers may in theory open up more doors, it may start them off on an unequal footing, especially relative to candidates who have personal connections to the industry.[21]

The people I spoke with thought the social ties formed at prestigious universities and high-status investment banks provide access to better jobs than those provided by headhunters. While prospective investment analysts pursue technical training in financial research, modeling, and sales at the leading investment banks, many—but not all—form networks through social bonding rituals and working long hours. Interviewees described these networks as tribes or fraternities, a clue to how gender, race, and social class shape who is included or excluded, as in the social circle track tied to one's upbringing. Once a person gains insider status, it provides connections through shared colleagues and friends to people who have advanced from investment banking to hedge funds.

The Trading Track: It's a "Rat Race"

On the trading track, a person runs orders between stockbrokers and floor traders on the New York Stock Exchange. After proving oneself on the floor, they receive an offer on a hedge fund trading desk. This track to the industry captures the masculine icon of the scrappy trader who earns riches through speed, dexterity, and aggression on the trading floor. The trading track is one of the few avenues through which working- and middle-class opportunists, mostly men, without elite pedigrees can enter the inner workings of Wall Street, albeit a fragile and tenuous entrance. During the age of electronic markets, however, this path has become less feasible and, as a result, the industry is even more elite.

Today, few traders work on the stock exchange floor.[21] When I toured the New York Mercantile Exchange, a commodities future exchange the size and feel of a basketball arena lit with screens and bright lights, each pit had only a dozen traders at most. As we passed the large trading pits, my tour guide, Dennis, a white man in his sixties, said twenty years ago the pits "would have been packed with 100 guys"—and a few women. On that day, men casually walked about and leaned back in their chairs talking with one another and looking around at the screens. I noticed only one woman who brought coffee to a man on the floor. Dennis joked about the informal attire, mostly slacks and even jeans: "It's more like a beach scene with the way people are lounging about."

When Dennis traded in the 1980s and 1990s, he wore more formal attire. Back then, Dennis learned the hard way through trial and error on the floor because he didn't know anyone who would teach him how to trade. According to Dennis, most floor traders learned the ropes from having a broker dealer father or trader friends. The floor operated around these social circles, he said, and it was hard to break into these "cliques," but some people, like himself, did so by proving themselves.[22] Industry insiders considered this path unachievable in the age of electronic markets when most traders work at investment banks.

Manny, a second-generation Dominican American who grew up on Long Island, provides another example of the trading track. He recounted his own journey to a hedge fund over lunch at an Italian restaurant on the West Side of Manhattan. Manny's social ease was apparent in his relaxed, warm demeanor. After graduating with a degree in finance from a small liberal arts school in the Northeast, he was working for his parents' small business when he ran into a family friend who asked him, "Wouldn't you rather be on Wall Street?" He responded, "Yeah, of course I'd rather be on Wall Street, but I don't know anybody there. I didn't go to Stanford."

The woman's daughter worked in a training program at what is now the New York Stock Exchange. The following day, Manny met with the head of the firm, who took his résumé, barely looked at it, and then quickly scanned to the "extracurricular activities" at the bottom.[23] "Really? You played rugby for four years and didn't kill yourself?" he asked, gesturing to Manny's smaller stature. After talking about rugby for thirty minutes, the boss invited him to start work two hours later. Manny recalled, "The next day I was a clerk on the American Stock Exchange floor." Rugby signaled that Manny could hold his own on the trading floor, which requires someone who can handle pressure, get physical, and be aggressive—all repertoires for masculinity associated with working-class and racial minority men.[24]

Manny's starting salary as a clerk in the early 1990s was $19,000 a year—half that of a competing offer that he received for a job at an insurance company. Despite the low pay and long commute, and to his parents' dismay, Manny took the job. Within six months, his gamble paid off: he was hired into a training program for traders. Before he completed that program, he took a job as a trader at a midsize firm. Like Joseph, Manny hoped that this break would be his ticket to the top of the social class ladder.

Manny attributed his success to his ability to do rapid math in his head and to his ability to read people socially:

I'm not in Mensa. I wouldn't say that I'm the strongest mathematician in the world. My gift is I can do third grade math really fast. And as a market-maker, in general, that's all you really need to do. The smarter math whiz in the crowd can usually figure out the risk in a position or the risk in a trade better than I can, let's say, but during the time period that I was trading on the floor, a lot of that stuff flew out the window.

Manny explained how, back then, the trading floor required simple math because there was "so much more edge in a trade" and "more cushion with regard to the risk involved." But today's electronic markets require more sophisticated mathematical tools that make money off of small margins on the high volumes of trades.

In those early days, Manny said: "Your social skills were huge." The most skilled trader was one who understood how traders and brokers interacted on the stock exchange floor. Manny said he had to effectively read and build relationships with brokers. Otherwise, he said, "If you couldn't read a broker's body language, if you weren't aggressive enough but likeable enough to ingratiate yourself to the crowd and to the brokers, to be able to go back and forth and have them work with you as a market maker, you were pretty much out of the game."

When he first started trading, as a twenty-three-year-old from a non-elite background, Manny gleaned satisfaction from besting men who graduated from elite universities:

[I was] a little cocky because I felt like I had done well in my training program, and then I know that I come from a little college in upstate New York, and I'm standing next to these Harvard, Wharton, Penn, all these MBAs, these really smart guys, and I'm absolutely beating them on trades, because they are overanalyzing the positions . . . and I'm beating them by like 2–3 steps.

Manny, and others like him, relished having the skills and savvy to outperform elites.

After working a turbulent fifteen years as a trader, Manny was recruited by a billion-dollar hedge fund to develop a new portfolio in his area of expertise, which was apparently of substantial value (even though Manny downplayed his own skill set). At the time, Manny recalled, "I went to that firm feeling like I had made it to the mountaintop." He remembered settling into an office on the highest floor of a skyscraper in lower Manhattan. Looking out at the Statue of Liberty, he thought, "I'm finally here." He had a full salary—as opposed to entirely commission-based income—and benefits for the first time in his career. As the son of middle-class Dominican immigrants, Manny reflects the rags-to-riches narrative of the trading floor as a meritocracy where anyone could succeed on Wall Street.

But only six months later, the firm laid off Manny. Manny said he was hired "to teach them how to play the game." According to Manny, once he had taught them his specialized knowledge from nearly two decades trading in that area, the firm replaced him with two junior men who were paid less. Even though Manny reached the "mountaintop," he found that his expertise was easily replaceable—hedged out—because he lacked an elite pedigree and networks. These are forms of institutional and social capital that are simultaneously classed and racialized. "Game over," Manny said.

As a trader, Manny had to take on considerable professional risk and financial instability. He worked at several unstable firms—one collapsed after the manager faced insider trading charges—which placed pressure on his family, who relied on him to be the breadwinner. So, instead of returning to a risky career in trading, Manny accepted a friend's job offer at a trading software company that provided the stability he felt he needed as a husband and father. While this move was a step backward in his career, and a failure to comply with elite masculinity, it preserved his masculine status within his family as the stable breadwinner.

Manny's experience demonstrates the precarious nature of skill and expertise on Wall Street. Manny's mastery and lengthy experience as a trader gained him access to an upper-level job at a top-tier hedge fund. But, to return to the analogy of the "hedge" as a risk management strategy, Manny made an investment in developing know-how, and this knowledge was transferable, which does not hedge against the competitive and uncertain labor market. However, an elite pedigree and the resulting networks are nontransferable, so they provide a hedge that protects the person from the risks involved in this career path. If you build your hedge out of transferable assets, the hedge is always vulnerable. Because of this, Manny was easily replaced—he was hedged out.

Achieving hedgemonic masculinity can be tenuous and fleeting, especially for men like Manny. Thus, a path that is more open to men lacking racial and class privilege (relatively speaking) is even more volatile, making it less likely that they will succeed, or even stay in the game. Without racial and class privilege, Manny struggled to simultaneously uphold the normative masculinity of the trading floor (requiring bravado and social savvy), the hedgemonic masculinity of elite finance (requiring financial risk-taking and career turbulence), and the breadwinner masculinity of a husband and father (requiring financial and professional stability).

The paths of Manny and Dennis reflect a bygone era on Wall Street. Yet, many insisted that the self-starter path was true in the hedge fund industry's early days, when "two guys and a Bloomberg" (the leading stock market analysis and electronic trading platform) could launch a hedge fund out of their garage. This story reflects a common origin myth and its association with men.

In the past, Craig said an average "guy" who graduated from a state school could get a start on the stock exchange floor, make it rich, and launch a hedge fund. To Craig, this was what made the industry remarkable: "For every hotshot that gets written up in Trader Magazine, there are 10 guys who are walking in the street right now wearing khakis and street jeans, or at my firm t-shirts and shorts, who have 10 times as much money." Today, he said, it has become institutionalized and dominated by the graduates of elite universities. Craig, for one, has a PhD in molecular biology from Stanford University—a staple in today's hedge fund ranks.

The Academic Track: It's "Elementary Physics"

In the academic track, the fourth and final track to a hedge fund, a person starts off in a nonfinancial field in academia or law, often with a degree from a prestigious university. For example, a graduate with a PhD in artificial intelligence becomes disillusioned with academia, or Congress cuts funding for a postdoctoral fellowship. A tip from a friend or mentor leads the academic to apply their mathematical skills to the stock market.

The academic track benefits class-privileged white men in particular. In the United States, white men comprise 43 percent of doctorates and 44 percent of professional degrees, yet only 31 percent of the adult population. Moreover, these graduates are more likely to be class privileged, with parents who also attained doctorates and professional degrees. Since the degrees most sought after in finance are even more disproportionately attained by white men, they have an edge in following this path, which brings considerable prestige and recognition, fast-tracking them to success.[25]

While working as a postdoctoral fellow at the University of Wisconsin at Madison, Craig was recruited by a high school friend for a trading job on Wall Street that paid six figures. At first, he declined because, he said laughing, "I had just gotten my doctorate and was making big money, you know $20,000 a year." When the friend explained how much money Craig would make, he reconsidered and moved to New York to trade on the New York Stock Exchange. He recalled: "I was a floor trader standing around in crowds waving my arms up and down yelling for contracts." After five years, Craig transitioned to proprietary trading—where a firm manages its own money—and then to hedge funds. While Craig followed the same path as Manny, he had elite social and cultural capital—a clue to why his career thrived while Manny's petered out. Other people I spoke with bypassed the trading floor altogether because their networks and credentials took them to an investment bank or directly to a hedge fund, like Andrew in the social circle track.

Craig and others with graduate degrees in nonfinance fields emphasized that it was a shame that their skill sets would not be put to the betterment of society. Anselm, a white Austrian with a doctorate in physical chemistry, lost his job at NASA when his department underwent funding cuts. Unsure about what to do next, he sought advice from a friend in finance who convinced him that the mathematical tools he learned in graduate school would lead to a successful career in finance. When I met Anselm at a conference, he was raising money to launch his own hedge fund. Tall, trim, and blonde, Anselm had a cautious and thoughtful demeanor that seemed out of place during the boisterous social hour. As we talked, he looked around with wide eyes, explaining how he was there to network and find client investors.

Similarly, I met Arjun at an event with a lineup of hedge fund managers who paid thousands of dollars to make pitches to an audience of prospective investors. "It's a complete waste!" Arjun exclaimed with a big grin and lighthearted laugh as he described the societal value of having so many people with doctorates working in finance, including himself. He said, "They are a drain on the economy when they could be doing such better things, like building bridges. But instead, they are in finance where they make nothing."

Of course, hedge fund workers make money, but his meaning was clear: they don't contribute to society. Born in India, Arjun moved to the United States for college and then earned a doctorate in applied math. He wrote his dissertation on artificial intelligence in the early 1990s when "there was nothing to do with it." Arjun laughed as he said this, gesturing to how valuable it would be to society today.

Other PhDs shared this sentiment that the work wasn't always as intellectually thrilling as the industry hype suggested. When I asked Albert how he became a hedge fund manager, he looked me straight in the eyes, smiled, and said in jest, "failed academic." Albert is a white British man in his forties with a frank yet charming demeanor reminiscent of Pierce Brosnan. He has a doctorate in polymer chemistry from Cambridge University. Like Craig, Albert became "a little disillusioned about academia" while in a low-paying postdoctoral research position. He stressed how the departmental politics, career risk, and solitary work made it an unappealing path.

A former colleague who left academia for Wall Street advised Albert to follow suit. As Albert recalled, "He said finance is every bit as analytically challenging as what you're currently doing, which was eye-opening to me." This led Albert to read up on the industry:

> I started to read some books on finance, derivatives, and the like. A lot of the stuff in derivatives, Black Scholes,[26] and option pricing, is frankly a heat diffusion equation except that they call the variables by different terms. So, I thought, well, finance is just undergrad physics. I can do this. And so, with that very ignorant approach—not knowing anything more—I set up some interviews and the rest is history.

Albert applied for nine investment banking jobs, interviewed for eight, and received all eight offers. Two were in different units of the most prestigious firm at the time. He selected the one that offered strong mentorship, he said, attributing the decision to his ignorance.

The other offer was in a unit that would later break off to be one of the most successful hedge funds of all time. In retrospect, Albert remarked, "I really, in reality, I chose the wrong job. If I had chosen the other career track, I would potentially have been far more successful financially."

After more than fifteen years at three different investment firms and locations across three continents, Albert had the opportunity to spin off his current unit and start his own hedge fund during the aftermath of the 2008 financial crisis, as I return to in chapter 6. The difficulty of starting a firm in this environment was still apparent when I interviewed him seven years later. However, Albert's staying power was perhaps indicative of the attractiveness of his pedigree—filled with elite universities and high-status investment banks—to potential investors, even twenty years out of school.

Like other people on the academic track, and Margaret on the investment banking track, Albert's elite credentials afforded him both economic and symbolic value, providing a path inside the hedge. A doctorate confers status more valuable than technical training. At hedge funds, the particularities of each fund's strategy require that most training be done on the job. Business schools rarely provide courses on hedge fund investments, although more are becoming available as the industry's reputation grows. People explained how firms favor workers who are perceived as highly intelligent and critical thinkers, because they will be more easily molded into the firm's investment tradition. A high-status degree signaled desirable characteristics: the ability to learn on the job, be groomed into a firm's practice, and gain access to elite networks. This is indicative of how patrimonialism operates in this industry.

The experiences of Craig, Anselm, Arjun, and Albert were more common among the people I met than the bootstrapping narratives of Manny and Joseph. Yet, both reflect the prospects and limitations posed by the recent proliferation of hedge funds. For workers, the industry represents both the lucrative opportunities of a free market and the shortcomings of a society that fails to invest in fields that advance medical science, aerospace research, and artificial intelligence. These accounts are also revealing of how masculinity operates in this industry. The hedge fund manager as a scientific, market theorist is the new archetype of elite, white masculinity in finance. This new icon of masculinity legitimizes how gender, race, and class guide access to rewards and opportunities.

. . .

While the dominant discourse of upward class mobility in the hedge fund industry reflects a meritocratic, self-starter ideology, the common tracks people take to enter the industry reveal the importance of elite networks and prestigious credentials. Of the four common paths to working at hedge funds, the social circle track appeared the most common track and yet also the most difficult to access, especially for people without wealthy families or elite private schooling.

The tracks people take heavily rely on recruiting through social circles built around wealthy families, elite degrees, and high-status firms. These social circles allow hedge fund managers to carefully select employees in ways that fortify their own power and autonomy within their firms. As we will explore further in the coming chapters, the normative practices and beliefs that reinforce the hedge's boundaries also legitimize a social organization that bolsters the authority of the manager relative to that of their workers. This becomes even more apparent in the hiring and interview process. Drawing from my own firsthand experience with on-site interviews at hedge funds, and those of my interviewees, the next chapter walks us through an interview at a hedge fund.

3   Getting the Job

I awoke before my alarm went off at six o'clock. The excitement of the day had me on edge. I would be interviewed for a job at one of the world's largest hedge funds. The night before, I had traveled from Austin, Texas, where I was in graduate school, to a rural region about an hour's drive outside New York City for my on-site interview.

As I got ready for my interview, I wondered: What would the firm be like? Was it a cult, as the rumors said? Did it actually foster the culture of "extreme openness" featured in the recruiting materials?[1] The firm had a reputation for an investigatory, even interrogative, interview style to solicit applicants' honest reflections about their own strengths and weaknesses, especially failures. As an ethnographer trying to establish rapport to secure a field site, I wanted to be honest—to uphold their culture and my scholarly integrity—and solicit their trust. Would the interviewers question my interest or, even worse, my intentions?

Having worked late shuttling employees to and from the firm's annual pool party, Fred, a middle-aged Latinx man, arrived promptly at 7:30 a.m. to chauffeur me to the campus. As he told me about the firm, I remembered that elite firms often use drivers to elicit information on applicants' intentions and backstage manners. While being careful about what I said and how I behaved, I too used this as an opportunity to coax out his thoughts on the firm.

Fred ran his own car service, and the hedge fund accounted for about 80 percent of his business. He was one of many workers whose labor is outsourced by hedge funds to minimize who shares in the benefits and profit pool. Because the labor force is racially segregated, people of color often work in the low-wage service sector. Hedge funds reflect this social stratification with firms employing mostly white professional workers and then contracting service workers who are more likely to be people of color.

Before entering the campus, we stopped at a security station. As the security guard, a Black man who was also likely a contract worker, carefully checked the driver's ID, Fred explained that I was a guest. Sitting in the back of the high-end town car all by myself, I wondered if this is what it's like to be part of the wealthy elite. It felt uncomfortable and removed to have a chauffeur speaking on my behalf. The job was a communications analyst, so I knew not to get used to this kind of treatment. The grand hotel and town car were to give me a sense of what life is like at the top—the kind of life I might, in theory, achieve if I worked there.

An hour later, I found myself immersed in the "culture" interview—the first in-person hurdle to accessing the hedge fund lifestyle. This interview stood out that day as the only one where I was put on the spot about why I wanted the job. The interviewer, a white man named Jake, was trim with good posture, had short balding blond hair, and wore gray slacks paired with a simple white buttoned-down shirt. Although nice, he was not overly accommodating like the receptionist and recruiter. In his early thirties, Jake said he joined the hedge fund a decade ago, back when it employed fewer than 150 people (compared to over 1,000 today). As an associate on the "culture" team, he would have been at my peer level had I stayed in the industry.

With a welcoming tone, Jake started with an easy question: "What makes you interested in working here?" I responded honestly. I had studied the financial services industry—and hedge funds in particular—and wanted to learn about our changing economy. On the cutting edge of innovative workplaces, his firm was an ideal place to gain firsthand experience.

"I can see why you'd be interested in the culture," Jake mused. "In fact, it could even make for an interesting thing to study." He said this casually, as though helping to brainstorm ideas for my research. But the deliberate manner in which he asked questions and carefully watched my responses gave me the sense he was studying me. I smiled and nodded in agreement, "Yes, it would."

Jake then shifted to a more inquisitive, but not aggressive, demeanor—in keeping with the politeness of upper-class masculinity. He leaned back in his chair in observation while asking pointed questions. Was I quitting my PhD? Was I only motivated by the money? His tone wasn't rude or combative, but questioning, as though he was trying to solve a puzzle. "Are you not doing well in school?" He asked carefully, avoiding the word failing. His delivery reflected the courteous yet confrontational firm culture of extreme openness.

Then he explained, "I don't understand why you would want to leave school for this job. I've been wondering if it's that you just want to make a lot of money." I knew to tread carefully on the topic of money, as my interviewees stressed the need to be motivated by the work, rather than the money. The firm likely screened every applicant to ensure money wasn't their sole motive.

He repeated, "It just doesn't make sense why you would want to leave the academic track." Then he asked for the second time, "What makes you want to work here?" As we continued back and forth, I realized he was struggling to create a narrative about my career. It wasn't straightforward, as is expected in the industry, which implied I lacked passion or direction.

Knowing that I had to pull my own weight, I redirected the questioning back at him. This is part of the script for interviews in this industry. The applicant must come informed with questions demonstrating that they, too, are evaluating their options. At this firm, I had read, you should be candid and inquisitive, so I asked about the firm culture and his own path: "When you described your experience here, I noticed that you have transitioned between several roles, and I was wondering if you could provide some insight into what prompted that process?"

"Sure," Jake said, his manner changing as he moved to the hotseat. He shifted in his chair and looked around the room, collecting his thoughts as he spoke. Each job, he explained, evaluates you for your performance *and* aptitudes. If it seems like you are better suited for another role, he said, management changes your job to make the most of your ability. On investor calls, he struggled to engage the audience without sounding scripted, so they elevated him to a manager role—some might call this "failing up," a glass escalator for white men who fail, whether in feminine-typed jobs or not.[2] When management proved less suitable for him, too, he moved to his current role.

Despite the firm's emphasis on reflexivity, I couldn't help but notice how Jake's answer revealed a moment of tension in the firm's cultural script. Even after a decade in a culture that promoted extreme openness and personal growth, he rushed through explaining why previous positions were not the "best fit"—careful not to divulge his own shortcomings.

Twice Jake asked for examples of times when I had called out someone or pushed back on an idea. I had prepared to talk about my own receptiveness to feedback, because the hiring materials fixated on the shortcomings of people who resisted constructive criticism (perhaps telling of Wall Street's penchant for arrogance). But I wasn't prepared to show my ability to confront someone else, a necessity for challenging others to grow, according to the firm.

I gave a generic example of how my graduate mentor taught her students to question each other's ideas, point out logical fallacies, and identify analytical gaps. Jake didn't look satisfied with this answer. I described my advisor in neutral terms, yet he responded in a way that is revealing of stereotypes of women leaders. "Your mentor sounds like a strong personality," he said. "Have you ever really pushed back when you have disagreed with her?"

"Yes. For this [job application]." I said, grinning. "She didn't think I should apply, but I explained why it was an important opportunity."

Jake's shoulders relaxed and his gaze softened, expressing curiosity. This got to the heart of his reservations about me. "What were her concerns?"

"She is worried I won't finish my dissertation," I said. "She doesn't want my energy diverted after I have made it this far."

"And how did you convince her?"

"I told her my reasons and made a plan for writing it in the next year."

"And she agreed to it?"

"She agreed to considering it further," I said. "She seemed to think my plan was reasonable." I did my best to embrace the culture of extreme openness.

· · ·

In the last chapter, we explored the supply-side factors that funnel people into this industry. Now, I investigate the demand-side of this equation: how and why people get hired within the industry's particular labor market. While dominant industry discourses reinforce a rags-to-riches story of upward class mobility, behind this tale are accounts of the importance of elite networks, prestigious credentials, and family ties—much like the tracks to the industry in chapter 2.

I find that elite social and cultural capital more easily secures access for white men while hindering the advancement of women and minority men.[3] I call this dynamic a voucher for hedgemonic masculinity, because gatekeepers at firms vouch for new hires based on shared social networks and cultural capital. This hedges the risks involved in hiring someone perceived as an "unknown," that is, without personal connections. Indicative of a system in which people are hedged out, these hiring practices construct social boundaries around who does and does not gain access to the industry.

The Hiring Process

The people I interviewed recounted lengthy job searches and application processes. Julie, a thirty-something Asian American woman, said she submitted over two hundred applications to find her last job. Others confirmed that her experience is the industry norm, even when the market is good. Several stressed how it was always better to apply for a job when you already had one. Those currently unemployed described longer job hunts and less appealing prospects.

Once a person's résumé rises to the top of the large stack of applications, the person may be invited for a series of interviews, a hedging process framed as determining "fit." Fit is a euphemism for social class[4] but also contains implicit meanings about gender and race. It became clear that this discourse of fit reinforces inclusion based on homophily: the tendency to favor people like you.[5] And, as I show here, "fit" also serves as a cover for more overt forms of exclusion.

The Chemistry Aspect

Consistent with my own experience interviewing at hedge funds, the people I spoke with described the process as primarily concerned with whether the person is a "good fit." In general, people recounted interviews in gender, class, and race neutral terms, saying that interviews allow the employer and candidate alike to determine if the position is a good fit. Several defined this in ambiguous terms: someone who "clicked" or sparked "chemistry." In reality, perceptions of sameness, shaped by gender, race, and, class, determined who fit and who didn't.

A former successful hedge fund manager who sold his firm, Vincent now advises hedge fund clients at a large investment bank. Because of the long hours and close working conditions, Vincent stressed the importance of "chemistry" in hiring:

> The hiring decision at a hedge fund is very much a people decision, like there's a chemistry aspect to it. There's a connection between the interviewer and the interviewee, which goes something like, "I could work with that person every day. I'm going to spend a lot of time—probably more time than I spend with my wife—so I need to be able to get along with that person."

In her book *Pedigree,* Lauren Rivera finds that top-tier investment banks, consulting agencies, and law firms largely select entry-level hires based on perceptions of cultural fit, such as expressions of passion for work and hobbies. High-status credentials (an Ivy League graduate, for example) open access to elite firms. In hiring, these forms of cultural capital solicit recognition—often on a subconscious, emotional level—from prospective employers. Even among graduates of high-status universities, Rivera finds that recruiters make their selections in ways that privilege those from elite backgrounds.[6] While homophily enables some people to get in the door and build trust with future colleagues, it also forecloses opportunities to people perceived as different.

A shared sense of passion was used as a litmus test to screen out applicants who were only interested in the industry's money and status. To understand applicants' motives, Wayne, a forty-something Asian American founder, said he asked them, "Why do you want to be in quantitative finance?" To me, he said, "I think, in general, you have to be truly passionate about what you're doing and not doing it just because you wanna make a lot of money. I try and fish that out when I interview people. I don't hire people who I think just want the money. Actually, usually if they mention money at all, I cross 'em off the list." Indicative of a culture of work infatuation and overwork, Wayne valued passion for financial modeling.

Reflecting on the hiring process, Margaret too said an applicant must be excited for the detail-oriented and all-consuming work. She said, "Whenever you walk into a hedge fund interview for a job, the most important thing that you can demonstrate is that you genuinely like looking at securities, and that is absolutely critical, because this is not a job where you can get up and walk away and call it a day. It is always, always happening." Here, Margaret used the word "like" to describe financial analysis. At other times, she used the word "love," as did many other people I spoke with who thought this made the industry's long hours and high demands bearable. This discourse of passion reflects an upper-class ideal for pursuing a vocation—work that you enjoy and find purpose in.

Margaret, and other women, embraced this industry discourse of liking, even loving, financial analysis. Yet, it was common during interviews and at events for people to attribute the low numbers of women to a "pipeline problem." That is, they thought women lacked interest in financial analysis and didn't pursue the field. For instance, a white woman, who had left finance to work in tech, referred me to her friend Steven, a thirty-something Asian American man. Not knowing that she began her career in finance, he cited her as an example of the "pipeline problem." He said she didn't share his passion for financial analysis, enjoyed fashion and the arts instead, and thus would never pursue a career in finance. When I asked if he knew she had previously worked in financial analysis, he expressed surprise, backtracked, but then reasserted his stance, "Oh, no, I didn't realize that. But still, not many women enter finance." Although the passion discourse appears gender neutral, it actually reflects gendered biases about interests and ability,[7] even though men and women alike expressed passion for the work (refer to chapter 5).

In probing the idea of "good fit," interviewees provided insight into how hiring is gendered and racialized. Nicole was hired as the only woman on an eighty-person investment team. A twenty-something white woman, Nicole cited a recent time when she strongly advocated for a woman candidate: "I knew that she would be pretty heavily penalized in fit for, you know, being different." Countering the norm for hiring men at Nicole's firm, women stand out and appear not to "fit." In contrast, Nicole said, men blend in more and are routinely endorsed by other men, which is naturalized and framed as fit:

> In recruiting, I have to push so hard to get a woman ranked in the top five, because what happens is, they ask around the room, "Does anyone know these *guys?*" [my emphasis] We'll rank them 1–10 and one of the big factors is if anyone knows about these guys from college, because it's all on-campus recruiting. And the guys are like, "Yeah, he was on the same sports team I was on. I'm sure he's a good guy." It's like even if they don't know them personally, they'll still vouch for them as part of their extended social network. But if the girls are on different sports teams or don't have as much friend overlap, nobody will vouch for them.

Nicole noted how college social networks and extracurricular activities such as sports teams are gender specific, and racially and class coded, as the target colleges are predominantly white with affluent students.[8] Even if the hiring committee members have no formal experience with the candidate, men vouch for other men in alumni, fraternity, and sports networks, which are used as a proxy for merit. Meanwhile, Nicole said, "I used an incredible amount of political capital to get the one intern in." This voucher for elite masculinity reveals how gender, race, and class shape evaluations of merit in hiring.[9]

At Nicole's firm, this voucher is then confirmed through an interactional process in which the interviewer and interviewee talk informally about their interests and leisure activities. Nicole described how this thirty-minute interview on "fit"—much like the culture interview I encountered—penalizes applicants who had less common ground with the interviewer. Questions included: "What do you do on the weekends? What sports do you play? Who are your friends? What do they like to do?" And so, Nicole said, "I've actually been on the phone for a lot of these, and the ones that work the best are the guys that come in and say, 'I played football or lacrosse or soccer,' and someone else in the office will be like, 'Me too! Do you know so and so?' And they'll just talk about their mutual friends from college for a half an hour." According to Nicole, a "good fit" is evaluated based on shared social and cultural experiences. These shared experiences may be based on gender-typed sports, racially segregated activities, and class-structured access to elite universities or prep schools.

Nicole then explained how this focus on hobbies may exclude people, "The people who don't have that point of reference flounder, because it's really hard to build a conversation that's built around the interviewer where it's like, 'What do you like to do on the weekends?' 'Oh, I like to run.' And the interviewer's response is, 'Oh, I don't think we have any other runners here.'"

Nicole's firm is dominated by people who grew up in upper-middle-class communities in the Northeast, attended elite boarding schools, and graduated from Ivies. Nicole said this became an implicit criterion: "the other thing [they look for] is where people are from and where they went to high school, specifically." With a middle-class upbringing, Nicole believed her employment was contingent on having an elite degree.

In addition to her pedigree, Nicole said, she was hired to increase gender diversity on an eighty-person team in which it was altogether absent. Before she joined, the sole woman analyst had moved to a client services role when she got married. The team's managing director, Nicole said, assumed that the woman would soon start having children and need a job that allowed her more time and energy to mother. According to Nicole, he asked that woman to "take over recruiting" because "we need to hire women." The woman hired Nicole to take on this sizable task, and as a junior analyst no less. Nicole said, "So I was hired to be the first woman and to start this push into hiring a more diverse class."

Margaret thought that despite these efforts to hire a limited number of women, the industry "doesn't really try" to make it more attractive to women. She said, "The industry tries to find women who can fit within the parameters of the culture as opposed to changing the culture to fit the parameters of women. . . . They don't even think that that's what they are doing, but that is absolutely what happens."

I wondered what hedge funds look for in women who fit within the culture. "Those who are not easily offended," Margaret replied. "Women who engage like men." Talking about one's personal life and feelings were discouraged, she said. Then she added, "Women who are willing to work really, really, really long hours, and place their careers the clear and obvious number one priority." According to Margaret, women encountered a high bar for entry; they must conform to the industry's expectations for masculinity even though they don't incur the same benefits as men. The problem, Margaret said, was a lack of impetus to "change the system" itself.

Similarly, Sharon spoke of the resistance to change, especially in small businesses. A forty-something white woman, Sharon gave the example of being the owner of a small stationary store: "[If] somebody came in and said, you have to hire these five people, I'd go, 'Huh? I am going to hire my mother, brother.'" Sharon expressed defeat, saying, "I don't know how you change small businesses," but then identified how client investors, especially large institutions, could put pressure on hedge funds to diversify their ranks.

The hiring process at these small firms opened or prevented access to jobs based on a narrow and ambiguous definition of "good fit." A voucher for hedgemonic masculinity and whiteness conferred extra social and cultural capital to white men with elite credentials, giving them gold stars as top candidates. Once inside, these industry insiders could then extend a voucher for new hires, obscuring the preference for hiring white men and rendering it as the result of networks, credentials, and cultural fit. These processes built boundaries around who is let in and who is hedged out.

Not a "Good Mix"

Homophily can't fully account for who these elite firms hire and who is hedged out. Insiders believed that firms outright excluded some people, especially mothers. For instance, Paul Tudor Jones, the billionaire founder of long-standing Tudor Investment Corporation, incited controversy when he said women weren't as committed to the work. Of the assumed all-consuming passion of mothering, he said, "Every single investment idea . . . every desire to understand what is going to make this go up or go down is going to be overwhelmed by the most beautiful experience . . . which a man will never share, about a mode of connection between that mother and that baby. And I've just seen it happen over and over." Because of motherhood, he argued, "You will never see as many great women investors or traders as men—period, end of story. And the reason why is not because they are not capable. They are very capable."[10] Jones captures how, as sociologist Mary Blair-Loy finds, an expectation for complete devotion to mothering conflicts with an expectation for a total devotion to work.[11]

Afterward, several people I spoke with referenced Paul Tudor Jones's comments as evidence of persistent discrimination against women. Sharon lamented how Jones's sexist comments validated rampant sexism at other firms. Sharon, like many others, cited hedge fund managers she knew who never hire women on principle. She said, "He brought out of the closet what we all know still exists. If you're a hedge fund, and it's your company, you can do whatever you please. If you're Goldman Sachs, you have to be a little more politically correct." According to Sharon, hedge fund managers have considerable discretion over whom they hire, fire, and mentor, allowing women fewer opportunities as traders or fund managers. She said, "I've actually sat next to a hedge fund guy who told me that he doesn't hire any woman, because he really doesn't like women in the workplace. And that was just three years ago."

Because the industry is small and reputation-based, candidates have limited options to pursue recourse for discrimination—and hedge fund managers rarely face consequences for doing so. The fear of being labeled a troublemaker made people I spoke with hesitant to give specifics, yet they often confirmed that they witnessed and experienced these types of discrimination throughout their own careers. Because Sharon held a senior role and was her own boss, she could speak more freely about these obstacles and gave many illustrative examples.

I wondered how the mentality expressed by Jones influenced her own career. Sharon, who is not a parent, recalled a time when a colleague left, leaving a big client "up for grabs":

> I was next in line to really get this client. And one of the guys who also covered the client went to my boss and said, "They don't like women. And they don't particularly like Jews, so I don't think you should give

them blah blah blah." And so, my boss comes up to me and says I don't think you should cover them. I don't think it's a good mix.

Hiring people, and matching them with clients, based on gender, race, or class, as Sharon recounted, is discriminatory. While Sharon's example is more overt, these forms of sexism and racism were often translated in coded language like "fit" and "a good mix" by other interviewees.

In another example, Sharon recounted a time when the hedge fund manager denied her a promotion because he "needed" to hire a colleague's brother:

Even some of my closest male colleagues would still love me, tell me things, and then make different decisions because, "Oh wait, I am sorry but so and so's brother needed to get hired. Shit happens." I don't think that's just reflective of working on Wall Street or at hedge funds or in venture capital, but when there's big money, greed, power, people protect their own. And sometimes it's the guy in the parish, the guy in the corner, the guy in the whatever.

Because of the high monetary stakes in this industry, according to Sharon, hedge fund managers relied on trust and loyalty-based networks—familial, religious, or local communities—when conducting business deals and hiring employees. People restricted access to resources and opportunities for themselves and their personal networks.

And these tight-knit networks were hard to break into. As a woman in trading, Sharon recalled: "It was very clear that being a woman on the trading floor on Wall Street, even though you were top-five salesperson, ran the group, that life is not a meritocracy. I don't golf. I don't live in Connecticut. I don't go to all of the same clubs. All those things matter. And those are great disappointments."

For younger women, however, a sense of similarity could work against them. Outside recruiters may create obstacles to entry for younger women because recruiters, Margaret said, "always appear in the form of young, twenty-something year-old girls who look just like you (for many younger women)." Margaret warned, "Recruiters are not your friends—not a friend of the candidate, anyway." The recruiters, she said, "are fun" and "you think that they are your friend":

> So, you tell them everything. You're like, "Oh, I don't like this part of my job. I hate this part of my job." And then, they write that all down. . . . Their goal is to filter out as many candidates as possible and pick out the best batch for the people who do pay them, which is the firms. I think a lot of young people fall into the trap of seeing somebody who looks like them across the table, spilling their guts, and then getting dinged for the fact that they just told them a bunch of things that are negatives.

Margaret provides insight into how hiring can disadvantage women: "They get filtered out." Since recruiters at headhunting firms are largely young women, women candidates were placed at a disadvantage because they are more likely to trust one another as peers. In this case, homophily does not necessarily privilege candidates and can instead expose their vulnerabilities in ways that may lower their chances of getting the job. Others mentioned how finding jobs through recruiters could imply that the person can't build the right networks, casting the applicant as less well-connected and trustworthy.

Hedge fund managers can basically do what they please when it comes to hiring. Some even explicitly justified excluding women with the belief that motherhood prevents women from performing in a demanding job as a trader or fund manager. At other times, leadership practiced favoritism, giving preference to family or friends when hiring or promoting, and blocking opportunities for others. Hedge fund managers faced few pressures to change their exclusionary ways, especially in firms too small to even have human resources personnel. By exercising unbridled discretion over personnel decisions, especially hiring and mentoring, managers hedge people out in an environment lacking scrutiny or repercussions for discriminatory employment practices.

. . .

It was clear that the hiring and interview processes at hedge funds often led people to be included and excluded in systematic ways. While Lauren Rivera foregrounds how cultural capital in hiring creates social class homophily at elite firms, I find that gender, race, and class simultaneously frame who is determined to be a good or bad "fit." Especially in a patrimonial system, cultural fit is about more than homophily; it is about hedging some people in and other people out to create an organization with few checks and balances for power holders' authority.

A voucher for hedgemonic masculinity hedges hiring risks by privileging the social and cultural capital of high-status, white men. Successful applicants bruised a knee playing rugby, were hazed at Dartmouth's Alpha Delta Phi fraternity, and cruised on a yacht in the Hamptons. And this process all but precludes access to someone perceived as an "unknown"—without ties to this elite social world. For those lacking gender, racial, and class privilege, access to the industry is granted yet contingent on conforming to hedgemonic masculinity, at least to the extent it was accessible to them. This made employment for women and lower-status men more insecure and unpredictable.

Embracing Extreme Openness

As for my own prospects of getting a job, the rest of my interview went much smoother. After the "culture interview" came the "team interview" with two white women, my potential supervisors, who were the same age and rank I was when I left the industry five years earlier. As the interview went on, I grasped why Jake "didn't understand" why I would apply for this role: it's considered a "red flag" when an applicant applies for a job below their skill level. I would essentially be starting from the beginning all over again.

Next was the interview finale: a group debate on a public issue. This surprise interview hadn't been listed on the day's schedule, perhaps to catch the candidate off guard. The recruiter brought in two men: the first was an employee to mediate and the second was another applicant competing with me for the job. The mediator, a South Asian American man in his mid-thirties, wore a polo shirt with a sports team logo and had a warm, relaxed demeanor, smiling generously. The other applicant, a tall, thin white man in his mid-twenties, had an affable and casual air about him reflected in his appearance: He wore a relaxed blazer and chinos and sported glasses with thick, black plastic frames. The man worked in publishing in New York City and "wanted to try something new"—likely something that better afforded city life.

I had anticipated this interview, having read about it on online forums, like Glass Door and Wall Street Oasis, where applicants anonymously disclosed their experiences of heated debates and awkward interrogations at this firm. I imagined a group of people all jockeying to look superior. The reality clashed with my expectations. As the mediator explained, the goal wasn't to attack the other candidate's views, but to have an honest, open, and constructive debate.

The mediator read us the prompt, "Is television harmful for US society?" Then he left us to brainstorm ideas together. I wondered if it would be better to catch the other applicant off guard, but decided against that approach. He seemed like a nice and thoughtful guy, and the goal was to work together as a team to reach a more nuanced and logical understanding of the issue.

When the mediator returned, the other applicant started the discussion. He claimed that television didn't influence society but reflected it, as in the case of reality TV. My mind immediately jumped to teaching reflection theory in Introduction to Sociology and the leading critiques of that theory. I held myself back, thinking that I had an unfair advantage and that I might come off as arrogant or, perhaps worse, that I could not form an original stance. Instead, I said that TV prompted viewers to empathize with someone different or challenge their assumptions about a social issue, giving the example of how *Orange Is the New Black* forced its audience to question the prison system.

As the discussion continued, we each took turns reflecting on the topic, posing questions, and brainstorming counterfactuals. At one point, the mediator asked me to clarify a point I made, and I forgot where I was for a minute, talking as though I was in the classroom. I cited how the Black Lives Matter protests in Ferguson and Baltimore spread around the country in part because *The Wire* helped a wider audience understand the context of police violence. I immediately realized I had crossed into dangerous interview territory, especially at a hedge fund in one of the nation's wealthiest counties, by discussing antiracist politics.

In the end, I didn't get the job. I don't know if it was mentioning Black Lives Matter, dominating the conversation, or applying for a job below my education and experience level. Or maybe, the extent to which I embraced their call for extreme openness was a little too open and a bit too extreme. My attempts to enact hedgemonic masculinity felt unconvincing and forced. Embracing the culture of extreme openness was perhaps easier for the other applicant, a white man, than for me as a white woman. But either way, the outcome assuaged my mentor's concerns that the industry would be too difficult to leave a second time.

4 *Inside the Firm*

"What do you think determines success in this industry?"

Albert pressed his fingers together, leaned back in his chair, and told me, "Ultimately, the business is very, very simple. . . . If you make money, you can dictate your own terms, and if you don't make money, you're perennially going to be going cap in hand to management." He calculated his successes in terms of individual merit measured in profit. The ability to make money allowed Albert to set his own terms, ascend the ranks at an investment bank, and eventually found his own hedge fund. "It is pure, absolute commercialism."

When he was starting out in investment banking, Albert recalled working in a "flat" group where "everyone was pulling together as a team." He appreciated that "it was not people crawling over the backs of everyone else to get further up the ladder." Over time, though, as the firm incentivized top performers—perhaps those who dictated their own terms—hierarchies became clear. "You give them titles and fiefdoms," he said, "and so a very, very flat structure became quite pyramidal."

Albert believed his own hedge fund captured the culture he'd appreciated in his early career: individualism within a collective culture. Everyone could contribute within a "fairly transparent, fairly level playing field." He told me he paid the first six employees almost equally to encourage them to compete together for the firm's bottom line. Their goals reflected an organizational value, collectivism, and a neoliberal one, individualism. In reality, Albert's firm was "flat" because it lacked middle managers and human resources roles—both feminized jobs supporting the well-being, rights, and growth of employees.

Preoccupied with profits, hedge funds are designed to maximize value for investors. In this way, they embody the ideals of finance capitalism. Under neoliberalism, executives no longer understand a company's primary purpose as the exchange of goods and services to consumers but the provision of value to shareholders. By this logic, layers of managers and bureaucracy detract from creating profit; hedge fund executives instead streamline their staff and embrace laissez-faire economics to better orient on the whims of the market and deliver returns on investment.

With relish, hedge fund executives and their employees praised their firms as "flat" and "lean" (relative to investment banks) and suggested these qualities were what afforded their firms the flexibility to adapt to and withstand abrupt market changes. Flattening firms, they said, enabled employees to openly communicate and fully participate in achieving a unified goal. Yet, without managerial roles, there was, in fact, a much steeper social hierarchy at play: the executive alone was empowered to make final decisions and wield authority. The rhetoric of flatness made that authority seem natural or necessary. And the pervasive ideology of whiteness and masculinity legitimized the leader's power. Whatever the executives might say, their hedge funds were anything but fair and level playing fields.

In the last two chapters, I established how people get through the organizational boundary or hedge to gain a foothold in these firms. Now inside, it's time to see which hedge fund employees gain access to status, money, and power—and which ones fail. When executives strip away layers of bureaucracy and management in new, supposedly flat organizational forms, what are the consequences for inequality?

To answer this question, we will dive into the underlying assumptions and everyday practices of hedge funds that tip the balance of power to executives like Albert. As in other firms, organizational logic—the rules, job descriptions, performance evaluations, and compensation systems—encodes shared expectations for workers. These beliefs are *implicitly* gendered, racialized, and classed, ensuring that inequalities endure over time.[1]

The Key Man

Hedge funds are designed to establish a flatter organization structure, but the operating agreements, drafted for prospective investors, reveal the concentration of executive power. "Key personnel" sections profile the chief investment, executive, operations, and compliance officers (who often hold multiple roles). These underscore the chief investment officer's (CIO) role as the primary investment decision maker. The fact that marketing materials and legal agreements promote these "key" personnel in part explains why the firms favor elite credentials, which confer legitimacy and encourage prospective investors to entrust their money to one firm over another.

Operating agreements emphasize the firm's ability to retain its stable slate of key personnel. A "key man" clause is often included, allowing client investors to withdraw their money should specific key personnel, usually the CIO, become incapacitated or leave the firm. Its existence signals that firms' operation is, in practice, dependent on one or two executives (assumed to be men). Potential investors also find disclosures about potential conflicts of interest. They are given avenues to request information about how much money a firm's chief executives have personally invested in the fund—that is, how much of a stake the top team has in its fund's performance.

And finally, the legal documents specify the firm's fee structure, usually in the form of the *management fee* and the *performance fee*. The management fee covers the firm's basic operating costs (equipment, office space, and salaries) and is usually 1–2 percent of the fund's net assets. The performance fee distinguishes hedge funds from other investment firms. The idea is that the firm should receive a certain percentage of its investment returns (20 percent is the industry standard) to motivate it to perform well. This bonus for the firm also allows hedge fund managers to claim not income taxes, but the lower-rate capital gains taxes, a crucial factor in their astronomical incomes.

My interviewees cited all these practices as part of their organizations' "flatness." In practice, however, the structure was acutely hierarchical and gendered, as in the "key man" clauses. The contracts created boundaries, or hedges, affirming the autonomy, authority, and value of firms' "key men." Within these boundaries, hedge funds establish their own norms for managing money, employees, and workplace culture.

Flattening the Firm

A workplace culture fixated on flatness, in effect, upheld a neoliberal ideology of maximizing efficiency and profit. Embracing this culture, the people I met repeatedly noted the firm's sizeable assets as a more important status marker than the number of employees. As Diane, a fifty-something white founder, said, "We've made a lot of money; we have billions and billions of dollars under management. We have hands down one of the best hedge fund track records. And, again, the process has just been so flat." That flatness, in turn, made success traceable to each employee's ability to self-manage: "Everybody here is an adult, so they require very little supervision." Clearly, Diane prides herself on managing huge amounts with smaller payrolls than other firms: "Neither my partner nor I have a desire to manage a lot of people. I think we have a desire to run a lot of capital, but not build some monstrosity of an organization." Over and over, executives lauded maximizing profit, managing voluminous assets, and employing few people as evidence of their firms' exceptionalism.

Executives touted the two-tiered employee structure, partners and support staff, intended to create a collaborative workplace and foster employee autonomy at the same time. Executives studiously avoided hiring—and paying—personnel they perceived as extraneous, such as middle managers and human resources officers. In this way, flatness was not about lowering hierarchy. Rather, flatness assigned multiple job functions, urged self-management, and outsourced all other roles. There were few opportunities for advancement. The smallest firms employed just one lead investment manager; a set of partners who covered noninvestment functions, such as legal, compliance, and client services; and outsourced contractors to handle information technology and payroll services. Deborah, a fifty-something white founder, said of staffing, "I considered how many hats one person can wear and what were the right mix of hats that any person can fill. For instance, can the accountant also be the receptionist? Can they book tickets?"

Within this structure, hedge funds divide labor between what is called the "front" and "back" office (though in a literal sense, most operate within chic, open-plan offices). These terms correspond to the firm's core functions: soliciting investors and investing their money. Personnel who bring in or invest the money work in the front office. And back office personnel handle tasks like operations, compliance, and administration.

Implicitly, the front office holds more importance than the back office. The people I interviewed deemed market-oriented and client-facing tasks higher-value work because support roles neither

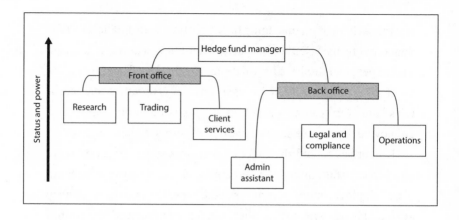

FIGURE 1. Hedge Fund Organizational Chart.

bring in money (sales positions) nor directly generate money (investment positions). This perception justified higher front-office pay.
Within the front office, they noted a secondary division in which investment teams earned more than client services teams. Through
the gender-typing I have described, which sorted men into investment jobs and women into client-facing jobs, it seemed "natural" for
men to out-earn women. My interviewees confirmed this gender division, describing firms marked by mostly men on investment teams
but more women in client services.[2] The back office, then, tended to
be more diverse in terms of race, gender, and class. But these positions presented fewer opportunities for promotion and leadership
roles (there is usually only one executive-level back office position in
a hedge fund, compared to several in the front office). The typical division of labor indicated that white men tended to dominate hedge
funds in numbers, status, authority, and income.

Gendered and Racialized Assignments

Even within the front office investment teams, assignments were often patterned by gender, race, ethnicity, and nationality. White men

usually began their hedge fund careers within expertise areas called "generalist" or perceived as technical (say, industrials or distressed debt). White women recounted gendered assignments, such as retail.

The only woman among eight incoming analysts, Nicole recalled her first impressions of a hedge fund. She told me "it was just very strange" to be "immediately identified as 'the girl.'" And it affected her assignment on the investment team:

> I was the only one there who had majored in the sciences, and I had written a senior thesis in biology and studied geology as my second major. So, I was in a unique situation to cover health care or biotech or energy or metals and mining or something. [Instead] I was assigned to cover retail, because I was "the girl." And they put two guys who had never taken a geology course in their life on metals and mining and energy.

Nicole thought her supervisors failed to make the most of her skill set, and she lost the chance to further hone her expertise in her field of interest, all because of her gender.

Margaret was also the only woman on her firm's investment team. Though she had a degree in science, her work focused on retail and industrial investments. It was isolating, she said, that there were seven men for every woman in a firm of just forty employees; the other women were an office manager and three admin assistants. Within her own team, gender affected the dynamics to the degree that she said it was the biggest challenge of her career. For instance, Margaret cited how men communicated in ways (like hogging airtime) that prevented her from contributing to team decisions.

Meanwhile, people of color tended to specialize in a geographic area loosely related to their race, ethnicity, and/or nationality. Foreign- and US-born people alike experienced this racial sorting, especially Asian Americans who were often typecast regardless of their birth country. Lisa, who is Taiwanese and in her thirties, managed one of her midsized firm's portfolios focused on "emerging markets" (economies in the Global South). Yet, "her" area included Korea and Taiwan, which the World Bank calls developed. The fact that US investors nonetheless considered them "emerging" seemed tied to beliefs about Western superiority against a world economy witnessing Asian ascendency.[3]

Lisa's racialized portfolio, consisting of smaller-economy emerging and frontier markets, triggered what Lisa called "perception arbitrage" in which predominantly white, Western-born industry peers and investors thought her investments were riskier than others':

> I manage what people say is a high-risk portfolio, but to me it's basically a perception arbitrage, because some countries in my portfolio have, I would say, less risk than many of the markets in the developed markets. For example, Saudi Arabia, that's my highest conviction area. And year-to-date, it's made pretty good money for me. It's a very stable government balance sheet, very compelling world story . . . and vastly under-covered by most of the brokerage firms. I think there is a very interesting perception arbitrage [of] Saudi Arabia.

Such racialized specializations appeared to make it harder for analysts of color to reach the C-suite. Even for those of Asian descent, who had higher numbers in entry-level positions than other people of color, these racist beliefs seemed to make them less likely than white colleagues to build the asset-rich networks required to become executives. That is, unless they had access to transnational investment networks (refer to chapter 6).

Hedge funds that specialized in quantitative strategies—those developed around algorithmic and systematic trading models as opposed to discretionary trading strategies—appeared to go against the typical gender- and race-typing of the industry but were not race-neutral. Because the quantitative strategies are math-based, it seemed they were racially typed according to stereotypes about the mathematical abilities of Asians and Asian Americans. Wayne, who is Asian American, described quantitative finance as a more level playing field than other specializations: "Most of the people I hired were women." When it came to racial composition, however, he mused: "I don't know what's in the water in China. They're all mainland Chinese. . . . Most of the résumés I get are mainland Chinese, and most of my hires were mainland Chinese. I don't know what's going on." Continuing, Wayne said, Chinese students moved to the United States to study mathematics, physics, and finance, then went on to pursue careers in finance.

The "model minority" and mathematical prowess myths may seem almost positive. But here and elsewhere, these myths tokenize Asian Americans and don't help to push them into the C-suite.[4] West Coast–based Wayne and Linda, a hedge fund's head of operations, were two exceptions. This is consistent with research in both the finance and technology sectors, where Asian Americans are often perceived as especially technically competent while their leadership potential is overlooked. Margaret Chin identifies corporate America's "bamboo ceiling," a barrier constructed by what these organizations fail to provide Asian American workers: role models, colleague trust, and leadership support.[5]

Over time, racialized specializations type-casted the expertise of people of color and limited their opportunities to advance. White supremacy, as a system, leaves white people in an "unmarked" referent category, with non-white people framed as stigmatized deviations from that norm.[6] In elite finance, predominantly white leadership and client investors transformed this worldview into a preference for US- and European-focused funds. Insiders insisted that the preference is based on perceived risk and a disinclination to invest in niche funds. All this meant investments in the Global South were usually considered higher risk. And these distinctions shaped how firms distributed pay, status, and authority.

This was not only true for Asian-heritage employees. I met people of color whose specialties lay in the regions perceived to match their race and ethnicity, regardless of where they were born. Assignments reflected an assumption that people of color are inherently more knowledgeable about other people of color.[7] At a conference, I met a Senegalese woman whose early mentor—a white man—explicitly advised her not to specialize in investments anywhere in Africa. She needed, he said, to counteract the stigma of being African and highlight her varied expertise. And so, she started out specializing in countries in Latin America, reifying the notion that those from the Global South simply aren't suited to expertise in Western investments. These specializations capture how racialized tasks, knowledge, and labor construct status hierarchies in even ostensibly flat organizations and industries—especially when they are predominantly white.[8]

The Parent Tracks

The "mommy track" is a term for workplaces pushing women into jobs perceived as more suitable for mothers (regardless of actual parental status).[9] But this dynamic played out through a double standard: fathers were seen as particularly in need of higher-paying executive positions that gave them breadwinner wages as well as control over their schedules and availability for quality parenting, such as going to soccer games and on family vacations. Meanwhile, the people I interviewed considered client services a better career for women, because these jobs were perceived as more "family-friendly."[10] A number of women brought up managers who encouraged them, after getting married or starting a family, to transfer into client services—

and embrace the "mommy track." Others shared that, under the management assumption that they would *eventually* have children, they too were pushed into client-facing roles.

To be sure, workers on the investment team and in client services were required to put in long hours and considerable effort. Client services team members described working long hours, hosting client dinners that wound late into the evening, and making themselves always available for investors' calls and emails. These were not the shorter or more predictable work hours believed to accommodate mothers.

I found precious few hedge funds with any standardized accommodations for parents at all. It was telling that while my interviewees explicitly regarded client-facing roles as being more compatible with mothering, no one identified client-facing roles as being better for men or fathers. Instead, several executive men indicated how their jobs gave them control over when and where they worked, allowing them to have families. Justin, who is white, ran a hedge fund out of his house. Twice, he expressed appreciation for being able to play a more central role in raising his daughters: "It's a great industry if you care about your family, because you can do your work from home. It's actually one that lends itself to having a family." Justin's wife, who had financially supported the family during the startup phase of Justin's hedge fund, worked long hours in private equity, so their family relied heavily on paid childcare, even though he worked from home and touted his ability to be present for his kids.

Of being a father while running a hedge fund, Scott said, "It helps being the boss." Scott, also a white forty-something, described having a schedule he largely controlled: "On a day-to-day basis, yeah, ultimately I'm the boss, so if people need to meet with me, I can just tell them when they're going to meet with me, and if there's some trip on the horizon, I can schedule it." Pausing, he continued, "But the joke about entrepreneurs and the great thing about entrepreneurship is that you get to pick those 120 hours a week that you work. And that's pretty much my life. I work very hard . . . but I do have some say in when I do what I do." Scott cited taking a call on Saturday morning at his child's soccer match as proof of his readiness to work whenever global markets trade or investors call (he was, perhaps, unaware he was describing fathering as measured in parent presence or "quality time" rather than care work).

Sole breadwinner Deborah was the only woman CIO I interviewed who was also a mother. Her story actually confirmed the gendered reliance on a spouse as a driver of success in running a hedge fund. As she put it, having four children while running a hedge fund would not have been possible had her husband worked. He was the family's homemaker. When she launched her firm, Deborah said, there were years in which she worked at least twelve or thirteen hours a day, including weekends and holidays. "I worked *all* the time," she emphasized, even sometimes going home to put her kids to bed and read them stories, then return to the office to work into the wee hours. "So, I really mean *all* the time." That was the commitment required of a finance industry executive.

Executives Scott, Justin, and Deborah all had demanding schedules, but only Deborah perceived these hours as inconducive to family life. This even though she was also the only one of the three with a homemaker spouse (Scott and Justin both had wives who held corporate jobs). Deborah likely perceived the long hours differently, because mothers face greater cultural expectations regarding selfless devotion to the responsibilities associated with the care work of parenting, as opposed to the "quality time" associated with being a good father.[11]

As I looked deeper into the "mommy track," I saw how common it was that women actually *began* their careers on the investment team, then later transferred to client services. Recall how, in chapter 3, Nicole was hired to replace a woman who was advised to make the switch after getting married (to better accommodate a mother's responsibilities). Similarly, Amanda, in her thirties, began her career on an investment team at a prestigious investment bank. Back then, a woman mentor told Amanda that, to become an asset manager, she would need to hire a full-time, live-in domestic care worker—one who would likely be a low-paid, woman of color, given the racialized division of US household labor.[12] Instead, Amanda transferred to client services at a large hedge fund and sent her baby to day care (for the socialization, not the money, she said). The expectation and norm of overwork required parents to outsource care work. But even with this paid support, parenting, or the expectation of it, tended to hedge women out of the investment team.

When we met, Amanda had just returned from three months of maternity leave at half pay. Even though she worked at a large hedge fund founded in the 1990s, Amanda was the first employee to request and establish a leave policy. During the leave, she said:

> I stayed pretty engaged . . . I knew I would be checking my emails anyway, so I figured I might as well log hours. I was working on a few big pieces of business that I wanted to make sure I was moving along. And then, because we don't have a ton of people [on staff], there's some stuff only I know, so people would have to call me and ask me.

Even in a client services role, Amanda felt obligated to continue working about five hours a week while she was on maternity leave.

After her leave, primary breadwinner Amanda negotiated for reduced hours and travel. Not including after-hours emails and calls, Amanda had worked fifty hours a week and hoped to move to forty. And where she'd previously traveled twice a month for client meetings in the United States and overseas, she was able to negotiate only a two-month travel break (a compromise after she initially requested a fourth month of full maternity leave). Amanda wasn't optimistic about future reductions in travel.

Amanda, who is white with an upper-middle-class upbringing, was married to a public service attorney. Because of his work's social impact, they had Amanda's work subsidize his; should Amanda change jobs in the future, they expected that her husband would go back to higher paying corporate law. Farrah and Sasha, both women of color from working-class backgrounds, also earned the primary incomes in their households, though they described it as a necessity, not a choice. Each recounted how various periods of unemployment had added urgency to their job searches—they had to provide for their families—as well as how being the breadwinner made them risk averse in their careers.[13] They never pursued alternate career paths, even when it meant putting up with workplaces rife with bullying and discrimination.

Pervasive industry beliefs about working hours and flexibility for parents cast client services as the ideal jobs for mothers and reserve executive roles for fathers. That is, heteronormative divisions of household labor created parallel divisions of firm labor. But contrary to this ideal, workers on both teams logged long hours and worked on demand. Effectively, the double standard sorted men into higher status roles and then rationalized their dominant position in the industry. It hedged women out of the C-suite, placing women lacking class and race privilege at even greater risk of mistreatment and foreclosing alternatives should it occur.

Outcomes at the Top

Consistent with the more hierarchical investment banks, the flatter hedge funds featured striking gender and racial segregation at the tops of their organizations because of the gender- and racial-typing of roles.[14] Scott, for instance, described his average-sized firm of fifteen employees this way: "It's a small team, and it's very flat. Everyone collaborates at one level. There are a few of us elevated above that level: myself, [man's name], and [man's name]." The executives were all white men, as in many other hedge funds. Outlining the organization of work among his partners, Scott differentiated his own role as CEO from his partners, who ran the investments: "I keep my finger on the pulse of the business, more importantly than anything. I'm checking the vital signs of the business. I oversee all aspects of what we do that don't involve investment decisions." As CEO, Scott oversaw the firm's day-to-day business operations.[15] This executive role was the top of the client services and operations career paths. Although Scott was relatively new to the hedge fund world, his legal background expedited his upward ascent relative to colleagues with client-facing and operational roles.

The gender- and racial-typing of jobs even affected firms organized as equal partnerships. Several interviewees described their firms' founding partners as having equal standing at the outset, with support staff hired later as needed. Within that formalized shared ownership culture, however, differences in status and responsibilities made these "equal partnerships" unequal in practice. Women became more likely to hold lower-status partner roles in operations and client services, a fact that became especially detrimental to women's careers when firms turned over (refer to the conclusion for the case of Farrah's firm).

Across the board, hedge fund managers described their industry's flatter organizational structure and division of labor in gender-neutral terms, even though women hold only 17 percent of all roles and 11 percent of leadership positions in this financial sector.[16] It's unsurprising, then, that—even though I oversampled for women executives—I spoke to only two women who were the primary decision maker in their firm: Deborah and Diane. Deborah, whose twenty-employee firm boasted 60 percent women employees, mentioned that industry colleagues disparaged her anomalous firm as "the chick fund." For her part, Diane's ten-person team also employed a greater than average proportion of women (including her CFO). This pair of exceptions highlighted for me just how normative men-dominated firms and men-dominated C-suites are throughout the hedge fund world.

Organizing Chaos

In a culture they described as flexible, autonomous, and adaptive, executives told me that fewer middle managers and more flexible advancement criteria promoted meritocracy. Their employees reported holding multiple roles and having no supervisors (hints of cost-cutting), self-managing with little oversight and without standardized evaluations. Executives exercised considerable discretion in compensating, evaluating, and promoting employees, since performance was usually determined on an ad hoc basis through the negotiation of annual bonuses and raises.

Diane had a more playful way of describing the culture of her firm, laughingly dubbing it "entrepreneurial chaos." She thought informality allowed room for creativity: "I think one of the reasons why we've been successful for so long is that we think outside the box. No idea will be knocked down because it doesn't fit into our box. Our 'box' is thinking about where the opportunities are at and how we monetize them. So, I would say 'organized chaos.'" Standardized practices seemed, to her, time-consuming and ingenuity-stifling: "At a lot of places, they meet every week, and they get together, and they talk about ideas and blah, blah, blah. The velocity of ideas that we're seeing is so huge that I would be spending four out of five business days going through every single idea, so we have to be able to go through stuff really, really fast."[17]

As the leader of the organized chaos, Diane said, "I'm hands-off, but I'm not hands-off." She clarified, "So, the research process, I'm very hands-off. I'm the one who comes up with the big picture, sometimes a crazy idea, and then I want the team to go out and create the models that either support or refute my idea." Regardless of whether the models actually bolstered her thesis, Diane made the call: "When it comes to the actual direction I want the portfolio to go, I've already decided how that is going to occur, but I want them to do the analysis to support my thesis." Lisa, a portfolio manager, said this happened at her firm, too: "The CIO [chief investment officer], he's pretty open-minded, but he is the sole decision maker for what makes it in the portfolio. I can make recommendations, and if he decides that he doesn't like what I recommended, then it cannot make it in the portfolio." As I found with other executives, Diane indicated that the firm's flat structure encouraged creativity and innovation, which it may in fact do, yet it was clear that this culture often served to reinforce executives' decision-making power and authority.

But employees, too, championed the benefits of working at smaller firms. Amanda worked at a large firm by hedge fund standards. Comparing it to her last job, at an investment bank, she described: "Less face time definitely [at the bank]. At a big bank, you have a very narrow focus. You are like a cog in the machine. As long as you are turning your cog, that's all anybody cares about." She found herself appreciating how her current job allowed her to make meaningful contributions and build personal relationships: "Here you do get to wear more hats and be involved with more decisions. Like, the founder of the firm, he knows me by name. He knows my kid's name. It's just more personal, which I really like that about it." She cited her role in a project with their largest investor that, she said, would "be a huge change in the way that we do our business" as proof of her works' impact: "The analysis you do actually affects business decisions. It goes to the founder of the firm, and he will use the work that you do to make an important decision about the direction of the firm. You can really see the impact."

Still, Amanda thought informality created some role ambiguity and conflict among colleagues. Her two-hundred-person firm, she said, had a "flat" structure she defined as having no formal promotional procedures or titles in the name of promoting meritocracy: "The only way you feel like you are getting promoted is through comp[ensation]." Although she liked the culture overall, Amanda explicitly questioned this aspect of the organization: "It's supposed to promote a meritocracy, but I think sometimes people need those milestones to feel like they are progressing in their career." Compensation was employees' exclusive source for performance feedback, but because higher-ups gave no indications of how they calculated pay and bonuses, Amanda was frustrated when it came to getting constructive feedback on her overall performance.

In this context, tensions between managers and employees were fairly unavoidable. Once, both Amanda and a teammate (who, without a formal title, nonetheless acted as team lead and supervisor) jockeyed for the same account; in the end, her teammate deleted Amanda's name from the meeting notes and took sole credit for recruiting the investor. Frustrated, Amanda thought this "superior" should have instead acknowledged her accomplishment, which bolstered his own achievements as the team lead. But because their firm used quantitative metrics to determine compensation behind closed doors, there was heightened competition between people on the same team.

The informal structures also led some of my interviewees to describe executives as poorly equipped to provide training and mentoring. William, a fifty-something white hedge fund advisor, suggests that the executives had not, in fact, intentionally adopted informality. They were informal because they lacked prior experience as managers, he said: "You're asking people to run businesses, and they're trained stock pickers. It's almost a joke . . . [the] level of dysfunctionality, and communication is often not very good because these are, you know, finance guys. Guys mostly, I mean, are not great communicators—obviously this is a generalization." William contrasted this with large bureaucracies: "When people rise up the ranks in traditional corporations, they have certain skills they evolve at low-management, mid-management, and upper-management levels. In a lot of the finance world, it doesn't happen that way at all."

Executives believed eschewing titles and evaluations fostered meritocracy and creativity. Employees, however, said procedural ambiguity led to dysfunction, bias, and unnecessary competition. Instead of creating flexibility in job roles, informality exacerbated a sense of uncertainty and unpredictability. Organizations that espouse meritocratic ideology tend to be biased in ways that promote the advancement of men over women and workplace contexts featuring uncertainty and ambiguity exacerbate biases.[18] This suggests that informal management practices are amplifying the lack of women in these firms' leadership positions.

Too Radical Transparency

In lieu of separate human resources departments and other accountability structures, executives encouraged employees to communicate openly and take advantage of the transparency of a flat organizational structure. The goal was to foster a culture in which employees felt comfortable taking professional risks.[19] Some executives called for "radical transparency," a term used to capture openness in organizational process, data, and employment relations, and encouraged employees to give direct, candid feedback. The idea made it into one firm's recruiting materials, which detailed explicit expectations for transparency, and I read a founder's letter calling for open feedback between truth-telling colleagues. To tamp down rumors and secrecy, another firm required supervisors to include employees in any meetings that concerned them, and even had a library of audio recordings of its meetings, intentionally created so that employees could hear what colleagues said about them. Even so, many employees told me they felt uncomfortable speaking up. Those who reported issues recounted unwelcoming, even retaliatory, responses.

Sam, a hedge fund billionaire icon, was a featured speaker at a conference I attended. Championing the benefits of radical transparency, he drew a boundary between internal, collegial transparency and external, public transparency. Of his own firm, he said, "We're like a family inside. . . . Make it truthful on the inside and make it radically transparent, that's powerful . . . [we strive to create] an idea meritocracy that produces meaningful work and meaningful relationships. And the way to get there is radical transparency. You have to have trust to do it." Hedge funds restrict access to a select few, but once someone gains entrance to the firm, Sam said, they are family and share a bond of trust within which employees can push and disagree and force each other to develop and grow. This idea is indicative of how patrimonialism is built on trusting relationships—and it lay at the heart of Sam's dream of a meritocracy of ideas. He admitted, though, that his firm has a 30 percent turnover rate, indicating that not everyone felt part of the family and safe to share openly.

Similarly, Vincent told me that removing layers of bureaucracy and management makes firms more collaborative and less competitive. As a hedge fund founder, he described cultivating an environment that was "very flat," "quick to decisions," and accessible enough that his employees can "just walk in the room and ask a question" of him directly. Consistent with the boosters for open communication among tech executives,[20] Vincent believed that removing middle management promotes contact between executives and staff and streamlines decision making.

Even the physical organization of hedge funds was set up to eliminate barriers between executives and employees. When I interviewed Sebastian, a Middle Eastern American man in his thirties, at his twelve-person hedge fund with over a billion dollars in assets, the receptionist gave me a tour of the office space. As in the other small and midsize hedge funds I observed, Sebastian's employees worked in an open room with side-by-side trading desks lined up in two facing rows. There were only two small offices—for the executives—and even those sported glass walls looking out onto the main room. The optics matched the value of open communication and transparency but also obscured a steep social hierarchy and allowed workers to surveil each other's work ethic and dedication, as Michel Foucault theorized.[21]

My interviews revealed some reticence about all this "openness." Several people recounted being penalized for accepting the invitation to openness. Sasha's story was particularly memorable. When I first met Sasha in November, she said enthusiastically that she enjoyed her work and her colleagues. The following April, over Easter dinner, she told me she had since become frustrated with her job. The dynamics with two white women on her team (a teammate and their mutual supervisor) became a problem when Sasha learned that her teammate, less qualified than she in both credentials and tenure, made three times her base pay. Embracing the call for openness and transparency, Sasha requested a raise commensurate with her training and experience: "I should get paid market, and market is x y z." Sasha said her supervisor refused, telling Sasha to just be grateful for the job: "She might as well have called me the N-word. That's what it felt like."

While always conscious of her token status as a woman of color, this was the first time in Sasha's career when she felt "put in her place." Her supervisor, she said, had always commended her work—until she demanded equal pay. "That was hurtful," beyond not getting the raise she remembered, "because the things she said to me really showed her true colors, her real feelings." Sasha's attempt to point out inequality and advocate for herself within the supposed meritocracy instead reinforced her understanding of herself as "the one" Black person in the firm. She sighed, "I've never been so directly spoken to, put into place—like 'know your role'—as I was at that moment."

I was surprised when Sasha told me the "human resources manager" reached out after the incident to discuss what had transpired.
Even though I asked about it in every one of my interviews, no one
reported that a small or midsized firm had personnel designated exclusively for human resources. Their concession was the occasional
import of a psychologist (a "corporate shrink") to mediate interpersonal disputes and motivate employees, as portrayed by the character Wendy on the television hit *Billions*.

Sasha's "human resources" turned out to be her firm's CIO—the
top executive—in what appeared to be common practice among executives who stressed both open communication and the need to
"wear multiple hats" in their firms. He asked if she would press
charges for racial discrimination, and Sasha understandably assessed the meeting as nothing more than an attempt to prevent legal
action. The CIO acted to protect the firm's interests rather than her
rights as a worker. In a flatter organization, few protections balance
the interests of executives and employees when disputes arise, but
when the executives who tout transparency obscure processes like
earnings distributions and promotions, tensions are sure to flare. Sasha quit her job within a few months.

In this competitive, reputation-based industry, Sasha had few options to seek recourse for discrimination. In this way, it was like the
other stories I was told regarding harassment and discrimination at
hedge funds. Going to a "human resources" person—usually an investment executive—was futile. At times, it made things worse.
Pressing charges was called a "career-ender" and "professional suicide," because it tarnished the plaintiff's reputation; several of my
interviewees stressed that no firm would hire someone with a reputation for rocking the boat. Thus, my interviewees identified two viable
options: resolve the problem among themselves or seek employment
elsewhere. They identified the labor market as the proper mechanism for addressing racial or gender discrimination in their field.

At a networking event, one woman confided that, during layoffs at her previous employer, 60 percent of the women on the investment team were laid off. Not a single man lost his position. Pregnant at the time, she contacted an attorney to "look into her options," although she didn't intend to press charges. She accepted the severance package, had her baby, and started applying for jobs. She learned from a potential employer that, when they called her previous employer for a background check, they were warned to watch out because she had pressed charges against their firm—"Which wasn't even true!" she exclaimed, still angry years later. Unable to find a job, she finally pursued legal action and settled with the former employer out of court. Now unemployable in the industry, she used the settlement money to start a consulting firm (the settlement forbade her from sharing additional detail, which may explain why her lawsuit was the only one I encountered throughout my fieldwork and interviews).

Matthew was another interviewee who experienced discrimination on the job. During his twenty-year career in trading, Matthew upheld the norms of masculinity in financial services. He had an elite family and pedigree, but his colleagues treated him differently because Matthew was a Black man. Two white women reported him as "threatening." When I asked whether he filed a complaint, as he worked at a larger firm with human resources, he said he hadn't "because these HR departments are designed to actually support management—full stop. So, who am I going to complain to, right? If anything, that gives you a straight ticket to be managed-out, which is fine. Then give me a [severance] package." Amid organizational racism, Matthew distrusted human resources and took it on himself to deal with the racism in his work. Institutional recourse for discrimination wasn't a real option for him; instead, he sought employment elsewhere.

A bit later, Matthew expanded, saying, "My mentality is always that I am responsible for my own career. Now there is something very powerful about that if you take that on. If you are responsible for your own career, and you are not happy, whose fault is that?" He waited for me to answer.

"Your own?" I said hesitantly.

"If you're not getting paid what you think you should be getting paid, whose fault is that?"

Again, Matthew waited until I responded, "Your own."

"If you're not being recognized. All those things. If you're not getting the leadership opportunity. All those things," he continued. "Because if you accept that responsibility, then you will stop waiting for someone to hand you something."

Matthew deemed it unrealistic to expect others to acknowledge and address their own biases, which led him to join others in identifying the labor market as his only workable solution to interpersonal and organizational racism. In doing so, he attributed neoliberal logics to the labor market that echoed those applied to the stock market:

> Improvement on the situation is not going to be somebody waking up one day and being like, "Holy shit, I have perception bias." It's going to be people gravitating to places where they can be seen for who they really are, and those places would benefit from the type of talent that they attract. . . . I'm willing to make the commercial argument that if I'm drawing from a broader talent pool because I'm able to see people for who they are, I'm going to win.

Rather than waiting for people to change their racist ways, or having to do the work to teach them, Matthew took his talent elsewhere, stressing the "commercial" case for diversity: firms that discriminate lose valuable talent, like his. Indeed, this hews to a neoliberal ideology of individual responsibility that posits the labor market as the appropriate recourse for discriminatory practices—take your talents and walk, let them suffer the consequences. However, the low numbers of women and men of color in this industry, especially in leadership positions, suggests that the labor market does not effectively deter discrimination. Although industry research has found some strong performance among women- and minority-led firms, these firms account for only 3.3 percent of the industry today.[22]

I call Matthew's approach, trusting in the market to match likeminded employers and employees and leaving the discriminatory firms to lose valuable talent, "market-mediated recourse." Rather than place the onus of change on the organization, the person addresses the problem by withholding their labor. No one I spoke with ever referred to government or institutional recourse for discrimination in the workplace.

In addition to the negative consequences of the (lack of) policies for workers' protection, this approach both reflects and reinforces an unchecked, hierarchical environment in which executives regularly escape accountability. Executives encouraged openness, except when it challenged their authority, and this tight-knit, reputation-based industry composed of small firms foreclosed internal (HR) and external (legal) options for discrimination recourse, as scholars have found in large, bureaucratic organizations.[23] The structure of hedge fund firms upholds racial policing and gendered double standards, as is clear in Sasha's and Matthew's experiences, and protects the interests of executives and other white employees.

The uneven application of organizational practices and the minimalization of racism reported to me, as in pay negotiations and tepid human resources interventions, reveals that race is part of the organizing fabric of these firms, constructing social hierarchies and legitimating opportunity hoarding, as sociologist Victor Ray has theorized.[24] When racism is embedded into the organization itself, its targets (and their careers) suffer. The labor market solution only underscored the power imbalance between executives and employees in these flatter firms: executives wield considerable power over their employees, employees must cater to executives' demands, and executives may lose any sense of accountability to employees. Again, these practices fit into a workplace culture that enables hedge fund managers to avoid oversight from regulators and demand high fees from investors.

A Wager on Compensation

Hedge fund workers' outsized incomes are decoupled from a household's needs, allowing these workers to invest their own fortunes. In fact, it's an expectation, made apparent in the cultural logics with which they discuss compensation. Workers describe performance-based wages that consist of a base salary and a bonus structured on both firm and employee performance, a setup in which employment relations are akin to taking a partnership position. In exchange for assuming the risk of working at a small firm, and, to some extent assuming the firm's financial risk itself through performance-based bonuses, workers incur a stake in their firm's performance. Earnings, then, reflect what I call a *wager* between an employer and employee. Each actor risks money, time, and security for potential earnings, commensurate with the amount of risk involved. Workers wager on the firm's ability to generate revenue, while the firm, according to people who ran hedge funds, wagers on a worker's potential to raise funds from investors or earn returns in the market.

Hiring essentially formalizes this bet on an employee's future revenue-generating potential, and early salary negotiations operate like a futures exchange in which the parties agree on a contract to secure a price and hedge against future risk. The starting salary can be understood as a stake, or money designated at the onset of the bet to represent the employer's investment in an employee's potential. If the bet pays off—that is, the employee raises the firm's bottom line— the payout comes as a bonus. Thus, the firm appears to hedge against the risk of employees underperforming or departing by paying a base salary while reserving full compensation for *after* performance expectations are met or exceeded. Employees wager that the employment will lead to high bonuses based in the firm's success and allow for professional advancement. Negotiating the base salary asks workers to wager on anticipated gains and potential losses, while firms, my interviewees explained, make offers based on the possible revenue an employee can bring in *or* the money saved by their labor.

Fernando, a thirty-something Brazilian man, summed up the firm's evaluation:

> How much do they pay the employee versus how much benefit the employee brings? Either in terms of profit generation, if it's an employee that's in charge of bringing in profits with good investment decisions, or if it's an employee that is in more of the administrative side, how they are going to help the firm manage the operations more efficiently?

A worker's potential is assessed much like any other investment a hedge fund makes; it is measured in metrics like past performance, tenure, social connections, and credentials. Inexperienced workers are a riskier wager, but their access to elite networks and credentials can signal profitable potential; experienced workers with established valuable social capital can demand higher wages and better terms from the get-go.

Hedge fund workers are evaluated just like their funds: through financial statements. As Margaret commented appreciatively, "One of the beautiful things about hedge funds is that because they are small and they are flat, the metric of success is so objective: It's did you make money today? Is it green or is it red?" Gita, a Singaporean portfolio manager in her thirties, mused similarly, "If you do this awesome job, but it doesn't contribute to the bottom line, does it really matter?" Both had assimilated into the culture of hedge funds, where success means raising money from investors and generating investment returns. Any other contributions are entirely beside the point, Diane warned: "At the end of the day, it's your rate of return, because if you don't have one, you probably won't be in the industry." In theory, most white-collar employees' salaries are based on the expected outcome of their labor, while hedge fund workers expect their base pay will hinge on their perceived potential to generate financial profits.[25] Amid these value perceptions, workers managed their careers like assets, always focused on their impact on the firm's bottom line.

Missing from this bottom-line discourse is the fact that individual contributions to an investment team are subjectively determined, as are the values attached to lower-status support functions more often filled by women, racial minority men, and less class-privileged workers. Three of the most common compensation systems at hedge funds expose the subjective determinations behind these wagers— and the way firms in this fundamentally risky business distribute that risk among all employees.

Individualized Profits

Only one compensation system pegged profits directly to a percentage of individual performance (usually separated out by trader rather than by portfolio/investment team). The "no netting compensation system" functions as a way to transfer what is called the "netting risk" from the firm to the investor, who must pay performance fees to traders or portfolios that do well and incur losses on the underperformers. Its secondary risk transfer devolves the firm's risk tied to underperforming assets to the individuals whose bonuses are withheld should their trades or team portfolios flounder.

Craig recounted how this incentive system, in place at his last firm, pushed individual, rather than team-based, risk-taking:

It was what's called no netting, so each trader got to keep their own profits. If I made, if my positions made $5,000,000, I got 10 percent of that . . . even if the guy next to me lost $7,000,000. So, the firm could lose money and the investors could lose money, but the traders could still get paid. . . . From a trader's point of view, it was fantastic because you get to keep what you make. You don't necessarily care what the guy next to you is doing.

In this system, Craig admitted, he evaluated risk based on what he and his family personally could afford to lose. When it came to managing his trades, "The way I have to think about it is a way of keeping score. It's a number that measures how well I'm doing, like in a pinball game or a video game. If you make it a personal thing, then you can't sleep at night." Yet, Craig acknowledged it could become extremely personal: "It becomes personal when you've lost enough money where you're not going to get paid for a while." To manage his own personal risk, Craig made it a rule to not lose more money in a day than he could make in a month. "So, if I have a bunch of bad days in a row, it's going to take me three months at my average pace to grind back from that, and that's livable. But if it's three years, well then, this year's done. You've thrown it away. You can start over somewhere else."

Craig and traders like him earn enough money to save for months that might come with no pay; the system heightens these high-earners' perceptions of insecurity. Traders from less-privileged backgrounds described the risks of the no netting system as unsustainable over time and incompatible with supporting a family. This is what pushed Manny, in chapter 2, to leave trading to go into a more stable sales position at a trading software company.

Team Contributions

The second common compensation system was a performance-based system evaluated by perceived contribution to the firm's profits. This system had a profit-sharing component that distributed some of the firm's ownership and profits, but aside from bonus pay fluctuations, it didn't distribute the financial risks. This compensation reflected a neoliberal logic in which the market is understood as unbiased and quantitative metrics as pure tools—ways to measure merit in a supposedly meritocratic system. This same market logic guides the management practices at hedge funds, with executives describing performance-based pay as incentivizing employees and promoting meritocracy. Several employees, however, expressed reservations, noting that it was notoriously difficult to measure the individual contributions of team members. To them, it seemed like a system that only claimed objectivity.

Diane's firm determined pay based on her perception of how each person contributed to the team's performance. In particular, she thought her firm's lack of hierarchy allowed her to better evaluate individual performance: "It's really flat. I measure our success by our performance. It's not measured by the size of somebody's office or where they went to school or something like that. . . . There are no big egos." She added, "The ego is in the performance, not in the process itself. And it's flat." Diane evaluates the team all together, assuming that if one person's performance falters, the entire team will underperform. Yet anyone who has done a group project in junior high school can spot this trap: the most visible contributions will gain the most praise, regardless of their actual contribution to the end product. Because women's work tends to receive less recognition in all fields (formalized in hedge funds, where the gendered client, investment division explicitly devalues women's contributions), scholars have repeatedly found that evaluating employees based on teamwork disadvantages women working in men-dominant teams.[26]

Quantitative metrics—a proxy for merit—also informed beliefs about workplace diversity. Among my interviewees, a number told me that using quantitative metrics to determine advancement *eliminated* workplace inequality. Fernando, for instance, told me the stock market provided an objective measure of performance, so the balance sheet reflected individual merit alone: "ethnicity is a nonfactor." He continued:

> Ethnicity: people don't care. And it's because these funds are very PNL [profit and loss] oriented. They are there to make money. And they make money not by people's looks, . . . by how people talk, by people's accents, or where people are from . . . [or] usually by whether a person has a great social network. Hedge funds make money when the analysts, the portfolio managers, and the traders make good judgments on the investments.

Fernando stressed that diversity in his firm—"I usually see all types of ethnicities"—wasn't just about the company "trying to abide by the Department of Labor laws," and said, "I really think it's a function of meritocracy. If you're from India, from Asia, if you're Black or white, it really doesn't matter, as long as that person can produce."

This was echoed by Steven, who is Asian American: "Hedge funds are a more merit-based system than other industries. If you have an amazing investment idea, anybody will listen to you . . . if you can prove that you can make money and have good investment ideas, nobody cares what country you are from." Likewise, Wayne, also Asian American, used the best-idea-wins rhetoric that reified the transparency of quantitative finance and, to him, explained the greater diversity he saw there: "In quantitative finance, my take is that it's a lot more level of a playing field. It relies solely on your merits, which are exactly quantifiable. Everybody, your manager, your manager's manager wants profit. Whoever makes the good strategies does well."

Having heard this justification before, I asked, "If you're just supporting the person who makes the strategy, is it quantifiable?"

Wayne paused. "That's a good point. Probably much less so. Much less so."

The widely shared idea that quantification is intrinsically meritocratic obscured how other social factors—such as race, gender, and class—influenced the determination of performance and value on teams. In my research, explicit favoritism and implicit biases, even discrimination in Sasha's case, appeared to absolutely influence how executives evaluated an employee's performance, value, and compensation. Justin questioned the ambiguity of perceived contributions for this very reason: "Since it's quantitative, your numbers are your numbers. But this is only when you have your own firm, which is late in your career." Until then, he emphasized, individual effort is hard to evaluate because it contributes to the firm's performance. "A lot of this is gut instinct. You can't tell if it's implicit biases. You like 'em and you enjoy their company." I asked whether implicit bias influenced how he perceived other workers' contributions, and he had no hesitation: "100 percent."

Contrasting Sasha's account of requesting a raise, on the basis of her market value, and being denied and reminded to be "grateful for the job," with Andrew's experience negotiating his offer is instructive here. Andrew told me that, in his negotiations, he referenced his "personal market value," because "you need to manage that trade-off of showing that you're excited about having the opportunity but showing also that you know that your personal market value is higher, and if they are going to get you to take this job, that they are going to have to pay you what you think is your market value." As an upper-class white man, he was confident that executives respect employees who negotiate and that not doing it indicated "a lack of assertiveness, lack of self-confidence, maybe, I don't fully appreciate my worth." Andrew demanded symbolic and material recognition of his personal value.

Sasha, using a peer as a reference point, negotiated instead in relation to equity and fairness within her team, comparing herself to an abstract idea of market value, using her peer as a reference point. The difference in Andrew's and Sasha's approaches can be traced to the backlash Sasha, the only Black woman on her team (and at her firm), rightfully anticipated: in all sorts of business contexts, tokenized workers including women and racial minority men are highly visible and frequently sanctioned or penalized when they negotiate.[27] White men aren't only free to negotiate more assertively, employers *expect* them to do so (and make negative assumptions if they do not).[28]

For all the transparency talk, hedge funds discouraged colleagues from discussing their compensation packages. Of course, information still flowed within and across firms, and I came across several cases in which an employee discovered, like Sasha, they were underpaid relative to their colleagues. As Sharon said, "After my first bonus, I realized life wasn't a meritocracy."

One evening, at the end of a women's networking event, I sat among a small group of women lingering on the patio at a wine bar. Each woman shared her experience with negotiating raises. One had authored a lengthy report demonstrating her value to the firm, while another did the same, but only after her manager gave her an unsolicited raise because she wanted her achievements to be recognized. A younger trader recalled that the first time her supervisor asked her into his office to discuss her annual bonus, she walked out. Though she had no benchmark for her earnings (her peers, all men, were tight-lipped about their compensation packages with her), she was a relatively young trader and a South Asian American woman, so she assumed her supervisor would underestimate (or at least under-reward) her value. Her suspicion was confirmed when the supervisor returned with a substantially higher amount, and in subsequent years their compensation meetings operated very differently from that first one. With all these accounts on just one wine bar patio, it was plain that performance-based pay, throughout the industry, is subjectively determined and negotiated in what is, for the employee especially, a low-information environment.

Shared Ownership

In theory, the third common compensation system, shared owner-ship, should eliminate these discrepancies. Employees share in the firm's profits, reflected in their annual bonuses, fostering a positive sense of shared ownership. This is also a profit-sharing compensation system, as the firm's success translates into financial benefit for its employees, but if the firm flounders, employees incur the risks in the form of lower earnings. At the same time, the shared ownership stops at a certain point, as only executives have a say in the firm's management.

Scott said his firm had an "ownership culture" with a pay structure that ensured "we're all pulling for the same thing." Scott fostered this culture by sharing partnership interest (a percentage of profits and losses) among employees, literally giving each staffer a stake, while other hedge funds distributed funds via annual bonuses, paid out from the performance fees charged to investors, to confer a sense of, though not an actual stake in, ownership to their employees.

Since they were in their start-up phase, Albert and his partner's firm had chosen to pay their employees equally and take less compensation for themselves, since they owned equity. Albert recounted, "In terms of my partner and I getting to be paid less, hopefully that's just a period of transition we're in. But you know, we could give away a lot of the equity. . . our plan is to give away some of the equity in this next year, but as long as we're sitting on the equity, then the budget gets tighter." That is, when Albert and his partner eventually distribute equity shares, which help retain traders and reward their commitment to the firm, it will free up the firm's cash flow: compensation can come in a combination of direct pay and bonuses with equity shares. When their firm begins making real money, Albert said, figuring how best to determine earnings and distribute profit among the employees will be a "high-quality" problem (that he calls this a "problem" at all further indicates that designations of economic worth and value aren't as purely quantifiable as industry insiders might suggest).

As Albert explained all this, he caught himself. Albert acknowledged that there were exceptions to the firm's current practice of equal pay: two people received higher salaries to help accommodate expenses associated with having a family. Albert didn't initially mention their gender:

> We made some modest changes frankly only for two people and that was because they had families and personal situations and came to us. . . . it was to the tune of a couple of tens of thousands of dollars a year. . . . We've only done it twice and both of them . . . [were] associated with raising a family in New York.

Later, when I ask about the gender composition of his firm, I deduced that these were both men who received a "daddy bonus" to support a family, because the firm's only woman was *not* a parent (I had met her, too). Albert's careful account, in retrospect, revealed why executives may think fathers deserve more compensation: the expectation that fathers are solely responsible for financially supporting their families (an idea rooted in the outdated, if ever real, "nuclear family" model). It also revealed part of the story of why men, particularly white fathers, often out-earn women across employment fields.[29]

Other interviewees confirmed this man's breadwinner advantage at their firms, with women noting they gained no similar concessions. As Cynthia put it, "Your bonus and everything is based on: Do they like you? Do they think you are part of the team? Maybe they want to give more to this guy because, you know, they're like, 'This guy just had twins. Let's give him money, because you don't need it.' I mean it's totally subjective." In other words, a confluence of micro-level processes explains why fathers reap the highest rewards in finance. Similarly, in investment banking, Louise Roth finds that managers and coworkers view women with children as less dedicated to work—hence the tendency to shunt women regardless of parental status onto the "mommy track"—yet deem fathers to be more serious and accountable and reward them financially. Consequently, fathers, especially white fathers, in financial services are rewarded even beyond fathers' earnings in other high-paying industries.[30]

· · ·

Each of the three compensation systems results from the way hedge funds socialize workers into a culture of calculation and investment risk-taking. Employee and firm progress are evaluated in accordance with the fund's financial statements, yet this apparently objective system creates room for ambiguity and subjectivity, allowing bias to flourish.[31] That designations of financial worth and value are constructed through interpersonal interactions and organizational power dynamics suggests that compensation isn't nearly as tightly correlated to rational models of value and efficiency as industry insiders believe (or at least claim).

Documenting all these pay disparities reveals how, for elite finance workers, a living wage has been replaced with a wager, my term for the bet placed by a prospective employer and employee that determines shared rewards in the operating risks of the firm. While a worker wagers on a firm's prospects for generating revenue, firms wager on whether prospective employees will contribute to the bottom line. Base salaries reflect a stake in the wager, and payouts (bonuses) come when the wager pays off. Hedge funds lionize the image of entrepreneurial investment, with workers embracing risks to get ahead, which means that wages have become speculative, as Lisa Adkins theorizes.[32] When risk-taking fails, workers find they function as independent partners, and so they endeavor to manage their careers like their assets. Whether through increasing investment returns or attracting investor capital, they strive to increase their contribution to the bottom line, because that proxy of their value directly affects their earnings in the moment and in the future.

A Brave New Firm?

Hedge funds provide a cautionary tale of flatter firms' insistence that they create more inclusive and open workplaces. The organizational logic I observed and that was described by my interviewees legitimized and constructed social hierarchies that placed largely unchecked executives on top. The contracts had gendered terminology highlighting the importance of the top executive (and other "key men"). The everyday division of labor structured who gained access to opportunities for promotion, recognition, and compensation in relation to employees' gender, race, and parental status. Even in foundationally "equal" partnerships, the gendered and racial inequality underpinning the industry created a steeply hierarchical power imbalance with limited accountability. And the financialized wager of employment left workers sharing unevenly in the rewards of profit-seeking risk. Without human resources, middle managers, and formal protections, risks were transferred to employees, and there was little accountability.

Many empirical findings presented here are consistent with research on hierarchical companies. Flatter organizations, however, were designed to reduce hierarchy and therefore the status differences within hierarchies. Hedge funds show why this does not always happen. Unlike technology start-ups, where flexibility and informalization can make workplaces more open and equitable,[33] hedge funds, I find, convert the same qualities to tools of social closure and opportunity hoarding. These firms are just flexible and informal enough to manage a context high in both capital and insecurity by doling out uneven rewards based in hunches and stereotypes. Persistent inequalities find new ways of emerging in these flatter structures, and perhaps in more insidious ways, since hierarchy is more visible and salient in bureaucratic workplaces. Delayering hedge funds didn't necessarily promote equality. Often, it worsened the problem of inequality by heightening executives' discretion and legitimating their enormous compensation. After all, removing role hierarchies cannot obviate social hierarchies and the enduring inequalities inscribed into organizations.

5 Moving Up the Ranks

The key to success in the hedge fund industry, insiders confided, was to embrace uncertainty—in stock markets and their careers. The long hours, hard work, and cultivated tolerance for risk-taking, both personally and professionally, really did pay off, they told me. Vincent, a white man in his late forties, distinguished between the mediocre traders who clung to security and the stars who, he said,

> are willing to take a step or two out of their comfort zone and learn. Those who do okay, but never phenomenally, usually it's because they get in a comfort zone in the job they are in: "It's a really good job. I'm making a million dollars. I never dreamed I would make a million dollars. I'm going to be quiet, and I'm not going to risk a million dollars."

The standouts, he said—conceding "maybe it's just being overconfident"—declared instead, "I can do anything. Failing is not an option. I better push the envelope."

Vincent's mindset of rationalized risk isn't an anomaly, but the product of cultural changes among white-collar workers beginning in the late 1980s. About that time, management professor Charles Handy became a best-selling author advising savvy workers to trade stable employment for independence in a "portfolio career"—a lifetime of diverse skills, achievements, and jobs—rather than chasing the vanishing single-role career and full retirement ideal. With steady employment becoming less reliable, workers were encouraged to "manage" their futures by becoming entrepreneurial "career capitalists." Handy wrote, "We're not talking here about contractual security within an organization. . . . The new form of security will be very psychological and personal. The new security will be a belief that if this doesn't work out you could do something else. You are your own security."[1]

The Ideal Worker

Every profession has its own "ideal worker," an abstract notion of what and who a worker in that industry is expected to do and be, and it sets the standard for who gets recognized and promoted. These characteristics may not even be the ones that lead to work success; indeed, they often capture the characteristics of people who have been successful in the job in the past.

I find that hedge fund workers conceive of the ideal worker as a financialized product that must be cultivated and capitalized—I call this the *portfolio ideal*, in line with Handy's terminology.[2] The portfolio ideal requires a worker not only to fit with (or adapt to) the dominant ideology of white, class-privileged, hedgemonic masculinity that we have seen dominate finance, but to make ongoing investments in their resources, development, and management over time.

To explain why inequality persists in the workplace, Joan Acker theorized how an image of a "disembodied and universal" worker becomes attached to a job within the organizational logic of the workplace, for example, in the job descriptions. Thus, the concept of a white-collar job appears gender and race neutral but is premised on assumptions about an unencumbered worker with no responsibilities outside work—presumably because we are *actually* talking about a vision of a man who can count on the care work provided by his wife, a luxury largely reserved for white-collar, white men.³ This ostensibly neutral ideal stubbornly reflects gender, racial, and class ideologies that become ingrained into the organization's social fabric and affect the distribution of jobs, tasks, and rewards.⁴ That it is so deeply embedded in workplace structures reveals why social inequality in the workplace is so pernicious.

The portfolio ideal, embraced by the hedge fund industry, also captures a gendered, racialized, and classed image of a worker embedded in the organization. Though insiders largely spoke in ways that supported the widespread belief that both stock and labor markets are meritocratic and self-regulating forces, their rhetoric obscures the patrimonial system that organizes the industry and leaves so many hedged out.

Patrimonialism, rather than career management, eases access to opportunities, resources, and rewards, because patrimonialism is a system that manages risk through loyalty and personal connection. As the industry draws in new workers, it is those who fit the ideals of hedgemonic masculinity (both raced and classed) who have the connections to extend the system and pull each other up. Patrimonialism legitimizes the position of white men, in particular, and institutionalizes their privilege, because it hedges upper-class ideals by making them appear natural—the product of meritocratic and neoliberal markets that favor calculated risk-taking. Meanwhile, it maintains a closed industry, preventing access to rewards for those who cannot easily overlay onto the image of the ideal hedge fund worker, predominantly women and racialized minority men.

A Portfolio Ideal

The portfolio ideal and the social organization underpinning it are just as much the product of the industry's institutional context as its patrimonial structure. Organized around global markets, hedge funds are idealized as arenas of natural competition best left lightly regulated, so they feature hectic working conditions and insecure employment, tempered by the potentially enormous payouts the work can bring.[5] Even the most established firms must weather market instability and abrupt shifts in investor confidence. For instance, when I interviewed Kristen, a thirty-something white woman working at a large, top-rated hedge fund, she said she felt secure in her job. A year later, we bumped into each other again at an investor conference, where she was networking because her firm, having taken its first losses in fifteen years, had summarily sacked her entire office.

In this working environment, Scott intimated, your life is bound to the markets. "You really never have control," he explained. "Markets are going to do what they are going to do. If there's a market crisis, and suddenly we have to . . . [reach] out to every investor to talk to them about how we are handling it, that's going to happen at a moment's notice." Debunking any misconceptions that this could be a nine to five job, Scott said, "It actually never really ends anymore because we trade globally and there's always a market on somewhere other than a slim slice of time on Saturdays." He described feeling like he was on a "treadmill": "You need to work hard. It's too competitive . . . markets change too quickly and too dramatically . . . as soon as I retire or I die or whatever happens to me, it's not like markets are going to stop." A constant concern about potential failure amid cutthroat competition compelled Scott to keep up with market activity and investor demands, adapting to the industry's culture of overwork. It was that, or risk ending up like Kristen, laid off and looking for work.

The churn of employee and firm turnover pushed hedge fund workers to prove their dedication by working long hours. The bar was so high for this "commitment" that the people I spoke with consistently said things like Margaret, who indicated that her twelve-hour days allowed her to retain "balance" in her life. For how much workers

TABLE 2. The White-Collar Ideal vs. The Portfolio Ideal

Discourse	White-Collar Ideal	Portfolio Ideal
Identity	Firm identification	Personal brand
Cultural values	Devotion to employer	Passion for the work
Norms	Incremental advancement	Big leaps
Social capital	Loyalty to firm	Loyalty to networks

strived to profit for the firm and secure their place within it, they simultaneously prepared for the very real risks of downsizing, even firm collapse. When hedge funds survive and this risk pays off, workers can gain tremendous benefits: autonomy, wealth, and status—and with it, a portable reputation that may sustain them in down times. But living with and attempting to manage the organizational insecurity and the market intensification fueled by technology can be crushing. It adds to risk management in ways that amplify workers' insecurity.

Many of these working conditions are found across white-collar work sectors today.[6] The mid-twentieth century white-collar worker ideal was characterized by the "organization man" (refer to table 2).[7] The twenty-first-century white-collar worker, however, is prepared to repeatedly change jobs and firms, whether to advance or merely stay afloat.

Even at more stable hedge funds, the compressed organizational structure limits internal advancement, Sharon told me: "Hedge funds are fairly flat . . . so you're going to be getting paid a lot and unless something really awful happens, there's no up or down." Instead, workers advance through external labor markets in which they compete for positions at other firms that offer higher status and pay.[8] To show how they do this, and uphold the "portfolio worker" ideal, the following sections examine hedge fund workers' self-identity, cultural values, advancement norms, and networking strategies, all with reference to the "organization man" of the past.

Marketing a Personal Brand

High-status workers in the knowledge economy, from creative industries to the Silicon Valley, build personal brands.[9] Yet, hedge fund workers reveal how the personal brand—the cultivated professional reputation—is a neoliberal requirement to hedge against professional risk that implicitly converts a career path into an asset or product requiring investment. To gain industry recognition as experts, interviewees promoted their brands by posting on social media, blogging, writing e-newsletters, and presenting at conferences. Each helped build trust, rapport, and visibility with future colleagues, employers, and clients.

Key to the hedge fund worker's personal brand is a cogent and recognizable "investment thesis"—an individual theory of how to interpret the economy that sets hedge fund managers apart from "the herd" and suggests they are trendsetters, not trend followers. Renowned investment philosophies in this vein include George Soros's theory of reflexivity that strives to anticipate trading cycles driven by the hasty speculation of trend-followers (as in the 2006 US housing bubble). Another example is Ray Dalio's "All Weather" strategy, promoted through his books, YouTube videos, and email newsletters, that evaluates the changing relationships between different parts of economic systems. The individualized investment thesis reflects gendered and racialized assumptions about mastery, independent thinking, and self-confidence, all of which naturalize and perpetuate white men's dominating leadership positions in the field.

Unsurprisingly, then, the white men I interviewed frequently referred to building their personal brand and establishing a reputation for wholly unique expertise. Jeffrey, a white founder, told me what it takes to start a firm: "I want to carve out my niche and I have the confidence with which to do what I'm gonna do." An original, niche idea and confidence are the investor's warrants to launch a new fund, in his vision, which overlooks how these conditions are more readily accessible to white men than to others.[10] Another fifty-something white founder, Brian, repeatedly called himself an artist and preferred, accordingly, that I say he worked in "investments" rather than "finance"—as he put it, investments are about "independent thinking" distinct from the number-bound quantitative finance side. "It's an art, not a science," Brian told me. In general, descriptors about artistry, mastery, genius, or exceptionalism were more often applied to and by upper-class white men, consistent with research on beliefs about white men's exceptionalism.[11]

Portfolio management overall was described in explicitly individualistic and gendered terms, even by women. Lisa's words evoked Brian's, for example, as she said, "To make money, you have to have independent thinking, you have to have a variant perception of a strategy, a single name, or a stock idea." Variant perception refers to a distinct or innovative stance, a productive and profitable nonconformity that can sometimes stymie collaboration among colleagues. Using a martial, masculine metaphor, Lisa suggested that "there can only be one trigger puller for every portfolio"—any attempt at shared portfolio management was doomed, in her opinion. "You can't have a co-PM model. It rarely works out."

Still, Lisa identified how social networks influenced investment decisions and contradicted the value attached to independent thinking: "In reality, people talk to other people who are also in the same industry who also cover the same kind of investment universe. And therefore, you see some overlap between portfolios." Lisa cited the "Tiger Cubs," affiliated firms described in the introduction, as exemplifying how "even though people encourage independent thinking, sometimes they will talk to their friends to verify the idea. For instance, if I like Apple for a stock and I talk to my friends, 'Do you also like Apple?' That sort of contagion exists in the industry." Contagion, or herd behavior, is generally frowned on because it narrows profit margins and inhibits investment returns. Contagion can even signal illegal insider trading. At the same time, rapid price movements in the stock market are evidence that investors absolutely share ideas about stocks and strategies through their industry's social networks.

Women took a slightly different approach than the white men who described crafting their reputations around unique, individual investment theories and prowess. Women tended to stress the importance of intentionally building a professional reputation within their firms and in the industry. Gita's manager explicitly told her to focus on building the latter if she hoped to become a firm partner. To Gita, her career involved two jobs: "The job of making the cookie and the job of selling the cookie are two hugely different jobs—the job of actually doing your job and the job of selling yourself, telling people, 'this is what I've done,' and building that credibility." Excelling at her day-to-day duties was ultimately less beneficial for Gita's career than concerted self-promotion—recognition she was able to parlay into conference presentations, a published book, and a reputation as an industry expert. She made partner at her firm.

"By speaking at conferences and being out there and promoting, it reflects on the brand. That was a lot of how I was meeting people," commented Jennifer, whose twenty years of client networks dissipated in the 2008 financial crisis. It was an uncertain time, and she needed to rebuild her professional connections. She said, "I had to go back to that, putting myself out there and following through." She believed a strong personal brand garnered recognition in the industry and access to clients, both of which could provide a modicum of stability.

Despite these women's proactive accounts, I was told that women, in general, struggle to self-promote (a variation on the stereotype that women have low self-esteem).[12] Margaret, for instance, summarized a sense of caution among her peers: "Women are very much less willing to make statements unless they think that they are right," while men "just kind of spew things out."

For her part, Deborah thought women tended to both underestimate their own abilities and overestimate others'. Hiring an in-house accountant, Deborah invited a woman to apply: "She said, 'Well, sure but I doubt I'm qualified.'" Deborah recalled telling the applicant, "Well, your predecessor was a poet and you're an accountant, so it seems like you've got the qualifications needed." To her, recruiting women was always a good idea, because "a better employee is somebody who's not racing ahead claiming that they can do things that they really can't do." Yet Deborah noted that this show-don't-tell tendency "does hold women back." If other women didn't advocate for themselves, she thought, their talents were sure to be underutilized. Women might, she suggested, need to take risks in their careers, as she saw men doing: "You throw your hat in the ring, you argue for it, you know it's a step up in your career or a step forward in your career, and you're confident you'll figure it out when the time comes." Of course, when I asked why Deborah had sidestepped these gendered traps in her own career, she concluded, "I guess I don't have the same concerns that [other women] do."

Several men of color also described how they self-promote by building an online presence. Matthew, who is Black, distributed a newsletter with relevant articles on topics such as investor sentiment, stock market conditions, and political news. And Sokhom, a thirty-something Asian American man, recounted vigilance when it came to maintaining his networks and reputation. He wrote for news outlets and built an online forum.

The people of color and white women I interviewed spoke far more frequently of the self-promotion imperative; white men had no need for the practice of reputation-building since it was afforded via elite networks. As is often the case, the exceptions to the rule of white masculinity in this field make the prevailing norms and double standards more visible.

The "portfolio worker" mentality is tied up with the neoliberal concept of an independent economic agent—*homo economicus*—inextricable from sexist and racist ideas of who can be a steward of capital.[13] The personal brand rhetoric is an identity discourse that deters collaboration, fosters individualism, and transfers risks from firms to employees. More perniciously, it gives the impression that anyone can become established in the industry, so long as they do the hard work of reputation management via online platforms, professional associations, and durable relationships.

In reality, women and men of color may struggle to comply with a norm predicated on white masculinity. These interviewees described explicit strategies to self-promote and establish a brand, and how they believed women were disadvantaged because the efforts countered stereotypes about being communal (rather than individualist and agentic).[14] Women even shared specific stories of backlash when they upheld the masculine ideals for things like risk-taking. Meanwhile, men of color contend with racist stereotypes that differ for Black, Latinx, and Asian American men, who may, depending on race, be viewed as either too passive or too aggressive when self-promoting. The successful self-promoters among these men and women risked being viewed as competent but less than likable and hirable.

Only white men seemed to communicate their personal brand to me as an expression of confidence in their expertise. They spoke of themselves as artists and people who know their own market value. The emphasis on personal identity had material consequences—even though Gita is right that self-promotion might be ideal for selling but does not actually guarantee the quality of the product—including that white men were more able to convert recognition and reputation into opportunities such as jobs with higher pay and access to client investors. Again, I could see the patrimonial structure of the industry just beneath the meritocratic surface.

Investing with Passion

In the new economy, ~~skills and experience~~ aren't enough. Workers must also express and convey *passion*. The rise of employment flexibility has replaced the "organization man's" devotion to his firm with passion for the work, transportable across firms. As I asked hedge fund workers what they found rewarding about their work, alongside the high compensation, they emphasized a love for investing as a fast-paced, variable, and stimulating job. Jay, who is Latinx and in his thirties, said: "Really, it's the passion. Don't get me wrong, we're all doing it for the money, but there are obviously many times when it's not all glamour like in the movies, but you do it because of . . . the intellectual aspect of it." His own fixation on the puzzle, the game of investing, traced back to Jay's high school absorption in the movie "Wall Street."

Similarly, Wayne described building a financial model and executing a trade as gratifying, even thrilling. He said, "Finance is an area where you can apply your models and get your results instantaneously. How well it fit is exactly quantifiable. . . . Having a sense of accomplishment and using your quantitative skills to build something that describes reality . . . certainly feeds our pride." When Wayne described the relish with which he watched his models play out in real time, he began to evince Jay's passion: "A trade that goes the right way on you is more exciting than sex. It's very exciting. It's thrilling. It's a thrill—the biggest thrill I know of."[15]

"What makes it so exciting?" I asked.

"Probably some addictive nature that you need a thrill," he replied. "You've made all this work, and it's unfolding exactly or reasonably, as close as reasonably expected, exactly to what you expected.

You nailed it. You're a fucking hero. . . . It feels like you've conquered the market."

Wayne's eyes grew big as he associated mastering the market with heroic, conquering masculinity. To put his comments in perspective, Wayne's strategy might involve as much as a billion dollars in a set of trades playing out over a single day. Of course it's exciting! For his own hedge fund, Wayne had spent a full year developing and testing the model, only then raising investor funds. As he talked about finally executing these trades, I imagined him like a mad scientist watching his lab experiment in real time. When I asked if there was a team element to the thrill, Wayne brushed off the thought. "It's personal," he said, embracing an individual sense of accomplishment.

I approached Diane after a conference panel as she walked briskly toward the exit. She apologized—no time to talk, she had a flight to catch. As promised, though, we sat down for an interview months later in her office. I asked Diane how many hours she worked in an average week, and she said with a twinkle, "I don't know if I want to know what the number is!" Tapping her smartphone—"this little guy is with me all the time"—she said that her labor didn't require physical presence in the office (though she put in a lot of office hours, too). Her long hours working nights and weekends, Diane told me, were actually her preference: "Investing for me is not my job; it's my passion. It's my extracurricular activities, so it's not even work. I feel sorry for people who don't love what they do. I can't imagine going through life not loving my job . . . I never really turn it off, because I don't want to because I love it so much." Overwork was positioned as a true labor of love.

A performative element imbued the way hedge fund workers spoke of love and passion. It seemed their accounts served to prove to me—even to themselves—that their work really did involve meaning, purpose, and conviction rather than the pure monetary motivation two interviewees espoused (just one man and one woman, both white, admitted they do the work for the money, no reservations). But I also learned it was a response to an industry norm that distributed hiring, training, and investing opportunities. "Passion" or a lack thereof was part of the sorting of industry workers into gender- and race-segregated roles (recall the retail, regional, and quantitative typecasting in the last chapter). Demonstrating sufficient passion could somewhat offset firms' "mommy tracking" tendencies for women employees. A woman's passion, that is, was ultimately a tool for expressing her overarching commitment to the work and willingness to put in long hours—and to forego the stereotypical pulls of home and family. At the same time, when women cultivated expertise in topics that went against gender norms, they were nonetheless frequently reassigned to gender normative jobs.

Several interviewees cautioned that there is a downside to their passion: hedge fund workers can get caught up in infatuated, even addictive behavior. Wayne, for instance, told me about celebrating his thrilling trades and how he always won the drinking and eating competitions his team indulged in on those billion-dollar days. His "proudest" and "finest moment" came as he sat next to his boss's boss at dinner. Everyone had already had a couple of drinks, but when the waiter set down an open bottle, Wayne remembered with a smile, "I said, 'I feel like reaching over and drinking that bottle of wine.' [My boss's boss] said, 'Okay.'" Taking this as a challenge, "I grabbed it, and I chugged nonstop, the entire bottle of wine." As he gulped, Wayne's team cheered and took pictures. The night ended in barhopping, but Wayne blacked out. His colleagues told him it had involved him dancing by himself, then being poured into a cab. "Somehow, I got home," he said, amused.

Taking this in, I asked whether the blackout evening had affected his work the next day, but Wayne deadpanned: "When you're an alcoholic, you don't have hangovers." This may have been meant as a joke, though Wayne elaborated, "I would frequently not have any memory. I would function, but I don't have any memory [of it]." I pressed again: did these celebrations ever create problems for Wayne? "No, I loved it." As an Asian American man, participating in these celebratory bonding rituals may have been a way to help overcome stereotypes holding that Asian people are reserved or lightweight drinkers (both associated with femininity). It is extremely unlikely that this same strategy would have been successful for other men of color, especially Black men, or women of any race. Rather, these rituals could be seen as proof of stereotypes about being unpredictable and reckless.[16]

Self-harming behaviors came up in Albert's interview, too. At a leadership retreat, he had a realization: this career path's high demands had damaged some of his colleagues' marriages and nudged them toward addictions and vices. He said, "What became very apparent and an eye-opener for me is that nearly every single one of the senior managers had a dysfunctional family life, dysfunctional marriages, high percentages of divorce, and unfortunately I have to hold my hand up high in the air because I went through a divorce earlier in my career." Albert noticed, too, that "an incredible percentage" of his peers had a "vice, whether it's substance abuse, alcoholism, painkillers, they chase something or need a distraction or a stimulant of some other kind." Stimulus seeking is certainly part of the popular imagination of the "wired" hedge fund manager, fixated on—even addicted to—the stock market.

But Albert wanted something different. Instead of stimulants and depressants, Albert demarcated the end of his workday and the start of his family time with a daily martial arts practice:

> My wife would probably say it's a bad thing—is that I've sort of thrown myself at martial arts. I'm now a third-degree black belt and I will be absolutely gutted, humiliated, and check my ego at the door by my master [instructor] . . . but it's a good way to cleanse myself

mentally and emotionally and then keep everything [in] check and hopefully have a rich and untainted family life.

Albert thought that this ritual of masculine domination allowed him to transition from the role of hedge fund manager to that of husband and father.

Hedge fund workers, men and women alike, expressed a passion for their work that evoked romantic entanglements, infatuation, and addiction. Hidden in this expectation is the assumption that the expectation for devoted mothering makes mothers *less* passionate about their work (as expressed outright in chapter 3).[17] Importantly, that perceived mismatch of passion appeared to figure into the difficulty women had cultivating mentor relationships and client investors in this field. That will surely hold them back, given everything else we know about advancement. Moreover, the expression and reception of passion as an *emotion* versus an *action* is further shaped by race and social class status, as evident in the norms for workers' expressing emotions in risk-taking.[18]

Taking Big Leaps

The industry culture encourages, even requires, workers to take professional risks and change firms to increase their pay and status. Risk-taking is viewed as necessary to boost the firm's returns, advance one's career, and distinguish oneself from competitors. Vincent used a violent metaphor for career advancement: "This is a contact sport. You can't get through ten years in this business without having someone try to kill you or having to self-defend and kill somebody else career-wise. It's a negative." Vincent attributed his own success to being smarter than his competition, being audacious, fearless, and willing to accept risk—all expectations attached to the industry's hedgemonic masculinity. But a symbolic line separates rational, calculated risk-taking from recklessness. The hegemonic masculinity of a given context is defined in relation to marginalized masculinities and femininities,[19] so caution is associated with femininity, and extreme risk-taking captures a marginalized masculinity.

"Traders will always portray themselves as being the one who is looking out for risk," explained Craig, a white trader. "The first rule of risk management isn't so much whether you make or lose money, but *when* you lose money, do you lose as much money as you thought you would lose?" Craig understood risk-taking as the bailiwick of those with mastery and control. Using the pre-financial-crisis industry as an example, he went on to clarify the distinction between careful and careless risk-taking: "I think definitely the days of glorifying the big swing trader [a short-term, trend-based strategy] are gone to the extent of, 'Oh, that guy made a $100 million last year, isn't he great?' There's a little bit of skepticism. 'Did he just get lucky?'" The "guy" who gets rich quick in the ways that helped tank the economy in 2008 is no longer, Craig implied, a hero to hedge fund workers.

Craig's hypothetical guy used gendered terms that steered my thoughts to the norms around risk-taking. In planning her career, Margaret emphasized the importance of "putting on risk" by asserting herself in investment decisions—a risk for those who differ from the majority. She knew that making money advances careers; if you can't tolerate risk, she said, "You lose, and it's actually that final, because you don't get to make money unless you put on risk and if you never put on risk, you don't get to make money, in which case you don't get to go any further." Changing firms, making bold investments, or launching new funds are the risks perceived to incur the greatest rewards and great losses. Yet, drawing on gender stereotypes, Margaret theorized that risk-taking held women back: "It's very nonintuitive to women to make leaps, but leaps are what this business is about."

When it comes to risk-taking, gender-essentialist stereotypes present a paradox. On the one hand, my interviewees generally held that women are risk-averse and men are more risk-tolerant—a "fact" that could hinder women's long-term success.[20] On the other hand, people suggested risk-aversion made women more effective at managing investments. Justin, the forty-something white founder, claimed that women-led firms "did less poorly" during the financial crisis because "men take more risk," but he posited that the same tendency might lead to lower profits during market upturns. This is a fairly popular belief, even though there is no conclusive evidence that men and women have different tolerances for risk in financial services.[21]

Deborah, herself a white founder, characterized men as more daring and women as more prudent. To her, moving up in the hedge fund world took "a certain kind of leap of faith that I can figure this out. . . . And maybe that's a little bit more of a male trait of you know, you throw your hat in the ring." But, she said, "I think women like to stick in safer waters." Contradicting her generalizations about men's and women's risk-taking, Deborah described her own determination and preparedness in her firm's launch: like Wayne, she carefully spent a year modeling the financial instruments, calculating the systems requirements, and building her team before her launch.

Another founder, Diane echoed Deborah and gave an allegorical car race between a man and a woman. As their Lamborghinis approach a sign reading, "Dangerous Turn, Slow Down," the woman heeds the sign, but, Diane said:

> The man keeps going. He drives over a cliff. She never picks up speed. He gets a new car. He comes back onto the road. That was the only curve, and he drives really fast to the finish line and ends up getting there before she does. She saw the risk. She made the appropriate changes in her vehicle to not drive off the road. He drives one speed, which is fast. The problem is she prevented a car crash. That's the good news. The bad news is she never got out of second gear.

In finance, Diane thought, whether or not risk tolerance really was engendered by biology or socialization, women are likely to be penalized for being careful, while men can trust that even a spectacular failure won't ruin their careers.

Real stories in my interviews tended to anchor hypotheticals, which often exposed beliefs rather than reality. Diane shared her car race allegory after describing a peer regarded as a "risk-taker." Diane's partners had challenged her decision to invest in this woman's hedge fund: "She's got great numbers, but she's aggressive, like when you meet her personality-wise, and I think it freaked them out a little bit." Diane told her partners that her prior investments in the woman's fund performed well, but "they were like, 'But the drawdowns,' and I was like, 'Look at her track record. Every time she has a drawdown, you want to put money in.' And so mathematically the numbers ultimately bear out."

Following this anecdote with the car race allegory was a contradiction. If a woman is pigeonholed as overly aggressive when she follows industry norms for men, it would appear risk-taking is a penalty for women, and risk-aversion a potential boon. As has been found in other white-collar work, women in hedge funds may intentionally present themselves as risk-averse because they understand they are being held to a different standard than men.[22]

The dominant gender ideology in finance not only stereotypes women, it also reinforces the ideology of hedgemonic masculinity, defined in contrast to normative femininity and marginalized masculinity. To wit: I found *no* evidence to support interviewees' claims that women take fewer risks than men. Diane described herself as "guilty" of being overly risk-avoidant, but she also gave plenty of examples of learning to evaluate and take calculated risks. At another point, she said that weathering market downturns had taught her risk tolerance and risk management: "That's part of it, you get used to the turbulence. It doesn't crash the airplane. It's just annoying sometimes. And that takes time. I wish I could flip the switch and all of the woman in finance could become incredibly aggressive, but that takes time."

Others cited their first major market downturn or bad trade as an industry rite of passage. At one women's networking event, attendees traded tales about the first time they lost over a million dollars on a single trade. One South Asian American woman remembered her terror that she would be fired when she lost five million dollars, and her surprise when her team lead, a man, instead congratulated her and welcomed her to the club so to speak. She even learned there was a ritual for getting past the bad bet milestone: express frustration in the moment (your passion!), then blow off some steam over drinks with colleagues after work. Even the most cautious investors understood the occasional big loss as the cost of doing business.

But men brought up their "sweaty palm time[s]," as Wayne put it, earlier in their careers, too. Wayne said he was more nervous the first time he took a million-dollar trade than his first billion-dollar trade. When that worked, as did his first ten-million-dollar trade, he gained confidence. I asked him what went through his mind with those successful trades: "I researched it pretty thoroughly. It worked exactly how I thought it would. When you have 1, 2, 5, 10, 20, 30 of those, then you start to think, 'oh, I think maybe I know what I'm doing.' Then it became pretty routine. I guess the next big thing was when I had a billion-dollar trade." Wayne raised an eyebrow, saying, "That became exciting just because of the number. It's an interesting number," then grew quiet, contemplating the size and possibility of *one billion*.

Over time, Wayne developed an ability to compartmentalize the scale of the money only in relation to the model he built rather than as a risk on the line, like a bet, but getting there was a "roller-coaster." He toggled between trusting and second-guessing his models:

I thought, "Okay, it's just not complete yet. You're not there yet. This is not fully it. You shouldn't be scared." [And then] I'd think, "Oh, no.

It's not working." I'd still have that in my mind. That made for an emotional roller coaster. . . . I've worked with these things for long enough that I'm a bit more used to it or trusting in it that I know what to expect. I know what it's gonna look like. I think I have less of those fears, particularly because this is so quantifiable of an industry.

Building a tolerance for investment risk took time and involved hesitation, even for portfolio managers with successful track records.

While interviewees had similar accounts of gaining comfort with taking risks, women were not the only ones who reported being responded to differently when they engaged in risk-taking behavior like their white men colleagues. Matthew spoke with a commanding presence typical of finance's elite circles, yet colleagues called him "arrogant." Matthew attributed this to the perceived incongruity of having an elite upbringing as a Black man. His colleagues also reacted differently when Matthew upheld traders' masculine, and evidently white, norms for aggression and competitiveness: two white women reported him as "threatening." Though traders are expected to act aggressively and express anger when trades fail,[23] in a sense performing their passion for the work, Matthew had to contend with what Adia Harvey Wingfield theorizes as the "specter of the angry black man" and attenuate his displays of masculinity.[24] The portfolio worker ideal is so implicitly typed as white, masculine, and elite that being two out of three was still not enough to allow Matthew to embody the ideal.

The ideal hedge fund worker is a risk-taking enterpriser invested in the neoliberal economy of self. But because perceptions of professional and investment risk-taking are shaped by gender, race, and social class status, not everyone is read as a natural fit for the ideal. Deviations are converted to exceptions to the norm such that women can be called out as either too risk-averse (because of gender stereotypes) *or* too risky (should they violate gender norms to uphold industry norms around risk-taking). And a Black man can be penalized for enacting the passion lauded among other workers, while an Asian American man can build his reputation positively by getting black-out drunk with his colleagues. Against a norm predicated on an ideal, hedgemonic masculinity, and an industry in which compensation is based on perceived contributions and subjective evaluations, perceptions of risk-taking and actual risk-taking have material consequences. The broader transfer of risks to workers in the new economy may place a particular burden on those who lack class, gender, or racial privilege.

Leveraging Patrimonial Networks

As I suggested earlier, in anticipation of layoffs and firm turnover, these workers endeavor to build durable networks both inside and outside the firm to ease the search for future job opportunities, investors, and institutional support. This allows patrimonialism, and its privileging of white men, to flourish in the hedge fund industry. It's all about the social capital—the resources and benefits provided by one's location in a social network.[25] Social capital provides access to promotions, job opportunities, client investors, and other institutional supports, yet it is a paradox in this context of insecurity. Although workers are expected to operate as independent, autonomous agents—personal brands—they are reliant on their social connections when they seek to advance through external labor markets.

People "grow their networks" outside their firm by attending the types of conferences and social hours I frequented during my fieldwork. During first introductions, people often asked one another, "What can I help you with?" or more directly, "What do you need?" Exchanging favors like personal introductions or investment advice is normative behavior. As one person described, there is a "pay-it-forward mentality" in the industry. People are eager to extend a hand in anticipation that it will be reciprocated. Thus, I saw people exchange business cards in a flurry, then follow up promptly with an email to establish a channel of communication and demonstrate their professionalism. Several people stressed how this helped to establish the trust and credibility that builds professional relationships.

Specifically, interviewees told me that, according to this social capital mindset, you do not build, but invest in a network. Workers with access to the white men's dominant networks recounted more job protection and opportunities. Their networks allowed them to take professional risks, like taking a job at a startup or launching their own firm. Social capital can also provide protection during an economic crisis, as Vincent experienced working at a large investment bank when the Great Recession hit. During the financial crisis, he drew on his vast and lucrative networks from his time as a hedge fund manager, and his "Rolodex" became valuable to the bank. He could source potential investors and business deals that helped keep his company afloat. Other people I spoke with intimated that women in hedge funds all but automatically lacked the social capital required for retention during times of turnover.[26]

And people stressed the need to "leverage"—to maximize the potential return on their investment in their networks. Recall that Jennifer, laid off during the financial crisis, said she "had been pretty successful at leveraging speaking at conferences" to reassert her personal brand, find clients, and rebuild her network. Leverage, in the financial sense, refers to a strategy where the investor borrows money or capital to generate higher returns. Because it uses borrowed capital, leveraging amplifies gains or losses (that is, the risks involved). Moreover, leveraging is often used to make investments in speculative assets, such as an early-stage technology startup, which are riskier yet. In that context, my informants' use of the term *leverage* implied a need to take social risks and capitalize on social networks.

Gita strived toward a network that she could leverage to advance professionally, prioritizing formal networking such as conferences in order to get face time with contacts: "In terms of building your credibility, part of it is just being in front of people, because they see you, they know who you are . . . be there and be present." Certainly, this involved some finesse and social skill: "You have to carry yourself well and professionally. And a combination of being charming and pleasant and at the same time, knowing your stuff and being aware of the market and understanding the dynamics of whatever it is, the area you cover. And those are all the things I am trying to leverage, that I can pull, in terms of building my network." Notably, Gita evoked the "soft skills" associated with upper-class femininity when she used the words "charming" and "pleasant." Women in finance, as we have established, are concentrated in client services roles and expected to manage relationships with wealthy investors on the basis of their interpersonal skills that uphold upper-class femininity.

As a new mother, Gita didn't have time to socialize with her colleagues after work, and so, she said, "I have to be creative in terms of thinking about other ways to basically get in front of people." This important task was "challenging for women," because, Gita noted, "Guys have a lot of ways to get together. For example, fantasy football, to drink and hang out or to go see a game or something. A lot of it is drinking. And for women—I don't want to do that. There are limits as to how much socialization I can do." Her limited time away from work was already spoken for by family, but Gita understood that social bonding and networking were taking place after official working hours. Because these activities matter for building mentoring relationships and making important business decisions, she sought to find other avenues for networking with her coworkers.

A women's association intentionally designed its events to contrast with popular men's-only events like the charity poker hedge fund events in which it was said men brokered deals, shared insider information, and formed bonds. Women needed their own events to create networks and provide opportunities like job leads and access to investment capital, and the group responded. However, it became clear that the association's events were understood to provide less valuable social capital than the men's events or deemed a last resort for networking in the industry (an insult consistently applied to the women's associations in other lucrative industries, as well).[27]

One event I attended with Erica, a white woman in her thirties, featured a speaker who was an author and the daughter of a business mogul. After the talk, in an old theater building in Midtown, a swarm of brightly dressed younger women rushed to introduce themselves to the famous speaker. Amid the flurry and noisy activity, we ran into Sasha, who was on the cusp of leaving her job after experiencing discrimination (see chapter 4). To manage the risk of leaving her firm, she was making a concerted effort to network with other women.

As the three of us talked, Erica gestured to the women around us, commenting how these events were "just full of women desperate to find a job." "No, really?" Sasha asked, raising her eyebrows.

The last time we had met, at another event hosted by the women's association, Sasha had wondered whether it was worth paying the extra fee—$1,200 (donated to charity)—to attend a hosted breakfast with the speaker. It would provide an opportunity to meet the speaker and mingle with a smaller group of women. Now it seemed she'd become even less sure about this "investment" in her portfolio career, because a white woman had denigrated the social networking value of those opportunities available to her. Meanwhile, Sasha didn't attend the Wall Street events and associations for Black professionals or people of color because she wanted to avoid tokenization. She had told me, "I don't want to be in that box. I'm trying to get out of that box." In this moment, chatting in a crowd of her eager competitors, Sasha seemed to realize she'd stepped into a trap.

Networks have always been important in professional development, and so they constitute a key driver of social inequality in finance.[28] In the neoliberal, new economy, the financial logics applied to social capital can be traced to the structural obstacles posed by downsizing and layoffs: increased job competition increases the value of your networks. Hedge funds have high-turnover rates, and insiders told me that women and racial minority men were the first to go during the 2008 financial crisis and other turbulent periods. Their social capital became more literal, as these workers sought to capitalize on—leverage—their social networks to manage the risk associated with employment insecurity.

But for those experiencing discrimination or harassment, access to these network-based safety nets is less reliable or may worsen their exposure to harm. And, unfortunately, women and racial minority men were denied access to the highest-value networks: those composed of elite white men. The social capital they could create was, as it were, discounted in the same way as their expertise, risk tolerance, and revenue-generating potential so often were.[29] These perceptions of social value in a capitalist economy have tangible implications for the structure of professional networks and the path of people's careers, especially in contexts of uncertainty in which people tend be more guarded and clannish.[30]

WORKING LIKE A FAMILY

Gaining know-how is crucial to those working within this unpredictable but high-reward industry, and much of that, insiders told me, happens through the close-knit networks and master/apprentice relationships that characterize their patrimonial field. Throughout my fieldwork and interviews, people referred to hedge fund managers as "chiefs" or "kings." One man even specified, "I intentionally said 'king' because it's always a man." These monikers indicated the primacy of particularly men hedge fund managers, their foundational investment philosophies, and their ability to anoint heirs apparent and spawn hedge fund dynasties (think, here, of the "Tiger Cub" firms founded by Tiger Management protégés).

The chiefs and kings weren't only gendered roles but racialized, too. Industry insiders described hedge fund culture as like "fraternities," implying racial homogeneity (fraternities tend to be racially segregated with Black fraternities labeled as such and white fraternities unmarked). The racial connotation becomes even more apparent in references to firms spun off from larger institutions like investment banks. People sometimes referred to these firms, often predominantly white, as "tribes" to describe the practice of a successful investment manager who would leave to start a separate firm—often funded by money raised from the previous firm and investors—and brings along their entire team. As Weber theorized, a patrimonial "tribe" is often bound by race and a shared ethnic culture.[31] The terms *king, chief,* and *tribe* reflect how social ties are racialized in this industry.

Building the sense of a firm as a "tribe" means inculcating members to the firm's and the industry's normative behavior, building trust through a common cultural script. Firms encourage close social bonds through social activities such as dinners, fantasy football leagues, and team sports; I encountered one reputable firm that used karaoke bar outings and annual relay races, while others hosted off-site retreats that involved white-water rafting, alpine skiing, or charity gambling in coveted destinations. Of course, the base fact that the firms and patrimonialism generally are both gendered and racialized configures which workers felt comfortable in these spaces and forged deeper access to the inner circles.

A hedge fund manager must select just the right workers (from the manager's vantage), then groom those workers over time into their investment tradition. Jay's response to a question about his own training was instructive in that it turned immediately to the value of leveraging networks to pass along knowledge and know-how:

The business is very collegial. It feels like a family almost. One thing I learned immediately is there is a very strong mentorship environment. It's very patrilineal. What I noticed is, for example, my boss came from this place and he had been taught by this guy . . . a very strong sense of that mentorship and master/apprentice type of relationship. . . . One generation teaches the next generation who teaches the next generation. There's a strong sense of loyalty, there's a strong sense of kinship and family. It really does feel like a family.

When a manager takes on a protégé, a standout employee on the front office investment team, they are passing along an investment tradition the protégé will carry forward. This gift instills a sense of trust, loyalty, even kinship with the symbolic father-leader, whose status is socially and culturally, rather than biologically, determined.[32] The exchange of protégé loyalty for a mentor's skills and insight may even be rewarded, down the line, with the manager providing seed funding for the protégé to start their own fund.

When I met Jay at a networking event, he was surrounded by a group of younger men, noticeably composed of racial minority men in a sea of white men's faces. As we talked, Jay would pause intermittently to introduce one or more of these men to important contacts, then return to our chat. Later, I understood this group as Jay's protégés. When we sat down for a longer interview, Jay told me of developing these relationships: "As you get older, wiser, more experienced, you seek somebody that reminds you of you, who has that same ambition, that same passion, that same drive. And you teach them all that you know." *Somebody that reminds you of you*—Jay had unthinkingly confirmed that hiring *and* mentoring choices hinge on a sense of familiarity. His words indicated not only how elite structures are reproduced from one generation to the next but also why homophily is so hypervisible in this industry.

Jay underscored tradition, which, according to Weber, becomes a way to describe a taken-for-granted structure by which patrimonialism feels natural to its participants.[33] Jay, himself socialized into this system, naturalized his hiring and mentoring selections as "this organic process whereby you see people that have the same mentality, the same passion. It's very tough to explain from a data perspective, quantitatively, how do you quantify that? You just see it. You kind of feel it. It's organic." Like other cultivated and highly valued knowledge in the hedge fund industry, I was told that leaders develop *senses* and accumulate almost mystical know-how. The "chiefs" were understood as having innate and nearly unquestionable judgment.

As men of color, Jay and his protégés counter the norm for white-dominated networks but prove it at the same time. Jay provided insight into how these networks become segregated, noting that "people always try to place" him racially, as though he must be categorized. Even though his surname easily identifies him as Latinx—which he verified by mentioning being Mexican American and growing up in the southern borderlands—Jay described professional interactions stilted by others' need to mark him in order to understand his place in these elite, mostly white circles.

The emphasis on race as a primary status marker may make it difficult for people of color to build crucial relationships with white leaders. Matthew, whose white coworkers had called him "threatening," said, "The diversity problem is that you have no Black leadership. And when there aren't people in positions of power then the whole relationship game cannot be played." Within what sociologist Wendy Moore terms "a white space,"[34] familiarity is seen as a proxy for trustworthiness and loyalty, boxing out the "unfamiliar" and reproducing white power and privilege through patrimonial norms, values, beliefs, and social rituals. Over time, even seemingly harmless social activities can prevent people of color from building the relationships needed to advance—or even to just stay afloat.

Gita reflected on how her marginalization from white men's networks hedged her out of untold industry know-how, investment deals, and job opportunities. Still, she described the "more subtle" exclusionary behavior in the industry:

> [This business] is about information advantage, right? I mean who you know, what you know, you need to know the place, and you need to know what are the motivations, what are they doing. . . . I think guys have a much more established network in this business, and they tell each other stuff. . . . They might be like golfing or like having dinner or going out drinking and [trading] these nuggets of information.

Being on the outside, she said, is "tough." Gita knew she was missing out on valuable investment advice and told me about once having discovered that her colleagues regularly shared investment advice and tips in the chat forum of their fantasy football website. "Women are still outside sort of like that inner circle," she said. "And you know, people like people like themselves. For whatever reason, there is a barrier."

Similarly, Linda, who is, like Gita, Asian American, recounted that she kept asking herself, "What would it be like if I were a man here right now?" and "What would it have been like if I were white?" When racism and sexism are cloaked by naturalized homophily, it makes it harder to identify and counteract. Those who are excluded bear the onus of either coping or trying to make the unseen processes seen—in ways that will make them seem even less like a natural member of the tribe. As the only woman in her firm—"a little bit like a frat house," Linda said—it seemed obvious that the team-building events were *men's* bonding events: "They can talk about, you know, sports, and they can talk about many other different things they won't feel comfortable talking about around women. It's the same thing as why golf clubs don't want that many women members."

When Sharon was the head of trading, she arrived at a meeting in her boss's office to find that all the men had agreed on their strategy decisions in the bathroom before the meeting. "'Oh, we talked about that already. Oh right, you weren't in the bathroom with us,'" they said. She recalled, "That still happens today."

When women *are* incorporated into the men's "inner circle," it is often in a familial or sexual way—at a cost to their careers. The socialization and premium on feeling "like a family" could extend to romance: the tendency for overwork meant the office was workers' primary place to meet people, and it was common for colleagues to date. A man I met at a conference told me that, at a friend's firm, "they are encouraged to sleep together," and the hiring materials feature married couples who met at the firm (a workplace extension of the "Greek" scene on campuses, which so effectively and proudly pair affluent white women with affluent white men).[35] At every co-ed event I attended, men commented on and assessed my appearance and asked me out on dates. An older man suggested at one point that I should meet his son and, at another, introduced me to his "handsome young business partner." The blurry boundaries between kin-like and kin-based relationships breed sexual harassment, as we explore in the next section.

Hinting at harassment, the women I interviewed stressed the need to "have a thick skin" amid "college boy stuff"—the prevalence of crude and sexualized jokes and banter in the office. Margaret described this as a requirement that women show they are not easily offended or risk being alienated. She elaborated,

It's a bunch of guys sitting together. The conversation eventually turns to their wives, which is always *interesting*—it could be good or bad. Sometimes it turns to sports. Sometimes it turns to lewd jokes, but in any case, it's very standard college boy stuff. You just have to be a girl who isn't pretending not to be offended by it but is truly not offended by it.

This type of banter, which Beth Quinn calls "chain yanking," is cloaked in ambiguous humor and fosters solidarity among men on work teams through the ostracizing of women.[36]

Similar dynamics were at work around race and ethnicity. For instance, one Latinx man had "nicknamed" his colleague of Middle Eastern descent "the Persian Rug." Many interviewees commented on "political correctness," leading me to suspect that white people also used these types of nicknames and jokes but perhaps in more coded language. I wondered whether they were perhaps ashamed to share specific examples of racist banter (whether their comments or ones directed at them). After all, research finds that Black professionals often disengage when they encounter racism at work; it is one way to resist and protect themselves from emotional injury without heightening stereotypes like, as Matthew indicated, the "angry Black man."[37] Clearly, these forms of banter create an unfriendly work environment that tokenizes and isolates gender and racial minorities; some, like Mathew and Sasha, will eventually be pushed out of their firms should the culture become unbearable.[38]

The social rituals of hedge fund "tribes," Margaret explained, include personal feedback delivered in team meetings—and often in offensive terms. "Very often the criticism is given not necessarily in the kindest or even the most PC way. You just have to accept that that's how the communication is being delivered, and it's not at all anything to do with you as a person." I pressed, asking Margaret how it felt in the moment, and she conceded, "It feels terrible. It feels absolutely terrible. And not letting it be something that's personal is very important." While candid criticism may have also felt terrible to the white men on Margaret's team, it was amplified for those who were tokenized, likely because insensitive and lewd language—codes for racism and sexism—specifically targets and isolates them.[39] Consistent with the trading floors of the 1980s and 1990s, the trading desk's definitions of competence and teamwork, giving and receiving criticism, and engaging in social banter often took sexualized, racialized, and especially demeaning forms.[40] By marginalizing femininity and non-white masculinities, this banter is key to constructing and shoring up the industry's hedgemonic masculinity.[41]

Relationship-based grooming practices at hedge funds affect who advances in this lucrative industry, and a deeper look provides a host of clues as to why white men not only dominate in the industry but also in its high-level positions. And the specialized, apprenticeship style of training allows them to demand a premium for their expertise.[42] While patrimonialism captures the industry's social organization, hedgemonic masculinity is the dominant ideology that justifies patrimonialism, as reflected in the portfolio ideal for workers.

Having a Million Dollars on the Line

In this networked industry, people "meet" constantly—for coffee, for lunch, for happy hour, and for dinner. It never ends, and I, for one, found it exhausting, as did many of the women I interviewed. But you don't know who is going to be helpful, usually in terms of leading to a job, a client investor, or an investment opportunity—or, for me, a research lead—and so you keep taking meetings. The problem is, women and minority men are more reliant on building connections to advance than are white men, and they are also more vulnerable to being harassed or put at risk should a meeting turn out not to be strictly professional. Interactions can cross the line so quickly and easily, and the "frat" culture of hedge funds excuses so much. The culture of overwork and meeting taking has different consequences for women than men.[43]

As feminist scholars have shown, sexual harassment is about power, not sex. It serves to secure power and domination in the workplace, and so it can be those women who are leaders, assertive, and independent within fields dominated by men who are most likely to be harassed.[44] Harassment puts people, especially women, in their place should they undermine the social hierarchy.

I found that industry expectations about women as polite and congenial, especially with men, left some women hesitant to label harassment as such. In my interviews, women more often termed a man's behavior "inappropriate" or said it made them "uncomfortable." Sexual harassment was explicitly tied to the expectations for upper-class femininity in a culture of hard work, sociability, and politeness. Women in elite social settings tend to be responsible for organizing social activities and ensuring that everyone gets along in a way that often caters to men.[45] And in the context of social networking, the ambiguity of whether or not the advance is, in fact, harassment is purposeful. It places the burden of proof on those being harassed who must then challenge the social hierarchy at work.

Women were expected to have strong social skills and an attractive appearance. The head of marketing and operations at her firm, Erica stood casually atop four-inch-high heels as she told me, "For investor relations, it sounds sexist, but it's helpful to be a woman because you have certain qualities that men don't have like we're more approachable. We listen better. And there's a gentler approach that lends itself well to investor relations." We have seen how the "soft skills" attributed to women are part of their gender sorting into roles that cater to affluent and institutional client investors who were mostly men. Women in sales are expected to be deferential, amicable, and attractive, and to settle comfortably into the power imbalance with their clients. All this made women especially vulnerable to overt comments about their bodies, ambiguous invitations for dates, and other sexualized interactions, which often made it difficult to do their jobs and earn respect from colleagues.[46] These habitual patterns of deference reinforced colleagues' view that women are "naturally" less technical, less authoritative, and more subservient—qualities better suited to client relations. It became an iterative process of stereotyping and subjugation.

Erica and other women in client services managed their physical presentation as carefully as their social relationships. I was struck by how often they seemed to do their work easily and confidently in formfitting dresses and towering high heels, and I was reminded when Erica, complimented me as "beautiful," that appearance is at a premium in the industry. Like the hostesses in Kimberly Hoang's research on financial dealings in Vietnam and the women whose bodies provide elite distinction in the VIP party scene Ashley Mears's investigates, women in hedge funds knew conventional sexual attractiveness was a form of currency.[47]

Erica denied that she had ever been harassed, but said, "You have to be kind of pleasant and sometimes guys take it the wrong way," implying that men had asked her on dates or made sexual comments. She laughed uncomfortably and again told me that, in sales "you have to be like nice and there's always gross guys out there, so . . . " She trailed off. I tried again to see whether there were examples of men who, she said, "respond not how you want them to" in professional interactions. She responded, "No real examples, just you know, the *flavor.*"

One evening in Manhattan, I got a better sense of this "flavor." I met Erica at an industry social hour held at an upscale cocktail bar atop a Fifth Avenue designer store. Though she said she'd fallen "out of the habit" of going to these kinds of events, we spent the night professional party hopping. I noted that Erica received unwanted attention from men throughout the evening, from older men walking up to compliment us at the cocktail bar (at which Erica, gracious and smiling with the men, occasionally rolled her eyes at me) to a persistent hedge fund attorney at an event in Bryant Park who doggedly attempted to engage with Erica, me, and one of Erica's friends (our evasion tactics failed, and though we moved to the patio, the man followed us outside).

Knowing the "flavor" of a vague sexual advance was a recurring theme in my interviews with women who interacted with client investors. It kept them constantly on edge. Women recounted clients whose invitations to dinner or coffee, whether by tone or informality, seemed to differ from a usual investor meeting, and clients who made sexual advances after business dinners. "When there's a million dollars on the line, what do you do?" sighed one woman who felt pressured not to make a big deal out of sexual harassment. The ambiguity and high stakes made it difficult to escalate unease to any kind of formal complaint.

Michelle, a forty-something white woman, had a more senior role and technical position in trading, which allowed her more control over harassing interactions. Nonetheless, she downplayed their effects on her. When a client invited her for a drink that felt "like it wasn't all about work," she said, "and I wouldn't call that harassment, but maybe, you know, a little uncomfortable." She said, "the most uncomfortable it's really ever gotten for me" was what she called, with an uncomfortable laugh, "client dates," which she insisted "I do not [purposely] go on," before saying, "It doesn't happen often. I'd say only a couple times a year maybe." While Michelle minimized these interactions, the frequency and the fact that she had a term for them suggested client overtures were both deeply uncomfortable *and* just part of the job.[48]

Recently, outside Michelle's hotel after a business dinner, a client asked, "May I come in for a drink?" She laughed, again uncomfortably, as she told me that she declined with a simple, "No. I'm too busy but thank you." The man left it at that, but Michelle did mention the interaction to the person on the account, who confronted the client, leading to an apology call to Michelle. She recalled, "he was just very upfront and kind of apologized if it came off the wrong way, and I said it really didn't. It was just funny—the timing or something. And then we moved on. And that's really the nature of this business."

That Michelle could expect her team to take inappropriate interactions seriously likely traces to her senior role. Women in junior roles often declined to share, even with me (let alone team members) any details of these kinds of interactions; perhaps their more precarious status at their firms puts them at more risk than their harassers might face. Nonetheless, sexual harassment was common, usually in the form of purportedly flattering but uncomfortable comments from clients and sexualized jokes and banter from colleagues, mostly men.[49]

It was *also* racist, women of color told me. Kim, an Asian American woman and more senior professional I met at a conference, lamented men's infantilizing, racialized, and sexualized comments about her appearance. Some mentioned that she looked unusually young, while one colleague, a man, astounded her by asking, "How to you keep so thin? Do you eat egg rolls?" Kim's jaw dropped and her eyebrows shot up as she shared her coworker's racist advances: "You wouldn't believe the things people say to me." As I had so often in my interviews, I had the distinct sense that the most egregious examples were withheld—perhaps too uncomfortable to share.

Only one woman said her firm acted in response to internal sexual harassment allegations. Linda shared that, earlier in her career as an accountant in operations, a senior colleague habitually pestered her with inappropriate questions, such as "How was your date last night? What kinds of things did you do? Did you go back to his house?" It felt risky to report the bad behavior of a senior colleague, so she kept it quiet for a long time.

Then, at a birthday celebration with her women colleagues, came a cascade of "me too" revelations. Linda recalled how, casually, one woman asked of the man, "Don't you think he's a little creepy?"

Another affirmed, "Yeah, actually, he's kind of sleazy. He said this to me the other day . . . " A third woman added, "Whoa, me too." Their conversation revealed that the man had said to one woman, "I bought my wife lingerie for her birthday. Do you wear lingerie?" and that, in another case, he had touched a woman's leg while they shared a ride to a work event. As the stories poured out, Linda remembered, one woman finally declared, "Well, I'm going to say something."

As a group, the women reported their experiences to leadership. The man wasn't terminated, Linda said with disappointment: "They were 'punitive' in that he didn't receive extra pay. There were no bonuses. He had to change seats to the center of the room, where the screens are available for everyone to see. He was being monitored. Another person was hired above him, but he stayed for, I think, another year or so after that." Claiming legal restrictions, leadership insisted he couldn't be fired, so they seemed to try to nudge him out, despite his unresponsiveness. Having to face another year of harassment is part of a dynamic that contributes to women's perception that reporting sexual harassment can be futile or worsen their work environments.[50] Often, there are repercussions for being the one to disrupt the "trust" and "loyalty" of the "tribe."

Of continuing to work with the man, Linda said, "It was a little bit awkward, but it seemed fine to me, better actually, because there wasn't side commentary. But other women didn't feel that way. He wasn't hostile. He was very polite to everybody, but I'm not sure how those individuals necessarily felt afterward." By avoiding hostility and maintaining politeness—in other words, class respectability— the man understood he could avoid accountability. Eventually, Linda said, he left to work at another firm, cycled through a series of hedge funds, and remained employed in the industry—it was a textbook example of the phenomenon called "passing the trash."

The response at Linda's firm both reflected and demonstrated how sexual harassment reinforces organizational and industry inequality and obscures the risks inherent in the industry's "meeting culture." Sexual harassment, in particular, often results in financial distress and obstacles to career attainment.[51] And by responding at all, Linda's firm was exceptional—likely because there were enough women to raise the issue as a group. At most hedge funds I came across in my research, women were fairly isolated, amplifying the risk of reporting discrimination or harassment, especially if an abuser was an executive (who, "wearing many hats," could turn out, as Sasha found in chapter 4, to be the firm's designated human resources officer). These dynamics were central to how relations of power and status operate at these firms and were upheld by the culture of overwork and meeting-taking.

The Capitalizable Person

Cultural ideals guide how high-status and high-paid workers respond to the hedge fund industry's employment insecurity and expectations of overwork. Often, they apply the strategies they use to hedge risk in the market to hedging risk in their own careers. The people I interviewed idealized an image of a worker as an innovative, passionate self-starter and active contributor to the firm's bottom line. They spoke of their own careers as a financial product or asset, requiring ongoing investments in resources, development, and management. I call this the portfolio ideal, a worker norm for building high value, high profile, and highly transportable skills. The underlying culture of insecurity that demands the cultivation of the portfolio ideal also reveals how gender, race, and social class, as systems of inequality, are a crucial part of the industry's social organization of *homo economicus*, the capitalizable person.[52]

The portfolio ideal worker appears class, gender, and race neutral yet legitimizes the dominance of hedgemonic masculinity in finance. The emphasis on a personal brand, for example, deters collaboration, fosters individualism, and reinforces notions of leadership reserved for white men. A value for passion for the work, again ostensibly neutral, serves to justify the work's intensity and long hours but appears incompatible with expectations for mothers, as well as for Black men for whom expressions of passion can be interpreted as arrogant or threatening. The norms for risk-taking reward people, mostly white men, who can leverage the most lucrative networks as safety nets hedging against investment and job loss. And the logics of financial markets are applied to investing in those social networks, where patrimonialism facilitates the accumulation of valuable social capital for men, especially those who are white, and discounts the power of networks formed by women and minority men. The portfolio ideal is, top to bottom, implicitly infused with positive beliefs that elite, white masculinity is the making of "natural" leaders within this system.

The portfolio ideal appears relevant in other fields, such as information technology and oil and gas, in which workers prepare to advance outside of their firm.[53] Market language, akin to leverage and branding, is part of a new ideal for masculinity in high-tech. Of the business literature, Steven Vallas and Christopher Prener conclude: "In the new flexible economy, free agents must approach their talents in the same manner as do finance capitalists, hedging their bets by engaging multiple clients instead of a single boss."[54] The decline of the "organization man" and the rise of the portfolio ideal seems to have spread well beyond Wall Street.

Hedge fund workers, then, provide an enormously influential case study of the transformation of the social organization of work since the mid-twentieth century. Firms no longer assume risks on behalf of their employees but transfer risk to them. In and beyond the new risk regime, cultural ideals are both symbolic and social forces that have very real lasting implications for individual workers, workplace structures, and the inequality they generate and exacerbate.

6 Reaching the Top

Hedge fund founders, the "chiefs" and "kings" who preside over investment acolytes and accrue astronomical incomes, fit well into the cultural ideal of the American Dream. Industry peers regard them as pathbreaking individualists sparked by an entrepreneurial spirit, their successes the market-approved result of a willingness to take risks and capitalize on their unique talent—genius, even—and their wealth the natural reward. Founders are seen as gurus and role models, and many of those I encountered throughout my research aspired to, or already boasted, founder status.

Thus far, we have seen how patrimonialism, which structures the industry, maintains race, class, and gender inequality. This system minimizes the presence of women and minority men within elite white men-dominated, flatter organizations and pushes them into the industry's less glamorous, less well compensated back-office roles. Now it's time to see who rises to the top, how they get there, and why founders and funders compose such a closed, classed network.

Like other entrepreneurial endeavors, founding a hedge fund requires considerable social, familial, and institutional forms of support. In particular, it means raising financial capital by cashing in on social capital. The average US hedge fund spends $75,000 in startup costs and $100,000 in operational costs over its first year, but those aren't the shocking numbers. To become *profitable,* hedge funds require an average of $85 million in assets from high-net-worth client investors. That means access to elite social networks is the surest indicator of which industry insiders have the potential to become founders, pulling themselves up by their Rolodexes rather than their bootstraps.

US Entrepreneurs

In 2016, twenty-seven million people in the United States founded a new business, but it was on an uneven field.[1] For instance, while women own four out of every ten US businesses and women of color account for 44 percent of those woman-owned businesses, men are more likely to start the businesses that garner big, private investments.[2] Women, facing gender penalties from investors and their networks, instead tend to rely on small business loans (with their more stringent requirements), and their entrepreneurial endeavors are accordingly smaller and less profitable over time.

Scholars have shown, time and again, how deeply held and socially constructed status beliefs cast men, particularly white class-advantaged men, as better entrepreneurs and more worthy of funding (stereotypes that are heightened in times of uncertainty like the Great Recession, when trust is paramount).[3] Women, sociologist Sarah Thébaud establishes, are seen instead as relatively less capable, their businesses less viable.[4] Others point out that, in finance, specifically, asset allocators consistently hold Black fund managers, even those with strong performance records, to a higher standard than their white peers when making their investment decisions.[5] All the intersecting social statuses I have explored thus far—gender, race, and social class—retain their power when it comes to who is recognized as an entrepreneur and how they obtain financing.

Overall, entrepreneurs who receive funding are more likely to be white men from higher-income families, whose upbringing has afforded them a consistent safety net and therefore the ability to engage in riskier endeavors.[6] In fact, they report having histories of engaging in disruptive, illicit activities as teens but also having higher self-esteem than others. By adulthood, it appears these class-advantaged white men feel more comfortable taking the professional risk of launching a business venture. Gender dynamics in heterosexual families also shape this outcome, given that sons remain more likely to inherit family businesses than daughters, who are less likely to be recognized for, let alone encouraged in building, their leadership skills.[7] Heterosexual couples tend to maintain breadwinner ideas for men, casting women's entrepreneurial endeavors as "side hustles" and hobbies. This gendered conditioning continues in workplaces, where white men incur fewer penalties than women and racial minority men for taking risks and sometimes, for failing, too.[8]

Entrepreneurial inequalities, I reasoned, would likely appear in my data on founders, even though I intentionally oversampled, in my interview recruitment, for women and minority men working in the industry in order to foreground their voices. And so, I began to look at the subset of my sample who had founded or cofounded a hedge fund.

The Funders

Made possible by financial sector deregulation, the hedge fund industry has for thirty years provided investors with a more lucrative alternative to investment banking. Traditionally, these investors are wealthy families, who remain 8 percent of hedge fund investors today, often in the form of "family offices,"[9] capital pools of family estates and trusts managed under a fund structure, used to fund philanthropic endeavors or establish wealth for subsequent generations. In some cases, a family member manages the fund, though this asset class has increasingly transferred its money into the management of hedge funds in order to increase returns.

The SEC requires that, to become accredited client investors in registered hedge funds, individuals must meet a financial threshold: a minimum net worth of $1 million (excluding their primary residence) and an annual income of $200,000.[10] Accredited investors are understood as having lower financial risk and warranting less regulatory protection than other investors, and only 13 percent of the US population qualifies (up from 2 percent in the 1980s). At the same time, many established hedge funds require a minimum investment ranging from $500,000 to $2.5 million.[11] This would indicate that only a very few Americans could invest in hedge funds, but institutional investors—say, teachers' unions—result in a wide segment of society having a stake in hedge funds.

For the affluent, of course, accredited investor status is an upper-class signifier, as visible as a private jet. Cynthia was chief operating officer of her first hedge fund, launched in the mid-1990s, and a second founded in the early 2000s. "By the time 2002–2003 came around, the biggest thing you could do when you went to a cocktail party is say, 'I'm a hedge fund investor,' because that meant you were accredited and had a lot of money," she recalled. Since people on Wall Street and in other elite circles know the SEC requirements for accreditation, those words became synonymous with "I am enormously wealthy."

Not only does starting a hedge fund require access to these elite social worlds, it requires entrance into and success within the patrimonial system of family-like trust networks that structures the hedge fund field. As we have observed, that access is attenuated, and social status is often the magic pass-code allowing predominantly upper-class white men to join the most lucrative networks. The industry terminology for early-stage investments—"seed" funding—even carries a distinctly reproductive connotation, reflecting the transfer of inherited, family wealth. For white men, gaining these networks' support involves entering another privileged "family" support system that cushions risk, amplifies financial rewards, and ensures successful founders' ability to pass along their own wealth and reputation.

Attracted by the prospect of making higher investment returns and diversifying their portfolios, wealthy investors, elite networks, and professional mentors provide founders with the seed money to launch hedge funds. In the following sections, I consider their demographic characteristics, then examine three influential factors that shaped how the founders in my research gained access to such patrimonial capital. The first features a manager providing both training and funding, and the second requires personal ties to wealthy investors. The third is a precipitating crisis, such as a poorly performing investment portfolio or a stock market crash, which provides an opportunity to spin off a business unit into an independent hedge fund. These paths aren't mutually exclusive, and several founders benefited from access to more than one.

The Founders

I spoke at length with eighteen people who had founded or co-founded a hedge fund. Of these, twelve people, three of them women, served as the primary investment decision maker for that fund: Albert, Brian, Eileen, Jamie, Jeffrey, Jerry, Justin, Ken, Vincent, Wayne, Diane, and Deborah. By contrast, the other six—Cynthia, Farrah, Margaret, Sharon, Linda, and Scott—had roles as head of research, operations, or compliance. Eleven founders were white, ten were men, and seven were white men.

Patrimonialism is a classed, gendered, and racialized system masquerading as a neutral meritocracy. It follows that the vast majority of the founders in my executive pool came from upper-middle-class or upper-class backgrounds but tended to describe themselves as middle-class. The idea that they didn't have class privilege was sometimes contradicted quickly, as they mentioned parents who were business or finance executives, for instance, while other times, a simple online news search revealed their privileged backgrounds. These people's self-categorizations are not anomalies. It is common in the United States for most people to identify as middle class and for elites to understand their position in relative terms, usually in comparison with people further above them on the class hierarchy.[12]

Vincent, Jamie, and Farrah were the exceptions to the norm, the only founders in my sample who came from working-class backgrounds, yet, as with Wayne (whose background was middle class), Vincent and Jamie also had law degrees. Elite educational attainment may have effectively bypassed their relative class disadvantage and given them another path into the elite networks that facilitate founding a firm. Margaret, who was, like Wayne, Asian American and raised middle class, boasted her own Ivy League education but wasn't a primary decision maker in the firm she founded. The difference may be that Wayne's elite network had been further boosted by his lengthy career at a large asset management firm, which brought him into contact with institutional investors and wealthy individuals.

It was less common, in my research, for people of color and white women founders who were born and raised in the United States, and lacked access to rich networks abroad, to occupy a hedge fund's top investment role—as the CIO or primary portfolio manager. Women founders, in particular, tended to hold the top back-office, or client services, role. For example, Farrah is of Middle Eastern American descent and the first generation in her family to attend college. She had a founder role as the head of client services. I gathered that her cofounders are elite because of the way she described their network and the fact that they didn't need to work after their hedge fund failed and shut down, and each went on to manage their own investments as a family office. Diane, Deborah, and Eileen were the only exceptions as women founders in top front-office roles.

Elite Social Ties

The "friends and family round" of funding is the first phase of starting a hedge fund. White men from elite backgrounds, like Ken, tended to take their proximity to such affluent, amenable networks for granted, framing this initial round of funding as a time of proving themselves in dogged trading with limited funds until they could amass enough capital to court institutional investors. Echoing other founders' stories, he told me, "It's that critical first $20 million then $50 million then $100 . . . only then you can approach institutional investors. Before that, I call it 'nickel and diming' it. You have to put your head down. . . . It's a long haul to do it."

As they had when describing their class backgrounds as "middle-class," those founders I interviewed, especially the elite white men, downplayed their access to first-round funding; instead, they emphasized the hard work that had gotten them where they were. Brian, who single-handedly ran his own hedge fund with $200 million under management, started his career in the early 1990s at a large investment firm. He spent a few years there in an introductory analyst job, stock picking, then left to launch his hedge fund. Despite having an MBA from an Ivy League university, Brian described himself at that point as a total industry outsider: "I didn't have the contacts in finance. I didn't know anybody."

Despite his supposed lack of contacts, Brian was able to raise $2 million in early investments from his personal and professional networks—including, he mentioned, a former girlfriend's father and "connections through my [other] exes"—as well as seed funding from his previous boss at the investment firm. His family and religious networks from his childhood community in the South, his graduate school contacts, and a colleague's father and his poker friends all invested in Brian's friends and family round, in his view, because he was just so "trustworthy." After our interview, I read in a news article that Brian's father had an over twenty-year tenure as the CEO of a public company and "plenty of friends in the business community" in Brian's hometown. I don't doubt his sincerity, but the fact that Brian perceived his vast wealthy networks as lower status than those in the industry could access captures how commonly those with race, class, and gender privilege take its relative ease for granted.

Within a decade, Brian's initial seed funding grew to $200 million, yet he took great pride in never hiring any employees (though he did outsource some tasks). He didn't want to achieve the scale and overhead of the large funds and preferred to keep his firm small: "Not one employee."

By the time we met, Brian was so embedded in the culture of Wall Street that he didn't recognize how the "old boy's network" he claimed to have rejected had evolved in the hedge fund era. He actually fit quite well with the new ideals of hedgemonic masculinity, such as valorizing the renegade. For example, Brian called himself as a "deep value guy," a term often used for activist investors,[13] then said, "Call me contrarian"—industry jargon for investors who go against popular practices in their stock picks—"but I prefer to be called independent minded." Brian emphasized innovation and creative thinking, telling me, "You find your own style. You make mistakes to refine your style. Hedge funds are like snowflakes: no two are alike. It's just about the guy or girl at the top and their brain." As a hedge fund manager, Brian described his own "unique investment style" that was "more based in psychology than in finance" and suggested it was the key to the trust his investors gave him.

Over and over again, Brian returned to the idea of himself as a creative artist, insisting "there is a lot of art to stock investment. It's not a science but an art." And to him, artists are independent, solitary geniuses. For instance, when I asked why Brian ran his hedge fund by himself, he looked around the small and mostly empty café before his eyes landed on a mass-produced piece of art on a wall nearby. Pointing to its bottom right corner, he asked me, "What would usually be there?"

Unsure where he was going with this, I guessed: "The artist's signature."

"How do you spell artist?" he asked.

Confused, I paused, then acquiesced: "A-R-T-I-S-T."

"You see, there's no 's' following that word," he said with satisfaction. "I don't want my ideas to get squashed. For some great ideas, there is no evidence. Artist not artists."

Brian reaffirms an ideology of hedgemonic masculinity that values individualism and originality and justifies designations of trust and loyalty—the currency of patrimonialism, a.k.a. the "old boys' network" made structural and durable.

When Brian's hedge fund collapsed amid the 2008 financial crisis, he was grateful that "my early investors stuck with me. I am an artist." Those who had "jumped on the bandwagon" in his high-profit years were the ones who withdrew their trust and cashed out in large numbers when he encountered difficulty during the crisis. Still, Brian spent the next five years unemployed—a fact he chalked up to his lack of Wall Street social connections: "the jobs are all about old boys' networks." As a "contrarian," he had worked from his home office outside the city and lamented that perhaps he had not sufficiently engaged in that "wining and dining" and "favors" side of the industry. Not long after, I learned from the business press that Brian had launched another hedge fund with initial-round funding from his original investors and their networks. Despite his sense that he was a maverick lacking in traditional connections, his wealthy networks provided the funding for his second act.

Women founders, like women in other industry roles, found building networks of valuable social capital tougher than white men had, though once they were in place, they could be just as lucrative. Funding from a wealthy family provided Sharon her first opportunity

to start a hedge fund in the 1990s. At first, she and two colleagues—
"one was a significant portfolio manager in the business" with access
to elite networks—invested money for this large family office, then,
similar to Brian, worked to build a track record before seeking more
investors. Sharon recalled, "We then used the track record and went
back to our roots. We went to large institutions, we went to consultants, went to other families and foundations." Recall that, in chapter
3, Sharon described building her Rolodex, establishing her social
capital, and how her boss denied her an account because the client
simply didn't "like" women or "Jews." Race, class, and gender were
all just as important in the formation of her network as anyone else's.
Of her team's ability to raise capital nonetheless, Sharon said it came
down to the networking and promotion: "If you come out of the institutional business, you understand the process of who are the gatekeepers and who are the direct buyers, so we just used our Rolodexes
and started calling. . . . That's how you build your business."

Other founders were able to tap into transnational flows of capital
from personal networks that extended abroad. In the 1990s, Jeffrey
cofounded a hedge fund with a client base of affluent European families. He recounted, "My partners were very, very wealthy European
families that were plugged into that world." Without his partners'
family connections, Jeffrey stressed, "There was no way you or I or
anybody was going to pick up the phone and [just] call these families." He referred to using the "network effect" to access these ultra-
high-net-worth investors, but consistent with how whiteness is often
left unmarked, didn't mention they were white families, a detail that
I verified through additional research into his firm.

In several cases, people of color demonstrated how access to
wealthy networks abroad could counteract the dominant racial hierarchies within US financial services. Jerry, who is Mexican American,
provided an exceptional case amid all these affluent white networks,
telling me that he used inherited wealth from his father and tapped

into high-net-worth networks to start his hedge fund in his late twenties. He identified the role of inherited wealth and high-net-worth networks. Jerry's early success at an investment bank allowed him to grow capital from his father's inheritance. He was also able to raise foreign assets through his family ties on both sides of the US-Mexico border. According to Jerry, he was able to "mobilize money from Mexican assets transferred across the border because of the conflict in northern Mexico, in places like Juárez." Jerry said he took a cautious approach to money management, because his client investors—whom he called his "partners"—were from his family's social networks. He felt both a personal and professional responsibility to do well. While that obligation may have pushed Jerry to make lower-risk investments, he had felt personally emboldened to take the entrepreneurial risk of starting his own firm. Jerry said the time was right because he was young, unmarried, and childless—if he failed, he wasn't jeopardizing a family's financial security.

Eileen, too, had international, non-white networks to thank for her hedge fund's capital base. At one investment conference, I met Eileen, a Chinese woman in her early thirties, who ran her own hedge fund out of New York and Shanghai, dividing her time between both locations. After graduating with an MBA from an Ivy League school, she began her career in investment banking and then specialized in Chinese equities at several hedge funds. Over the past decade, Chinese markets had opened up to foreign investors, which she called a tremendous opportunity. But, Eileen said, US investors were reluctant to invest in Chinese stocks and bonds because of the perceived lack of transparency: "There are corporate governance issues and fraudulent companies coming out of China, which leads all investors to [either] assume all Chinese companies are fraudulent or trust them all because they have no benchmarks for evaluating corporate governance." Eileen's extensive networks with Chinese executives and government officials gave her insight into investment opportunities and enabled her to assuage xenophobic fears of US investors and overcome their reticence to invest in foreign funds.

Although whiteness is associated with the dominant category of elites on Wall Street specifically, people of color with elite networks that extend abroad show how foreign investors can help to challenge white supremacy in finance. Such transnational elites capture the increasing global impact of financial investors in places like China, Hong Kong, and Singapore, as Kimberly Hoang's research demonstrates.[14] The United States remains the center of the hedge fund industry, managing three-fourths of assets under management worldwide, but the funds' investors are increasingly global.[15] In Asia today, high-net-worth individuals have double the wealth claimed by high-net-worth North Americans. And asset management in the Asia-Pacific region is growing at three times the rate found in North America. From 2016 to 2019, North America's share of global assets dropped from 55 percent to 50 percent, while the assets managed in Asia and the Pacific increased from $12 to nearly $18 trillion—a rapid closure of the asset management gap. The association with whiteness among US financial elites may become more tenuous, even disappear, in coming years.

As I mentioned, my interviews oversampled for people of color, and so my sample of interviewees and my subsample of founders is less white than the industry, in which assets are overwhelmingly held and controlled by white men.[16] For this reason, racial minority hedge fund founders who drew on wealthy transnational networks capture an important growing trend, yet still remain underrepresented. Access to affluent networks is most readily available to elite white men, a fact that did not escape my interviewees, some of whom specifically pointed to the need to gain access to rich white networks' capital as a major barrier to industry advancement for people of color.

Matthew, who wasn't among the founders in my sample but was one of the more senior Black men I met, cautioned against the pipeline explanation for the dearth of people of color in the industry (the idea that too few people of color study finance or pursue careers in financial services to have yet risen to the top ranks). Inviting me to imagine that two equally qualified people—one white and one Black—had the same idea for a hedge fund, Matthew said bluntly, "One of them is going to have access to people with capital. The other will not. And that's the difference between who can start a hedge fund and who can't. I think it flows from there. It's access to capital."

Matthew and the other Black men I met in hedge funds did eventually leave their firms, but as consultants or contractors—not to start their own funds. Matthew said his trading style was becoming obsolete, yet I couldn't help but wonder if his path would have been different if he had been white. In a study of a performance-based pay system, William Bielby found that Black financial advisers earned one-third to 40 percent less than their white colleagues. These gaps were, in part, attributed to Black workers' difficulty in generating commissions from white households, especially since personal referrals and social networks were a key mechanism in building a client base early on, and the gaps widened over the course of their careers.[17] Other research identifies how even high-performing Black fund managers are held to a higher standard of "success" than their white counterparts, revealing and resulting in racial biases in asset allocation.[18] I expect similar dynamics are at work at hedge funds, which require founders to have considerable personal financial capital to sustain themselves through the startup period and access to affluent investor networks that, in the US context, are predominantly white. Because of the systemic racism we explored in chapter 1, the amount of domestic wealth available from the networks of non-white investors is far lower. Thus, even though upper-class Matthew had vast networks built through his Ivy League education and long years working at elite financial firms, he never seriously considered launching a hedge fund.

A final, very closed network came up in some of my interviews: some founders, especially those lacking class privilege, described having to rely on financial support from their spouses in their startup phase. Wayne timed his departure from his stable investment firm job to coincide with his wife's benefits coming into effect at her job, and Justin pointed to his wife's income and benefits from her well-paid job in a private equity as enabling him to risk starting a hedge fund out of their home twenty years ago (he noted that they'd met as students at an Ivy League business school in the 1990s). Of his wife, Jamie said, "I couldn't do this without her"—nor her emotional, intellectual, and financial support as he started his hedge fund. Though he had worked in the corporate sector previously, it wasn't in finance and Jamie lacked the upper-class upbringing that might otherwise provide opportunities to find investors. Instead, after spending three years at home with the children, his wife returned to work to provide for the family as he chased his investment dreams. These accounts of specifically women's spousal support fit with studies of men in the technology and innovation fields whose wives support their families financially during periods of unemployment and entrepreneurship.[19]

Whether through professional or personal ties, access to wealthy networks and personal capital are necessary for launching a hedge fund. Initial investors are often located through familial, racial, ethnic, and religious networks, which reflect patrimonial structures enabled by trust networks and a shared sense of loyalty among families, friends, and colleagues. These patrimonial structures are predominantly organized around gendered and racialized relationships such that the founders who are women and racial minority men are relatively rare among hedge funds.

Cultivated Firms

Hedge fund founders provided valuable forms of mentorship, training, and seed funding to a select group of trustworthy, loyal protégés groomed to carry forward their investment tradition (see chapter 5). Should a protégé go on to start their own hedge fund, the apprentice-master relationship may lead to the transfer of large sums of seed money, cementing the familial—generally patrilineal—relationship while allowing the original founder to diversify investments and increase profits. A hedge fund founder may even seed a lineage of affiliated firms guided by shared investment principles and professional guidance, as the Tiger Cub firms evidence so clearly. Because another hedge fund seeds the firm and grooms its founder, I call these "cultivated firms."

At age eighteen, Ken started his first hedge fund. White and class-privileged, he told me that gathering seed funding was quite organic and spontaneous, as though the opportunity arose through sheer good luck, though his initial pool of $200,000 included $25,000 from each of several of his father's friends, an unspecified amount from his father (the dean of a business school who ran a hedge fund on the side), and $10,000 each from his mother and grandparents. It was too little money for him to need to register his hedge fund with the SEC, but it grew as he set a track record. By his early twenties, Ken had been featured in the *Wall Street Journal,* which called him the leading fund in his strategy and printed his phone number. Soon it was "ringing off the hook" and he had tens of millions in assets under management. When he hit twenty-five employees, Ken said, "Raising the capital was difficult," so he hired outside marketers to reach the "big investors"—large institutional investors.

The strategy the *WSJ* referred to was once a niche investment path that Ken's father had developed. "My dad just had a philosophy that he came up with," Ken remembered. Today, Ken and his father's practice is a mainstream investing strategy, but they are known as the first. Ken received other mentorship from his father's friends and contacts, including several traders—all white men—who would become hedge fund billionaires. Ticking off names I regularly see in *Forbes* and *New York Times* headlines, Ken told me, "I had the opportunity to invest with some of the greatest commodities traders and meet them and learn the industry professionalism from them." Without seeming self-conscious, he mentioned, "I met them when I was very young, one after the other." As a young teenager, Ken had observed well-established traders as they worked, asked them for tips, and read the books they suggested. Back in the 1980s, he recalled, a trader who is now a billionaire had just $10 million under management and would allow a rapt Ken to watch him in action, "trading and doing all this crazy yelling while he's doing stuff in the markets."

Ken's story had started out suggesting that he had almost stumbled into becoming a hedge fund founder, yet even at age eighteen, he had all the hallmarks of a typical founder: elite upper-class white networks saturated with money and trust and experienced mentors eager to train him in an investment tradition. His apparently exceptional backstory masks what was actually a quite standard cultivated firm.

Due to the large sums of money involved, extraordinarily successful hedge fund managers nearing retirement often groom their sons to take on the family business, transition their firms into family wealth offices tasked with managing their personal fortunes, or start their own hedge funds.[20] For instance, George Soros appointed his sons, Robert and Jonathan, to oversee investments at the Soros family wealth office converted from Soros's hedge fund. Warren Buffett also plans to transfer leadership of Berkshire Hathaway to his son, a farmer and philanthropist, on retirement. And Howard Marks of Oaktree Capital Management has provided his son, twenty-eight-year-old Andrew Marks, $200 million in seed investment to launch his fund.[21] There are many cases of founders investing in or passing their businesses down to a son, but I found only one anecdotal story of a hedge fund daughter anointed to carry on the family name.[22]

My interview with Justin, who manages $50 million in assets and is proud to have never hired an employee, is revealing. He has two adult daughters, one of whom works in finance, yet expressed ambivalence about them following his path: "Do I want to steer my daughters into this industry? I would help them out, but I don't know [if I want them to], because it's very much an old boys' industry." As he thought about his daughters' well-being within a men-dominant industry, he suggested, "Sooner than later, I would want them to get out on their own so that they don't have a boss. Then they don't have to get along with anyone, and they are not in a subservient position, except with investors." Justin apparently didn't consider training his daughters to take over *his* firm, which would have obviated his concerns about them working for men in the industry.

Most protégés get access to mentorship, training, and networks on the job, rather than through their own family. And, because a small asset base better sustains some investment strategies, larger hedge funds can gain new opportunities for revenue generation by seeding small firms. As I described in the introduction, Julian Robertson of Tiger Management has seeded an estimated 120 affiliated, protégé-founded firms known as the Tiger Cubs and Grand Cubs. Among them are fifty of the world's top hedge funds, and the total assets under management of just the sixty-two Cub firms registered with the SEC is over $250 billion, implying that the Tiger family's wealth is substantially larger.[23] That these firms feature similar investment philosophies, strategies, and performance outcomes suggests that Robertson groomed their founders to perform according to his model. In other words, they feature a shared investment tradition. Since 2006, Robertson's protégés have outperformed the Standard & Poor's 1500 Index by 53.9 percent, bolstering Robertson's wealth and status beyond his own firm. Today, Robertson manages his own family office atop a Park Avenue skyscraper called the "height of perfection."[24]

I didn't interview the founders of any of the "Tiger Cub" firms, though I spoke with several hedge fund founders who received partial or full seed funding from a previous hedge fund boss, past colleague, or a family member who worked in the industry. The hedge fund where Linda worked shut down when the founder transitioned to managing his own wealth, but not before investing some $50 million in seed money to support his employees' launch of their own new firm. Linda recounted that the new cofounders were "a team that was contributing a lot to the performance and kind of holding the [previous] firm up and together, so it made more sense, and the owner was ready to move on to his next chapter." In addition, she said, "some of the old investors from the prior firm came over as well." When we met, a few years later, Linda's new firm managed a couple of billion in assets—the support from their previous firm's founder, in financial and social capital, had enabled the firm to fundraise successfully.

As with Julian Robertson's Tiger Cubs, the previous firm's founder trusted Linda and her cofounders to invest his money because he had trained them into a particular investment tradition and business model that he endorsed. Of the transition, Linda said, "He supported us. It was a very unique transition because we took his people, the firm, the employees, as well as he gave us the equipment, the computers, even the leases, we took over. Some of the technology contracts . . . and so we were able to work together immediately." Building the firm out of an established model helped to ensure it ran smoothly. Linda identified the human and social capital of the employees as an important part of what made the transition feasible.

Farrah, one of the hedge fund cofounders who went on to hold a back-office, client services role at her fund, also partnered with colleagues from a previous hedge fund and raised funds from investors out of the client base she had built there and throughout her career. That her cofounder, the portfolio manager, had a strong reputation and track record that investors trusted eased the path to Farrah convincing people to provide early-stage funding. Interestingly, the dynamic between Farrah and her partner matched the common gendered division of labor at hedge funds described chapter 4: women are tracked into client-facing back-office positions while men work as investment decision makers, and may indicate that it's easier for a woman to become a hedge fund founder if she is willing to serve in those client services roles. That said, Farrah's career took a major hit on account of this decision when her fund eventually went under, which we will return to in the conclusion.

In another type of cultivated firm, entire units of investment banks break away to become a hedge fund. Sharon explained how this fosters the tight-knit bonds in the industry and makes it difficult for others to get in and get ahead. She said, "The point I want to make about the evolution out of trading floor to smaller firms [is] a lot of these hedge funds started as just a bunch of guys getting off of Goldman or Credit Suisse or Morgan's trading floor and starting a firm." Especially for women, a splinter like this led to very high pay but limited opportunities for advancement, especially in flatter firms:

> Some guy is the head of trading and some guy is the CEO, and they were best buddies on the trading floor and they've got a track record. And in the hedge fund . . . you're not going to get ahead. So you've got to be comfortable in whatever spot it is because you could be a 10-person firm and be running $5 million. You don't need a lot of people. So if you're head of [a department], and most women are the marketing person and very rarely are the trader, you're going to be getting paid a lot . . . [but] there's no up or down.

Investment bankers, in other words, can boost their earnings by seizing the opportunity to join colleagues starting a new hedge fund, but the relatively flat structure limits an upward career trajectory. Then the only way to advance is by founding your own firm, and that's less possible for women who are funneled into lower-status client-facing roles.

The apprenticeship style of education at hedge funds builds strong bonds between employees and with their managers, presenting opportunities to venture out and start one's own firm. When employees are groomed into an investment tradition, over time they receive access to training, investor funds, a reputation for association with the founder's investment philosophy, and even direct seed funding from founders that may enable them to start their own hedge funds.

Financial Distress

A third context in which founders typically launch their own firms is a counterintuitive one: financial distress at their previous firm, as in the event of a financial crisis. For potential founders, leveraging a crisis involves reducing the distressed firm's operating load by departing and taking some or all of the business unit and customer base to start a new fund. It can be quite seamless, because the new founder has access to the previous firm's wealthy investors for recruiting new client investors.

Vincent told me that founding his own hedge fund "was very opportunistic." He was working at a large investment bank, where he had created a new business unit: "I started in this firm and within eighteen months, I was running a desk [a business unit]. So, it was a rapid ascent. I started something they didn't have. I used my legal skills to expand on a concept." This novel investment business within the investment bank would become the foundation for his hedge fund when the opportunity arose with the Russian Debt Crisis in 1998. When management asked for voluntary resignations, Vincent "took a long shot and said, 'Would you be upset if I took this team out and created my own thing? I'll take care of all the clients. You'll never have a client issue. Clients love me. They'll travel.'" The bank didn't formally approve Vincent's plan, demurring, "'Well, we can't say yes.' But they winked or blinked or whatever and I did it." Looking the other way freed the investment bank from a source of financial distress, and it allowed Vincent to move his business unit "out of the investment bank, joined with a competitor, made a twice as large-sized firm." Over an eight-year period, Vincent's firm grew from $50 billion to over $200 billion in assets under management.

The financial crisis of 2008 provided many such founding opportunities. Two people in my study followed Vincent's path, with Deborah and Albert taking business platforms at investment banks and spinning them off into independent hedge funds. The mentorship and entrepreneurial culture of the investment banks, they said, prepared them to take advantage when the opportunity arose. Deborah grew up on a farm in the Rocky Mountain West and completed a doctorate in statistics at the University of Chicago. Rather than go into academia, she sought alternate career options. One professor suggested she head to New York City: "There are these investment banks that hire mathematicians. They're not rocket scientists, but it's pretty interesting work." It seemed worth a shot.

When Deborah moved to New York, "At that point in the mid-eighties, there were a lot of jobs available. Everyone was looking for people with my skill set as well as many other skill sets. It was just a boom time in the business." She started in research and modeling, which diverted her from the more popular trading path but prepared her for portfolio management. After a decade, she moved into and eventually ran the proprietary trading unit, overseeing the firm's money rather than investors'. This appointment, she recalled, was "meant to be an honor [the firm] gave people to prepare them to go to hedge funds." In 2008, the bank was forced to downsize, and Deborah was, in fact, ready to start a hedge fund:

> Luckily at [the investment bank], it was a very entrepreneurial, aggressive place, so I had been basically running my own business for a long time. Not just trading, but actually managing the expense side of the equation as well and hiring, so it wasn't that huge of a step to go to a hedge fund, but it's all incremental. It's kind of all an evolution of one's career.

Like Vincent, Deborah had first become an internal entrepreneur, building a business unit, then spun off the business as a separate hedge fund.

Feeling frustrated with the political dynamics of investment banking, Albert decided to capitalize on the skill set he had developed by leading business units using hedge fund strategies within investment banks as well as the regulatory changes that came after the financial crisis. The "permanent reduction in risk capital on the part of the banks," he explained, opened up investment opportunities he felt ready to grasp. "In my mind, if there was ever a time to really to take the gamble and see if you could build something by yourself, then it was then." Whereas the financial crisis provided an opportunity for Vincent and Deborah to leave firms in distress, Albert left to capitalize on investments related to the banks' exposure to risky capital and those underlying risky assets.

Wayne was initially inspired to launch his own hedge fund in 2008, yet he waited almost a decade to do so. In the moment, he remembered, he "just didn't have the guts." He didn't have the safety net, either. When I asked what amount he felt he needed to leave his firm, Wayne, who has a PhD in mathematics, described his thinking as unscientific: "I just pulled somewhat a round number out of the air. I stayed so long I ended up doubling that number." What was that initial number, I asked. "It was just a million bucks." As someone from a middle-class background, Wayne felt less secure in taking the risk of launching a hedge fund during the financial crisis and instead felt compelled to set aside considerable wealth to mitigate the risk of the transition.

For founders like these, financial distress and crisis provided an opportunity to start their own firms. However, these openings may have set them off on a less secure path, especially in the case of Deborah and Albert who launched during a recession. In general, women and racial minority men are more likely to assume leadership positions in organizations facing instability or crisis, which often sets them up to fail—a phenomenon called the "Glass Cliff."[25] While I didn't interview enough founders to discern whether people of color and white women were more likely to stay at failing companies but assume leadership roles or to leave to start their own hedge funds, it is certain that the founder's route is especially challenging for those without access to wealthy networks.

.   .   .

Hedge fund founders often attribute their success to having a high tolerance for risk and a strong drive to succeed. Yet, I found that success is most closely associated the social, familial, and institutional forms of support typical of America's elite upper class, particularly white-dominant elite networks. Three influential factors shaped how the hedge fund founders that I interviewed gained access to investment capital: having personal ties to wealthy investors, having a founder at a previous employer who provides training and funding, and/or having an opportunity arise from a previous employer's financial distress. The importance of familial and family-like ties that provide resources, training, and other forms of support categorizes these firms as "cultivated firms," grown within the patrimonial structure of high finance and furthering the transfer of US wealth among relatively closed networks.

Put differently, the paths that hedge fund founders take to entrepreneurship reflect the privileges more often afforded to elite white men by the gatekeepers who recruit and reward the people who "look like them." Whether it be through grooming practices, friends and family money, or a wife's support, upper-class white men more easily accessed the resources, support, and opportunities that enabled them to launch their own firms in the top position of chief investment officer.

7 View from the Top

"How do you like destroying the world?" The gregarious host of a Hamptons beach party teased Bradley, to his enduring chagrin. Feeling misunderstood, judged, and vilified was a common theme among the hedge fund workers I interviewed over the course of several years.

Bradley, a white analyst in his twenties, felt that hedge fund managers had become scapegoats for American inequality: "It's so easy for the media and for, you know, 99 percent of America to be like, 'Look at this guy's house.' It's like a $60 million apartment in New York City, or a $40 million house in the Hamptons, or x, y, and z. It's very easy for people to look at that and be like, 'Look at that excess! It's not fair! Why aren't they more equitable in their distribution of wealth?'"

Bradley understood that the opulence made people compare it to others' misfortune. But, he said, "I think that speaks to a much greater problem that we have in America rather than 'it's this person's fault.' I think people are looking for outlets to sort of place responsibility on certain people, and it's not fair." For him, the real injustice isn't the consumption practices of the exceedingly rich but the system that fails to provide basic support systems for the neediest and distribute resources more evenly among all. Further, Bradley suggested that hedge fund managers routinely redistribute their own wealth, the media and social critics just didn't pay attention to that side of the equation: "Most of these people are contributing a lot to charities . . . to further a lot of really good causes. Not to say that they are perfect, but, at the same time, I don't think the whole picture is being taken into account."

This, too, was a common theme in my interviews, reflecting a cultural premium on the act of "giving back" that is pervasive in the hedge fund industry and US society at large.[1] Yet citing the ability to engage in philanthropy as a reason for profit-seeking perpetuates the untenable but closely held idea that finance and other enormously compensated industries are, in fact, free-market meritocracies. I didn't doubt the sincerity of these scripts, as most of the hedge fund workers believed that a free market system with limited interventions rewarded those who worked the hardest and, in turn, as hardworkers, those who rose to the top were naturally best-equipped to decide how to distribute their riches to the rest of society (picking charities like so many stocks). Of course, the underlying implication is that the logic holds in both directions: that monetary success indicates personal merit and that having become hedge fund multimillionaires and billionaires justifies stewardship over the distribution of capital to those presumably not smart enough or hard-working enough to have accumulated their own wealth.

Although tax codes and deregulation allowed for the rise of hedge funds and their workers' astronomical incomes, my interviewees didn't identify taxation or financial market regulation as incompatible with the free-market ideal. They explained that, by investing the money of societies' largest institutions, including governments and public education, they could help to protect citizens from the potential excesses of a capitalist society. Consistent with hedge funds' obligation and commitment to serve their client investors, the people I interviewed said they *wanted* oversight to ensure the smooth functioning of financial markets. What varied in their accounts was the appropriate form of government interventions. Some told me regulators didn't accurately understand their work and added inefficiencies in financial markets. Some, worried about the individual workers whose retirements and pensions are invested in their funds via institutional ties, suggested regulators might take aim at the high firm fees and distribution of profits between investors and fund managers.

By and large, rather than "destroying the world," the people I spoke with saw themselves as saving at least some corner of it. They gained a sense of meaning from their work by building portfolios that could establish strong foundations for social institutions including governments, university endowments, pension funds, and arts foundations. When I asked about the social impact of their work, hedge fund workers prided themselves on helping middle-class families achieve financial security and described their desire to help average workers, those earning pensions or investing in 401(k)s, get ahead. Noting that her firm donates 10 percent of its profits to charities every year, Lisa told me, "Ultimately, if we make more money, the college endowments will be able to fund more scholarships and the pension funds can meet their funding requirements and the foundations can also make more grants for a certain project. That's the first and foremost mission."

"Most people kind of earn their salary and then spend it all on their life. That's it," said Scott. "But the way money and wealth are created and true value gets added in this world is when you take whatever money you've earned and invest it in something and get a return on that. And those returns are what create wealth. Those returns are what get donated to charity. Those returns are what build infrastructure and what build societies. So, being a part of that is really exciting." Scott understood financial investments as the building blocks of society.

That hedge fund workers translated making money in financial markets into making a positive impact on society perpetuates the logic of neoliberalism: the best way to address society's needs is for financial markets to allow enterprising individuals, rather than government, to accumulate and then redistribute resources, and so stripping away inefficiencies like bureaucracy and regulation is good for the people. Yet they also consistently placed a premium on their ability to support social institutions and workers only with protective regulatory oversight. They saw little contradiction in favoring both unfettered markets and crucial government oversight.

The Number

To be sure, when I asked what motivated their work, quite a few hedge fund workers readily admitted it was the money. Jeffrey suggested his peers had three primary motives—craving the action (recalling the "passion" discourse of the portfolio ideal), ego gratification (recalling the expectation to build a reputation as a savvy, independent-minded, and creative investor), and generating profit and income. That last one, Jeffrey said, was why he was in the game. He wanted to achieve "independence," which he saw as the ability to choose whether or not to work (see chapter 2 for more on the financial freedom discourse).

Sharon, too, wanted the high income but tied it to the ability to be altruistic and to function, in neoliberal terms, as a job creator: "I like money. I like things. I look at opportunities. I don't have a social consciousness to that, I want to do focused investing where I think I can have impact. I want to create markets. I want to create jobs." Through markets that distribute opportunities, Sharon explained, she can positively affect society while also getting rich.

Like Jeffrey, Jamie shared that he wanted to achieve financial freedom.[2] When I asked him what that position of security looks like to him, Jamie reflected on reaching "the number," or his conception of a sufficient financial safety net: "I don't know what number that is, because living standards change and inevitably when you have more, you kind of want more. But there's going to be a point where we've got everything we need. I guess you could say that we had everything we needed when we were in our suburban lifestyle, but it wasn't what we wanted. We felt like we wanted more." His previous work as a corporate attorney had, Jamie conceded, covered his family's needs, but their desires fueled his pursuit of upward mobility through investing. The very fact that he could not pinpoint a specific number that would be his dream "lottery ticket" provides a clue to why people strive to earn higher and higher incomes in this industry: lifestyle inflation. As people adjust their standard of living relative to increasingly wealthy peers, their expectations rise and rise. It also reminds us that the status conferred by hedgemonic masculinity is always relative.

Women were particularly likely to indicate that "the top of their career" would mean making enough money to be able to retire, leave the financial services industry, and do lower paid or entirely unpaid work on behalf of a social cause. Sasha, born in the Caribbean, indicated that, rather than keep working in finance, she'd rather pursue a doctorate in economics and work for the World Bank to promote sustainable development—yet her status as breadwinner for her family of four (a status more common to Black women like Sasha) prevented her from taking the leap.[3] Cynthia, on the other hand, suggested a path associated with white, upper-class women like her: she wanted to turn her philanthropic involvement with a children's cancer research initiative into a full-time pursuit.[4] Gita's main constraint was that, born and raised in Asia, her US visa was tied to working in finance, and so she couldn't realistically quit.[5]

The only man who idealized an alternative path in a feminized job was Andrew. He characterized his industry as a drain on society's human capital, pulling smart talented people away from lower-paid but more important work. If the money wasn't an issue, Andrew would rather make an impact as a teacher.

I think for society the risk [of the hedge fund industry] is, I mean, so much intellectual capital has flown into this space. Like, if you want to make a couple million bucks a year, there's no industry that's better . . . that's not even considered like exceptional income for my industry. That tends to get a lot of the top students excited about this industry and heading into this industry. And perhaps it would be better if the intellectual capital was a bit more broadly allocated into other areas. And I think, you know, our society would be a better place if that was the case.

I wondered where he thought these smart young people could make a better impact, where their "intellectual capital is needed."

"I mean science, education, those are like two obvious ones," Andrew responded. "If you gave me the same salary for doing what I do in teaching, I'd teach."

"Why is that?" I followed up.

"Um, I think I'd find it more rewarding, more personally gratifying," said Andrew. "I mean, it would be a hell of a lot less stressful."

Here, Andrew counters the dominant industry discourse of an intellectually stimulating field attracting the best and the brightest who have passion for their work. He also implicitly buys into the ethic of work infatuation, by assuming that his hedge fund work is more stressing and demanding than teaching—work that is arguably equally if not more demanding but devalued as feminized care work.[6] The only men I met who actually left the hedge fund industry did so to become tech entrepreneurs—upholding the expectations for elite masculinity rather than feminized, underpaid, and directly prosocial jobs like teaching, nursing, or social work.

The people I interviewed spoke about working toward financial freedom to achieve the ability to work instead for fulfillment or pleasure, but Andrew's words bring us back to the fact that, in the United States, "hard work" is a gendered concept. Rachel Sherman finds that the wealthy work, regardless of need, because it signifies their moral worth.[7] Thus, for hedge fund founders, the symbolic meaning of working without financial necessity reaffirms their strong dedication to the work and distances them from the feminized stigma attached to unpaid work, whether in the household or beyond, and care work of all kinds.

Regardless of their goals and motivations, the "number" that represented financial freedom varied across my interviews. One thought, for instance, that $50 million would be a modest amount with which to set up a trust for his family and support philanthropic causes. But as Jamie indicated, the "number" escalated as workers advanced in their careers. For the most part, it was always out of reach because of new thresholds: another raise, a bigger bonus, a wider profit margin, or more assets under management. Because eliteness and masculinity are always defined relative to one's peers, the standards are set higher and higher as you rise up the ranks.

To leave the industry, Craig told me, "I would have to wait for when my kids are out of college," pegging the idea to age and stress as well as money:

No one's in this gig to make, you know, $150,000 or $200,000 a year. [A salary that low is] not worth the instability or the stress. And there definitely is a feeling that, at some point, you've got to have made enough to cash out or at least move on to something a little less stressful than the day-to-day of trading. That [age] threshold moves. Maybe in the '80s and '90s, it was 35 and now it's 55, but I definitely don't see retiring in this job, because if you retire in this job, it's because you've made enough money to be done and be able to go on to your next career. . . . But it would probably have to be in a different part of the country, because it's too expensive to live out here unless you've got a six-figure a year job.

To Craig, hedge fund work is something one continues until they burn out or make enough money to do what they love. For him, the expenses associated with raising a family were his reasons for continuing as a hedge fund trader. His two children were in public schools, but he mentioned his property taxes alone were higher than most private school tuition.

Vincent was the one interviewee who told me that he had achieved the dream of financial freedom. In his early forties, Vincent sold his firm with $200 billion in assets under management, retiring to spend more time with his wife and children than he could as an active investor. But retirement bored him. Where he expected early retirement would be a time of leisure and recognition, he was volunteering on charity boards—surrounded by "blue-haired ladies"—a discomforting contrast with the elite, masculine world of the high-status hedge fund manager. He stayed retired for only a few years before returning to the industry.

As I explored in chapter 2, hedge fund workers expect money to indicate when it is time to retire, but move the goalposts beyond what many would consider a "reasonable" financial safety net and continue working in this field that has come to define them.[8] With sometimes hundreds of millions of dollars stored away, people often told me they kept working out of a "love" for the work (perhaps also a reflection of their sense of loyalty to and enjoyment of their colleagues). But the answer is inextricable from the recognition and status of this work specifically.

All this suggests that the neoliberal discourse of striving toward "achieving" financial freedom isn't just a rational response to economic uncertainty and fraying safety nets.[9] For this select group, a safety net in the millions—let alone tens of millions—is about mastering risk to ascribe to the elite status of hedgemonic masculinity defined by independence from wages and the ability to eschew the constraints of a corporate job. Thus, the financial security discourse rationalizes the pursuit of ever-larger fortunes; once salaries denoted elite financial status, but today, *wealth* is the meaningful term distinguishing the upper echelons of the class hierarchy from the working rich.[10] The amount of wealth that merits the distinction escalates as financial elites move up the class strata.

As captured in the accounts of hedge fund workers who want to work without needing to work, the emergence of the working rich is tied to cultural demands for long working hours and infatuation with work. That is, the working rich hew to the culture of overwork in the finance industry, understanding their top incomes as requiring long hours and complete dedication,[11] even though the new markers of social class distinction include transcending work. Whatever they told me about their "number," many of those I interviewed will continue work long past achieving reasonable financial security, because it is so deeply ingrained into their disposition as hedge fund workers. Currently, the feat of amassing enough wealth to manage their own money in a proprietary trading or family office firm structure, like Soros, is emerging as another status distinction of the working rich as it levels the status of some top-level fund managers with their high-net-worth investors.

The financial freedom dreams of hedge fund workers evoked images of workers on the other end of the economic scale: the low-wage, service-sector and gig economy workers whose incomes have stagnated and whose expectation of ever being able to retire is all but nonexistent. In an era when the top 1 percent drives extreme income inequality, I was struck that a sense of sufficient financial security appears, even for those rarified few, to be unattainable.

Good for the Public?

In contrast to the investment bankers, who believe that their vocation is to make companies and markets more efficient,[12] the people I interviewed believed their work helped to make markets more efficient, *and* they embraced a broader vocation of providing security in tumultuous financial markets and allowing for investments in society's future well-being. For some, this allowed them to morally disengage from the high fees for their clients.[13] These conceptions of the social value of their work informed how they either justified or critiqued the higher fees, lower taxes, and fewer restrictions for hedge funds relative to other financial firms. Their accounts generally upheld free market ideology, though the gaps and contradictions demonstrated a more complex understanding of financial markets, government interventions, and economic inequality than other research has uncovered.

The high earnings to which hedge fund workers aspire demonstrate how incomes have become speculative in a time when *wages* are decoupled from *labor.* Lisa Adkins theorizes how top incomes today stem from beliefs about who is worthy of being capitalized. High earners are capitalized with wages that allow them to invest, while low earners are noncapitalized and must use debt to subsidize stagnant wages.[14] The rich, controlling access to credit, are able to decide where and how to invest their money, and in doing so, shape the future of society and help to further entrench social and economic inequality over time.

Hedge fund investments and philanthropy certainly can contribute to the social good; there is no doubt, for instance, that continued growth is the only way public pension funds will survive and continue to benefit workers. At the same time, the rhetoric of redistribution and giving back ultimately masks how this system transforms money managers into multimillionaires while indebting the middle class and risking the scant financial security available to students and the working class. Most Americans face stagnant wages, mounting debts, and insecure jobs—that rarely come with retirement benefits—and this is directly tied to the rise of the financial services industry and the high earnings it demands.[15]

Regulation and Regulators

Throughout my research, I was fascinated with the tensions revealed by insiders who spoke with equal admiration for free markets, whose unfettered profits could fuel their altruistic impulses, and financial market regulation, often characterized as checks and balances, to ensure the markets run smoothly and prevent wrongdoing. Those who addressed their seemingly discordant ideas suggested several reasons for holding both views. Some told me free markets and regulatory restrictions weren't inherently in opposition, but the political climate—and politicians who benefited from easing reasonable regulations like Glass-Steagall—made it seem that way. Others said they, too, wanted reasonable financial protections, but thought that regulators with a poor understanding of their work made their jobs more challenging, created ambiguity around lawful activity, and aimed to end certain practices (such as short-selling) without logical bases. Regulators, in other words, added to the uncertainty hedge fund workers faced in their work and made them feel vulnerable to what they perceived as the whims of nonexperts. And stemming from this perception, I was told that regulators' work is ineffective and inadequate because regulators aren't sophisticated enough to understand this complex field (itself a belief attached to lower-paid work of all kinds, because, again, hedge fund workers adhere to the rhetoric of meritocracy and believe smarter people work hard and get rich).[16]

Sharon was in the first camp, describing herself as a laissez-faire capitalist who supported the 1933 Glass-Steagall Act (repealed in

1999 and subsequently included in the blame for the 2008 financial crisis) that separated commercial and investment banking activities and created the Federal Deposit Insurance Corporation to protect individuals' savings. She said:

> I think there should be pieces of Glass-Steagall. [But] you know, I'm a capitalist. . . . I believe in free economics. I have no problem with that. I have always felt that trading around loopholes isn't, that's not trading, that's just finding loopholes. To me, that's not the game that should be played. I also have a hard time blaming the financial institutions for the fall-down of economics when politicians drew-back, drew the lines back to make it better for everybody including themselves. . . . There is supposed to be a check and balance here. Now I could get into why politicians aren't doing their jobs. But that is what happened. The breaking down of Glass-Steagall, the free-for-all, I don't think that's capitalism; I think that's politics.

Sharon saw free economics as compatible with government intervention, attributing deteriorating regulatory restrictions and oversight to politicians acting in their own self-interest. At the same time, she decoupled capitalism and free economics from the broader sociopolitical context, as though people and institutions do not create the markets.

The second camp are those who expressed frustration with the way they believed regulatory uncertainty had prolonged financial market instability in the aftermath of the financial crisis. Margaret didn't believe the postcrisis regulations to promote "transparency" were "a bad thing" but said the "processes which need to be implemented to get you there are onerous, and generally, not clearly guided by regulatory bodies." Confident that the regulations would become clearer and improve over time, Margaret still resented the way they hindered her work in the short term.

"It's funny, when you read in the paper, people always just think that finance people don't like regulation," Margaret continued. To her, that stereotype was misleading:

> It's not really about regulations, but it's about *uncertainty*. If you want to implement regulation, that's absolutely fine, but you need to implement regulation immediately, and let us know what needs to be done . . . the point of the matter is that if regulation were implemented swiftly and with clarity, I don't think anybody—people will always moan—but I don't think it would be a problem. Whereas if it's something that's implemented over long, long periods of time during which there is significant amount of uncertainty, it causes difficulty and inefficienc[ies] within the business that influence and impact things negatively.

In some ways, this is a have-it-both-ways argument: regulation is needed to make financial markets more stable and efficient, but the way regulatory change is undertaken produces uncertainty that limited efficiency.

Craig recalled, specifically, that at the height of the 2008 crisis, the SEC had imposed a temporary ban on short-selling stocks on "expiration Friday" (the third Friday of the month when stock options expire). His trades that day were "long," but he planned to exercise options to buy and sell the stock throughout the day and was unsure if this would be considered "short-selling" given those options' automatic expiration. He called experts to try to verify the legality of his trades that day, "but no one will tell you whether that's allowed. All I wanted is someone to say, 'Yeah, that's fine.'"

This moment put Craig in an uncertain position. He might either lose several million on a trade or expose himself to SEC investigation if he misinterpreted the new regulatory ban. Craig got out of the trade, but years after still thought such ambiguity could lead to unde-

served sanctions against traders: "people don't want to make decisions that will come back to haunt them later. And then you're having
to balance what is the right thing to do and where you are going to get
burned later down the line." Comparing the imposition of unclear
regulations to other laws, Craig made the case that it could get ab-
surd: "We're lowering the speed limit, but we're not going to say what
it is. Just drive slow." How would you know whether you deserved a
speeding ticket? He wished there was a regulatory hotline, where
"you could call to give them a specific situation and say, 'I'm willing
to go on the record, this is what I want to do, is this illegal or not?'"

Even the portability of Craig's skills seemed limited by regulatory
uncertainty. When he was job searching, he had some interviews at
investment banks, which are more heavily regulated than hedge
funds. Craig explained, "Definitely that an entire industry can be at
risk based on what the regulatory environment is, so as I look at interviewing with banks, one of my worries is that next year Congress
does something or someone triggers something, and the bank will
just get out of the entire business because it's [not] worth it from a
regulatory view and they can't do it anymore."

When I asked whether Craig imagined anything could be done to
clear up the "gray areas," it became apparent that he thought regulators might be intentionally vague. Craig said, "It's tough because
they don't want to be specific because all of the banks and the hedge
funds have very smart people who are paid to get around rules. As
soon as they specify, hedge funds will find a loophole to get around
it." He acknowledged how hedge funds were explicitly designed to
exploit regulatory gaps and loopholes—the limited oversight serves
as a hedge, a protective boundary for their profit-seeking.

When I was conducting fieldwork at a leading industry conference, I attended a panel on regulation. The panel featured several
trade execution and regulatory specialists from the United States and
Germany who discussed a quirk of trading platforms, which in delays

of fractions of seconds can affect profits, spur traders to cancel trades, and appear to show market manipulation. The panelists alluded to market manipulation briefly, but brushed it aside as a lesser problem than inefficiencies in trade execution—still, it is hard to tell which is behind the anomalies regulators spot in the platform trades.

When regulatory oversight came up as a potentially complicating factor, Craig's allusion to the undereducated policy makers and regulators who simply didn't understand the business came up again. At this, a bearded panelist with long, curly hair (who stood out amid the short expensive haircuts and freshly shaved jawlines in the room) chimed in, "I'm a liberal from Berkeley and I support regulation, but these kinds of uninformed regulations do not make the industry run smoother. They just create difficulties and inefficiencies." He went on to advocate for a centralized system allowing for improved regulatory transparency in trade executions while also upholding the idea that poorly informed regulators and representatives frequently make misguided interventions into the hedge fund world. The insinuation is the hedge fund traders know better—they're richer, therefore smarter, after all, and they work within these systems and exploit loopholes every day.

Bob, a portfolio manager, told me that the SEC was unable to recruit talent from the industry, so regulators were never going to be aware of the real work of hedge funds. A forty-something white man, Bob specialized in an investment area that is difficult to evaluate according to the regulatory guidelines and required advanced accounting techniques. "Anyone doing quality forensic accounting won't be working for the SEC," he said, and so regulation was insufficient and the SEC unable to catch individual wrongdoing. Further, the esoteric investments so common to the industry have unspecified risk, complicating regulatory oversight. To gauge whether his own investments technically followed SEC regulations, Bob said he asked himself, "Would this meet the NYTimes test?" That is, if a potential trade might draw press scrutiny, then it was likely out of line.

A hedge fund billionaire, Sam agreed that outsiders couldn't parse his firm's sophisticated investments, justifying his firm's maintenance of an air of secrecy, hedging out external scrutiny. "We can be radically transparent inside," Sam acceded, "But we can't be radically transparent outside, because they wouldn't understand." Fund founder Brian went further, claiming "the regulations are so unfair" and that the oversight infringed on his proprietary trading secrets. His firm's assets fell just above the $100 million threshold, requiring him to register with the SEC and potentially reveal his strategies through the filing documents. Protectively, he told me, "Your stocks, your ideas are your secret formula. Coca-Cola doesn't have to reveal theirs." Again, we see a hedge of opacity behind which traders can exercise more freedom and leeway in their work.

Even so, Brian wanted "incompetence and negligence" weeded out of his industry, declared the meritocracy a farce, and claimed that illegal activities like "front running still goes on, which is when you tell someone that someone is going to dump a bunch of stocks so they can short them." These led, he thought, to negative media portrayals and further tarnished the industry's bad name, and *someone* needed to take care of it. Like most citizens, it appeared he was heavily in favor of some laws (the ones he followed but others didn't) and truly resented others (generally those that kept him from simply doing what he liked in his work).

Hedge fund workers might seem contradictory when they talk about regulation, but it's the same way most of us talk about laws: there are ones we think are crucial to follow and others we see as unjust. We don't all agree on which is which, because we have different priorities and interests. Whether it be a belief in free economics, concerns about uncertainty, or undermining regulators by calling them incompetent, these beliefs espoused by hedge fund industry insiders are indicative of their stake in minimizing oversight, another way of hedging out accountability.

High Fees and Low Taxes

Not too long ago, the California Public Employees' Retirement System divested from hedge funds, citing a common concern that the funds' performance did not warrant the high fees and risk. The industry debate over hedge funds' investor fees was reflected in my interviews, too, with interviewees sharing their view that the industry should be more mindful of the middle- and working-class workers whose pensions and retirement accounts pay those fees.[17]

When I asked Amanda how her firm contributes to society, she looked out over the city, taking in the skyscraper's expansive view, and said, "I mean, we do manage money for, like, public clients and things like that. I do think we provide an important service. [The stock market] is extremely volatile and not very good at capital preservation, and those are the kind of services that we provide."

Glancing toward the lobby to see if anyone was within earshot, Amanda lowered her voice, and quickly added, "I just think it's too expensive."

"In terms of the fees?" I asked.

Amanda nodded her head, smiled, and said with a laugh, "Just don't say that too loud here!"

Matthew, head of trading, imagined his end-client as the worker with a pension, which inspired caution in his stock market positions and a critique of the hedge funds' high fees: "The costs to the institutional investors are very important to me because the individual investor has been sold a bill of goods . . . that by putting money into your 401(k), your pensions, 529s, all of this stuff, you will be able to at some point in time retire if you just do what you are supposed to do." Of the current investment environment, Matthew concluded, "[It] creates a situation where essentially just the moving around of money makes a lot of people wealthy, but it doesn't serve the people who are actually committing the money to the market."

Espousing, perhaps, even more progressive views, he said, "the price of real wages, the price of education, and the price of real wage inflation have gone in opposite directions." That divergence is what we call income inequality: "Now you have a situation where a lot of people who are saving all of this money are finding that they are unable to retire or the money that supposedly was going to cover them can't cover the current expenses that they have. And I just think it's a shame."

Matthew suggested that, even if hedge funds lowered their fees, "People are still going to make money. Everybody is going to be fine. But you're not going to have guys who make $4 million a year [for] just picking up the phone"—a situation he deemed "ridiculous." Becoming more animated, he continued: "The service should be some reflection of the actual effort. How does that guy make $4 million a year? . . . He happens to be a salesperson that covers all of the big accounts for the big asset managers. Why does he cover all of those big asset managers? Because two of his frat brothers are portfolio managers at those asset managers. Kid you fucking not. That's the way it goes down."

Another reason our hypothetical $4 million man can get wealthy in this work is hedge funds' tax status, which allows hedge fund workers to claim the bulk of their compensation as capital gains, rather than income, in their taxes. The people I spoke with sometimes used ethical terms as they spoke about this tax break. Sharon, who earlier shared that she saw her work as creating jobs, returned to that logic: "I'm okay with tax breaks, if we're creating jobs." She then qualified her statement: "I'm not okay with tax breaks just so that we give people tax breaks. I think that sucks. I think people have personal responsibility, and I think the government has responsibility. I don't think it's my responsibility to build a bridge or . . . bail out the school system. But I will—I will help. Public-private ventures are really important."

At this point, Sharon doubled back again: "But I will help, because we've gotten so off track. . . . We're twenty-seventh in education in the world. All I'm saying is that I believe people have personal responsibilities, but I believe government has responsibility. Building the roads, building the bridges, responsibilities for educating our kids." It was as if I could see Sharon thinking through the competing ideologies surrounding the question of what makes a strong civic society. She weighed out one that values an individual responsibility to improve society by investing in the stock market as a means to create jobs and another that values a government that taxes the public to invest in improving society as a whole. Embracing neoliberal ideology, she settled on public-private partnerships as the only viable solution to social problems.

Brian, who thought regulations were unfair, also thought the lower-cost capital gains tax status of hedge funds was unfair. "It's different when you risk your own capital," he said, suggesting an asset manager would be justified in paying capital gains rather than income taxes if they only invested their own assets. Instead, "Hedge funds are making 20 percent on profits, and if it's long-term gains, they only pay 15 percent in taxes. Is that fair? It's just not fair," he said. "It's scandalous and shameful." Brian went on to talk about a restricted practice that was nonetheless alive and well among his peers: "short at the end of the year to work the capital gains tax." Basically, investors can take short positions on securities they already own (creating a zero-net effect) to cancel out their capital gains until the new year, allowing them to avoid paying taxes. Brian frowned on short-selling in general, calling it akin to "betting against the house," and thought that using short-selling to exploit capital gains was indicative of a "lack of integrity."

In general, Brian cited the existence of capital gains taxes (a.k.a. the carried interest loophole) as evidence of a "revolving table with Washington." He said, "People are just trying to make as much money as possible, but the whole system is flawed. [Hedge fund manager] Marc Lasry hired Chelsea Clinton. It's about access to politics." Brian further condemned the common practice of domiciling funds offshore to avoid paying domestic taxes, eased by the fact that "people in politics want jobs and donations, so they don't charge the higher taxes." As for the hedge fund managers, Brian said combatively, "They rationalize it by giving money to charity, but they're stealing money from the government."

Cynthia and other interviewees instead turned the tax discussion back toward the idea of accruing personal wealth in order to enact her altruism—and reasoned that paying no taxes at all was the best way to take care of society. The ability to give was her compensation's "true value" and "meaning of life," and Cynthia was unabashed in affirming: "So, I want to make a ton of money so that I can finance things, you better believe it." In particular she cared deeply about funding research into childhood leukemia. "But to me, I don't want to have my name on a plaque," she said. "If I could be there in that room when he [the doctor] can say to a mom, 'We've got the therapy. We're going to be able to.' I mean, what kind of greater victory can you have in the whole world?"

Cynthia's hypothetical was touching, but her reframing was telling:

> [The economist Paul] Samuelson said that we should pay no taxes, that we need to support charities, and we need to support funds, so we need to pay a certain amount and then we decide what we want to fund. So, if I decide I made 20 percent in a year, and I want it to go to pay welfare, you can do it. If you want to pay for cancer research, fine. If you want it to go say build more Ronald MacDonald houses, arthritis, whatever you want to do—"man on the moon," you know. So, I just think that's where the human spirit is. It's so exciting.

She brought us back to the neoliberal conception of redistribution,[18] with smart rich people (assumed to be smart because they're rich) deserving to choose how best to distribute capital. Interestingly, she was wrong in attributing this theory to economist Paul Samuelson, who had been an early hedge fund investor back in the 1960s but actually opposed the tax cuts enacted by George W. Bush.[19]

Jennifer provided a cautionary counterpoint, explaining why she found it alarming that hedge fund profits gave the industry a disproportionate ability to effect change. Beyond quibbles over fairness and the social good, Jennifer warned, the outsized renumeration may even undermine democracy. When we met back in 2013, she said, "I think about these guys that are making money—a lot of money—on the backs of pensions, and they're starting to look bad." Their charitable giving wasn't enough—could never be enough—to justify the high earnings they accrued investing money for the working class.

During the Great Recession, Jennifer reminded me, hedge fund billionaire John Paulson had gifted $100 million to the Central Park Conservancy. When she read the news, she said, she exclaimed aloud, "What an asshole?!" She elaborated, "He's lost so much fucking money [for his investors]. Right? And he [personally] has made all this money, and he's not making any money for his investors now, but he made boatloads of money . . . And he gives it to Central Park! Like, what the fuck? There are so many worse off people." This is a key point: it's not hard to imagine that the priorities of hedge fund managers may not align with the needs or wishes of most Americans.

"A lot these guys are making a lot of money with investments from endowments and pensions. These pensions are not making enough money, and they're not gonna make enough money from being in hedge funds" to support individual workers. Jennifer said, "So, it's this vicious cycle. It's a little like liberal fantasy land. I wish these guys would think more about their impact and, you know, how what they do is perceived, and whether they could be more gracious about how they've achieved their wealth and more helpful in how they redistribute it."

Rather than focus on the giving to high-profile causes, Jennifer thought, hedge fund managers should think about the students and workers affected by the endowment and pension money their firms manage, and they should lower their firms' profit margins to better support those people. Charitable giving was all well and good, but when it was only possible because hedge funds have "been able to make so much money by exploiting tax loopholes," it was breeding a new kind of resentment toward the industry and all the hedges it has erected to maintain the status quo.

Conclusion

Picking Winners and Losers

Carved out by a confluence of regulatory and tax conditions, the niche in which hedge fund workers—mostly elite white men—thrive is carefully surrounded by a thick, protective hedge against the incursion of "others." To be sure, women and racial minority men do make it into the hedge fund world, even to its dizzying heights, though more often they are funneled into less-glamorous support roles dressed up as partnerships within these flatter organizations. They can even be the tokenized exceptions who prove the rule. This is a space that facilitates the outlandish accumulation of elite white men's wealth and effectively hedges out everyone else.

Amid cutthroat competition to enter and stay inside this bounded sphere, aspirants are socialized into the habitus of the ideal hedge fund worker: the norms and practices that build and sustain wealth through patrimonial structures of access and advancement, durable networks of trust among high-net-worth individuals, and the portfolio worker imperative to build a transportable personal brand. Those able to embody this habitus, hedgemonic masculinity, and *homo economicus* can convert "failures" into soft landings in top-tier jobs, and even new funds that carry on an investment lineage.

Inequality created this rarefied class of financial worker, and, in turn, their work creates inequality. Inequality is amplified through the structure and function of risk and reward: the billions of dollars hedge funds manage, the steep fees they charge, and the tax quirks that insulate their profits. Workers espouse altruistic aspirations, noting that when they have "enough" they may retire or pursue lower-paid, prosocial, and feminized work like teaching. But even when that could be possible, their strong identification with the status of working at a hedge fund and the changing markers of class within the 1 percent keep pushing that magic number further out of reach. Those who do leave feel compelled to keep one foot in the game, or jump back in.

Scholars often look to the brutal results of inequality, rightfully telling the stories of the working poor; in this book, I have examined the beneficiaries of inequality through an in-depth study of the hedge fund industry and its working rich. How has this segment of the finance industry maintained its fiefdom, in which a tiny fraction of American workers—already socially privileged elite white men—can acquire riches by hedging out regulators and aspirants? Why is this elite group of white men so durable and how does its persistence enable the high incomes and wealth transfer among the "1 percent"?

In her foundational book *Masculinities,* Raewyn Connell identifies the myriad forces working against women gaining power, from legal exclusion to recruiting, to merit-based qualifications, to biases. Then, highlighting how power holders protect their elite advantage, she writes: "Behind these barriers to entry, at the upper reaches of power and only dimly visible from outside, are the self-reproducing strategies of power-holding elites. They include traffic in money and influence, the selection of successors, the mentoring of aides and allies, insistently selecting men for power." In *Hedged Out,* I have shifted our attention from the barriers to entry to put the spotlight on how exactly the inner workings of finance empower an elite group of white men.

Connell's words beautifully and brutally capture how some people are hedged out from, while others are hedged in the upper echelons of society, as I have uncovered among the financial elite. For instance, in US financial services, Asian, Black, and Latinx people hold 40 percent of entry-level jobs (the same as their representation in society) but are outnumbered nine to one in the C-suite.[1] These numbers are even more abysmal among women of color who account for 21 percent and 2 percent of entry-level and executive roles, respectively. And, overall, women hold 54 percent of jobs in finance today, yet only account for 22 percent of senior leadership roles (and merely half that at hedge funds). When asked why such low numbers of women of all races and men of color advance to high-level positions in finance, the people I interviewed for this book pointed to a tried-and-true dismissive argument: there are just too few members of these groups in the promotion pipeline or they aren't interested in finance careers. I have taken those low numbers as crucial evidence, as one way into understanding the social fabric of an industry that functions as both springboard and safety net for already privileged elite white men.

To call the upper echelons of business and government an "old boys' club" is to trivialize and naturalize the scope of white men's power in the United States. By observing the inner workings of hedge funds and talking to the workers on the inside, I have extended our understanding of financial elites and rising inequality in three important ways. First, I uncover how a system of patronage patterns the industry through discriminatory behavior masquerading as a preference for homophily. It captures the trust "naturally" afforded to those who share one's own class, gender, race, and other statuses and the tendency to transmit access, knowledge, and wealth along those lines. The people of color and white women who do gain access, even power, in this field sometimes benefit from the grooming processes that characterize patrimonialism, but they also carve opportunity out of crisis, as when firms restructure or the economy weathers a shock. These exceptions among hedge fund managers may suggest how hedge funds' patrimonial structures can be adapted or upended.

Second, I find that the social structure of hedge funds obscures durable hierarchies. The flatter, bureaucracy-free organization hedge funds champion in the name of nimble innovation is, in fact, a discourse rather than a practice. As a discourse, flatness obscures the authority of the key decision makers—the front-office executives with rock-star reputations and few checks and balances—who have become the "chiefs" and "kings" (and king-makers) of the industry. Removing bureaucracy and stripping away managers reduces the number of employees who share in the rewards, and heightens income, wealth, and social inequality. By examining social inequality in these proudly flatter organizations, I update theories of gender, racial, and class inequality in the workplace, which have tended to foreground fixed organizational structures, particularly within large bureaucratic firms.

Third, I theorize what it means to be hedged out: a form of boundary making around an elite status explicitly tied to masculinity and whiteness. Within this system, *hedgemonic masculinity* captures a distinct ideology embedded in the industry ideal of a creative, confident risk-taker and the ritualistic traditions that reinforce patrimonialism. People of all genders comply and contend with hedgemonic masculinity as they navigate the "meritocracy" and strive to fit the "portfolio ideal" norm. Combining entrepreneurial risk-taking, upper-class intellectualism, independent thinking, work infatuation, and investment passion, this track record can allow a worker to change firms or even, in the right circumstances, found their own hedge fund.

Hedgemonic masculinity legitimizes the practice of constructing a firm that is small and steeply hierarchical. In other industries, like technology, flatness is also valued. But as the business grows, these other firms become bigger and begin to add layers of bureaucracy.

Hedge funds, however, can stay small: with no physical product—only money to be managed—the business can grow without staffing up. This allows a hedge fund manager to reign with little scrutiny of the employment practices that privilege their interests and again naturalizes and normalizes the continued primacy of white men in leadership and among the highest compensated.

Who "Wins" and Who "Loses"

To further illuminate how patrimonialism, "flat" organizations, and hedgemonic masculinity hedge some people in and others out, I offer three cases of hedge fund founders who had closed a fund: one to retire, and two when mediocre performance caused investors to withdraw. Only the former came out a "winner." The latter two struggled, both personally and professionally, in the aftermath.

Vincent's Monetized Rolodex: The Patrimonial Safety Net

When a hedge fund worker achieves hedgemonic masculinity and proves themself a money maker, the patrimonial structures of the financial services industry facilitate their future success. Over the course of his career, Vincent, who is white, successfully rose to the top of an investment bank, launched his own firm, achieved financial freedom, retired to spend more time with his family, and returned to work on his own terms. He achieved what others dreamed, earning enough money to retire early and enough social capital to follow his passion and *return* to work for another successful go.

Vincent described launching his own fund as a youthful gamble that paid off: "It was completely opportunistic, and I was just young enough to take risk. I mean I had kids, but I was not that bright. I wasn't as fearful as I should have been." He elaborated:

Anytime you leave a cushy job . . . walk away from it and take the risk of starting something entrepreneurial, a lot of people would have said, "Don't do it." And a lot of people did. I attributed it to probably not having as much fear as I should have had. And we pulled it off. Knock on wood. I think if we tried that now, we would fail. But at that time, the stars aligned, the market environment was correct, there was plenty of liquidity out there, we were in a twenty-year bull market, we were good at what we did—there weren't that many obstacles and we blew it out. I don't know if that can be done today.

Vincent described how he took risk and prevailed, invested in himself and succeeded. Despite his success, Vincent warned others against following his path, reflecting the odds against a wager that most workers will fail to collect on.

Later, in his early forties, Vincent's firm managed $200 billion in assets and he'd acquired "enough" personal wealth ("a fair amount of money," in his demure estimation) to retire and finally spend more time with his family, even pursue charity work.[2] He recalled, "It was fun for six months, but pretty boring after that. I wasn't ready for the blue-haired lady boards. I love all that stuff, but I was just too young." Vincent felt his status dwindle among these older women doing largely unsung work, and it cued him to reclaim his vigor (read: masculinity) by reestablishing his career.

It wasn't tough for Vincent to leverage his old client networks to find a job—in fact, he *created* one. "I had made a lot of connections while running a business. I knew lots of constituents in the equation," he explained, and so he approached an investment bank and pitched a job, "So what I sold in was that I can be the adult in the room on any conversation, any subject matter, any part of the business of an investment bank or asset management." That role didn't exist, but Vincent "sold" it to the management on the strength of his personal brand. His track record of entrepreneurial success even allowed him to argue this new role was a high-level, senior position: "I was able to negotiate a senior relationship manager kind of role within a business. I was the senior statesman."

Vincent could demand the terms of his new position, and he told me he went in to the bank with "a couple conditions," which "shows you that I'm a man of conviction." At the same time, he indicated he didn't have anything to prove, didn't even really need the money: "I had no more ego left. I didn't feel the need to rise in the ranks of a bank again. I wanted a job. Money was tertiary. I knew I could make money. I've always made money. I could just come in and be a rainmaker" for the bank and attract investors. When he called himself a man of conviction, that conviction appeared to be his own unshakeable confidence in his worth, bargaining power, and security.

Within nine months, the 2008 financial crisis took hold and the investment bank started layoffs. Even so, new hire, high-salaried Vincent retained his position: "As things deteriorated, me as an individual became more important to them. I could be helpful in a lot of situations they never saw before, especially dealing with investors. I had a Rolodex, so I was able to help with keeping liquidity in the bank . . . from some large institutions." The vast networks that Vincent had amassed before launching his own hedge fund and refined in his career gave him a safety net allowing easy access to jobs and clients, which sustained his work and status during the financial crisis. The patrimonial structures in this industry extend beyond familial ties; relationships of exchange built on trust and loyalty underpin the relationships within and among financial institutions.

Equal Partners until the End: Farrah Finds the Flaw in Flatness

"We were equal partners," Farrah told me of her hedge fund's cofounders, "so there wasn't really, you know [a hierarchy]." Legally speaking, that was true, yet a flatter firm does not ensure founders equal footing in their future endeavors. Farrah described how there was a clear separation of responsibilities across the founders: "We kind of leaned on one partner, who sort of took on a lot of the running of the business. I did everything that was client-related, and he did everything that was more related to the business, and the other two guys were happy to let him do that." Each person held the legal title of partner, but their earnings and decision-making power at the firm were not on equal standing. With a loyal following of client investors, the portfolio manager's investment philosophy dictated how the partners ran the firm.

After five years, the fund's performance dropped and the firm went under. That was when Farrah saw the consequences of the gendered division of labor, in which she, a founder, took a feminized, "back office" role in client services. While her colleagues on the investment management side of the business could go on to manage their own money, Farrah struggled to find a comparable position at another firm. First she settled for a less senior position at another smaller firm, then, after the 2008 financial crisis, cycled through a series of short-term jobs in small, struggling firms.

Farrah blamed herself for founding a fund without having "enough" personal wealth to give her a safety net: "That's probably the mistake I made. Even though we did well for five years, we didn't make enough that I would never have to work again. And so, for me, it's been a struggle." She described how closing the doors on her hedge fund brought on a deep depression, even suicidal thoughts, intensified by the pressures of being her family's primary breadwinner, that recurred as the subsequent firms imploded. She caught herself before she could finish the phrase "I became unwanted," rephrasing that she was "not as marketable" in the industry.

Maybe, she lamented, if she'd had wealthy family ties or Ivy League credentials, it wouldn't be like this. Instead, Farrah had grown up in the South, the first in her family to graduate from college, and attended a local state school. Without an elite background, Farrah warned, "it is a big mistake for people to leave a big firm and go to any small firm, any small hedge fund, unless they've made so much money that they don't need another job. That's when you should go." In the end, she worked at an investment bank, with a salary half what she'd previously commanded. When I asked whether she would start a hedge fund again, she responded, "No. Would I go to a startup? Never."

Small organizations have few openings for people at the top of the organizational hierarchy, fewer still in flatter firms. And though a hedge fund founder may "wear multiple hats," it may be poor preparation for later periods on the job market. Further, for those more often hedged out—in Farrah's case a racial minority woman in a client-services rather than a "front office" portfolio manager position—attaining and losing founder status can seem like proof that elite white men are better suited to those top roles.

Cynthia and Bert's Bubble Bursts: Hedgemonic Masculinity Is Fragile, Too

In the late 1990s, Cynthia founded her first hedge fund with her friend Bert. As is the common gendered front/back office split, Bert served as the hedge fund manager, overseeing the investment portfolio, and Cynthia ran the marketing and operations side. The dot-com bubble allowed them to raise more than $100 million in capital in just a few years, but their investment strategy required a "critical mass" of at least $500 million. If their firm had survived the crash in 2001, Cynthia thought, she and Bert would have outperformed the market. But it didn't, and they had to return the money to investors before their long-term investment strategy could play out.

At this point, as we turned to the aftermath of their fund's failure, Cynthia spoke more slowly and carefully: "Unfortunately, Bert,

I didn't even know, he had a really bad drinking habit—I mean, I *knew,* but I didn't. He one day got drunk—this was after we closed the fund—on a bottle of vodka, went to his roof, and jumped right off. It was horrible. It still breaks my heart." Bert died by suicide, she thought, "because his whole identity" was wrapped up in their firm and his role as the hedge fund manager (a title Cynthia did not claim, as the head of business operations). Again, she shook her head, "And if we had just hung on, we'd be making a bazillion."

Hedgemonic masculinity confers high, but contingent, status and the depth of that identity blurs the boundaries between professional failures and personal shortcomings. Cynthia described the pride of the hedge fund manager identity and specifically tied it to men: "A hedge fund manager is like, 'I've got money. I'm smart. I'm an elite. I've got huge clients. I'm like the Vanderbilts. I'm the anointed.' There is really a lot of pride . . . it was so clubby. It was fun though. So yeah, [Bert's] identity was really tied into it. But that I think was true of any guy in this business. Definitely." Bert's suicide reflects the fragility of masculinity, in so many of its forms.

When a hedge fund manager fails, it seems like a failure of their very identity. Their friends and family are often directly affected, since it is common for investor funds to be sourced through personal ties. Their all-important professional reputation is tarnished in this small and interconnected industry, and it underscores the sense that their failure is on display to friends, family, and the entire industry. Acute shame is no surprise, and it amplifies the well-documented masculinity threat of failure in the workplace, which stems from cultural expectations that men will be defined in terms of their work and breadwinner status.[3]

While Cynthia also started on the investment side of the business, Bert and Cynthia's gendered roles as founders shaped how each identified with their work and coped with professional success and failure. Bert's more acute sense of irredeemable failure reflects the burden of upholding elite masculinity predicated on mastering investment and entrepreneurial risks. Recall, though, that under intense pressure as a breadwinner, Farrah also ideated suicide after failure, even though she held the same role as Cynthia, who didn't have children.

Later in my research, I had the opportunity to explore suicidal ideation among hedge fund managers. For instance, in chapter 5, I described Wayne's passion for mathematical modeling and how he built a tolerance for risk-taking over time by trusting his approach as he executed billion-dollar trades. But he also spoke of the downside of this passionate infatuation with his work: if it failed, the personal shame could be crushing.

Wayne told me at one point, "I hope I don't get a huge down year, but I could." I wondered what he thought he'd do if the "worst-case scenario" came to fruition, how he'd feel and how he'd cope. We had, by this point, met several times, and I felt confident that we knew each other well enough to delve into this potentially sensitive topic.

Looking me straight in the eye, and in an even tone, he replied, "Handcuff myself to the table so I don't jump out the window."

He looked away, pausing to think, then added, "I don't know. I'd talk to some friends."

I let that sit for a moment before continuing. "Is that worst-case scenario something you've thought about before?"

"Oh, yeah. All the time. I always think about the worst-case scenario."

"That *particular* response?" I asked, hinting at the suicidal impulse he'd revealed.

"Yeah. I'm sure it would flash in my mind. I think that's the cowardly response. I would think—I hope—that it wouldn't last more than two seconds in my head."

"Why do you think that that would be your response?"

"When I think about it—I'm trying to put my head in that space— I can feel that as a response. I guess it'd be—I feel there would be tremendous shame. All eyes would be looking at me, and I failed spectacularly." After a deep breath, Wayne said, "That's my worst fear."

"Why do you think [suicide] is a 'cowardly' response?"

"It's giving up." He took another pause to think about it, and then explained: "It's not wanting to face [failure] and make something of it—continue or do something again or do something different. It's giving up and burying your head in the sand, ultimately. I think it would be a cowardly response."

· · ·

In the hedge fund industry, who wins, who loses, and who is hedged out altogether shows that the mechanisms generating the reproduction of inequality are patterned by race, gender, and class. Each affects processes from entering the industry to rising up the ranks, founding a firm, and recovering from failure.

Moreover, class, gender, and race, as systems of social inequality, help explain why earnings metastasize and wealth consolidates in this industry. Past studies have considered the growth and persistence of the 1 percent but rarely consider gender and race's central role in how the working rich share resources. By taking a look at the relationship between income and wealth within an insular industry, I find that the social processes of elite earners' workplaces comprise the differentiating force that separates those who win from those who lose in this rarified strata of society.

The implications of these findings for inequality also pertain to studies of the US and global elite. Previous research has contradictory findings on solidarity among elites. Mark Mizruchi identifies a socially and politically fragmented US elite, while others attribute rising income and wealth to a national and global consolidation of elite networks. A study of local elites finds that the most influential feature is a high level of cohesion, with little less gender, racial, and class segregation among the wealthy and powerful.[4]

Focusing on one industry, however, reveals an interconnected—and likely politically mobilized—financial elite connected within a system of patrimonial structures. Patrimonialism engenders relationships among white class-advantaged men, particularly the most influential in the industry, but fragments ties with and among those with different gender, racial, and class statuses, even though they are present among the ranks of the working rich.

Implications for Democracy and the Economy

What happens in the hedge fund industry has enormous implications for global economies and governments. First, there is substantial overlap between government officials and Wall Street insiders, which allows the financial sector to expand its political might.[5] Investment banking is rife with household names: Goldman Sachs alone has been associated with former Treasury Secretary Henry Paulson, former Head of the SEC Arthur Levitt, former House Majority Leader Dick Gephardt, and former White House Chief Strategist Stephen Bannon.

So, too, are hedge funds. After Ben Bernanke completed his second term as chairman of the Federal Reserve, he was appointed senior advisor to $25 billion hedge fund Citadel. Bernanke's predecessor, Alan Greenspan, consulted with a number of hedge funds as well. And after leaving the White House, Barack Obama's chief of staff, Bill Daley, joined a hedge fund, too. The pipeline goes both ways, and so recently we can point to Robert Mercer, hedge fund manager of the $65 billion Renaissance Technologies, who invested millions in Donald Trump's presidential campaign and in Bannon's Breitbart News. Under Trump, hedge fund founder Anthony Scaramucci briefly served as communications director in 2017, and chief of staff Mark Mulvaney launched a hedge fund in 2020 that invests based on his regulatory expertise.[6]

I even specifically noted in my fieldwork that, at a hedge fund industry conference during the 2014 midterm elections, every keynote speaker was a notable financial lobbyist working in Washington, DC (and that all of them wrongly predicted who would win the presidency in 2016). The audience around me was chock-full of billionaires whose firms boasted political lobbying arms—one was, at the time, the wealthiest person in New York City. The revolving door between finance and the state swings smoothly,[7] ensuring that the former increases political power and influence alongside pecuniary rewards.

Second, hedge funds have a long history of collapsing currencies—as when George Soros "broke the Bank of England" by short-selling the British pound—and causing international financial crises, such as those in Asia in the late 1990s.[8] When category-5 Hurricane Maria devastated Puerto Rico and caused over 3,000 deaths, its recovery was stymied by the fact that the commonwealth was enormously indebted to hedge funds—to the tune of bankruptcy negotiations and $74 billion owed to sixty different hedge fund creditors. (The Puerto Rico Electric Power Authority owed $9 billion alone.) This debt had accrued when hedge funds flocked to Puerto Rico, where, because of its poor credit history, they could charge interest rates double those charged to other governments. Until 2016, US law even forbade Puerto Rico from filing for bankruptcy, meaning, in theory, it would be required to pay its debts. A financial crisis built, with borrowers and creditors contesting the terms of the debt in court as the island's 3.2 million inhabitants—all US citizens—grappled with 10.5 percent unemployment and an out-migration of 60,000 each year.[9] The hurricane was the last straw, collapsing the whole house of cards hedge funds had erected.

And third, hedge fund managers have become increasingly intertwined in international affairs. For example, hedge fund creditors led by billionaire Paul Singer of Elliott Management mobilized legal interventions to reclaim $100 billion of bonds lost in the 2001 Argentine default. Singer targeted its government assets, foreign exchange reserves, even prominent politicians' personal assets. He seized an Argentine naval vessel in 2012, holding it as collateral for the sovereign debt through an injunction issued by the superior court of Ghana, where the vessel was docked (the ship was released when the International Tribunal for the Law of the Sea intervened). By 2014, when the US Supreme Court ruled on behalf of the credit holders and prompted a second Argentine default, the Argentine president, Cristina Fernández de Kirchner, called the hedge funds extortionists guilty of "financial and economic terrorism."[10]

As Wall Street networks overlap with worldwide political systems, what happens on the trading desks at hedge funds and in their activities after hours affects economies and governments. And their inner workings help us understand how elites protect their interests and maintain their independence. As flashy media stories focus on individual cases of illegal activity, like insider trading and drug use, we hear little about the very real, global impacts of the industry's encroachment on government power, which chips away at a functioning democracy. To be sure, accounts of financial fraud are important and indicative of the entitlement afforded by eliteness, whiteness, and masculinity—the ease and luxury of making money in whatever way is most convenient and without the fear of devastating legal ramifications. Revelations about the ubiquity of illicit drugs show us that the culture of extreme overwork is another form of addiction and risk-taking. And reports of sexual harassment and assault are symptoms of a context in which masculinity is defined as powerful through the control of women and racially and class-marginalized men. We simply cannot overlook that all of the entitlement, control, and power threading through popular accounts accrue in the elites who so frequently straddle the boundary between Wall Street and

Washington. Hedge funds exploit and expand inequality, and they threaten democracy.

Inequality and Insecurity

Wall Street's high-risk, high-reward culture is an insufficient explanation for its astronomical incomes and prevailing leadership of upper-class, white men. Instead, the patrimonial structure organized around weathering risk restricts access to the rewards of financialization. The antibureaucratic sentiment espoused in the industry discourse of flatness, the contrarian ideals of hedgemonic masculinity, and the system of patrimonialism are all responses to the risk and uncertainty that characterize contemporary financial markets. Gender, race, and class become speculative metrics, figured into the hedge fund elites' discretionary choices of who is included and excluded from this lucrative world, yet hedged by the language of meritocracy. The resulting environment breeds favoritism, exclusion, and even authoritarianism, ensuring that inequality persists and is protected at the highest levels.

The implicit social hierarchies arising from networks built on trust and loyalty in hedge funds' flatter firms facilitate and legitimize the exceedingly high pay that exacerbates income and wealth inequality. As a result, a system of patronage allows a select group of elite white men to groom and transfer capital to one another. In this light, it's little wonder the top 1 percent is predominantly white and men.[11] The fortitude of patrimonial structures, like those on Wall Street, maintains this select group's claim to resources and further entrenches inequality among future generations.

It is often believed that the low numbers of women and racial minority men in the halls of power evidence a "pipeline problem" that can be solved through empowerment measures helping people of color and white women get interested in and maybe break into Wall

Street's C-suites. However, my six years of research in the hedge fund industry revealed a much different pipeline problem. The pool of aspirants is funneled into two *separate* pipelines. The patrimonial system, which rests on certain brands of white masculinity and moneyed networks, gives white, upper-class men a fast-track pipeline to the top. And everyone else must prove themselves equal to the hegemonic ideal in order to advance through a much more crowded, slower pipeline. Some of these "exceptional" people will make it, becoming high-profile traders and founders, yet this system most efficiently transfers power and resources from one generation of white men to the next. Economic inequality has accelerated in the United States not in spite of meritocracy, but because meritocracy is a myth—nowhere is that more evident than among the 1 percent.

Elites are empowered by the rising conditions of American insecurity. Increasing the gender and racial diversity of the power holders is no quick fix, because the criteria for and meanings of eliteness, whiteness, and masculinity are always shifting, and because inequality is both reason and result when it comes to Wall Street. Rather, change lies in transforming the economic and social systems of inequality that allow specific groups of people to garner such high pay for their labor while others struggle to make ends meet, all under the guise of a level playing field. Imagining alternatives is difficult work, enacting them more challenging still. Recognizing that the ultrarich, hedged in by the durability of race, class, and gender inequalities, play by different rules is a necessary if not sufficient first step toward a more fair and equitable distribution of resources in society.

Methodological Appendix
Studying Up

In-depth interviews and field observation allow scholars to learn about people's everyday lives—a necessity for understanding what happens in spaces less accessible to the public like elite social worlds. Like other groups featured in the news, elites tend to be polarizing because the public has preconceived notions about them.[1] This is especially true for a group like hedge fund managers and workers that has come to symbolize inequality. By observing them in their homes, workplaces, and social life, I gained a more nuanced understanding of their everyday lives. I learned how social hierarchies form, how resources and opportunities are divvied up, and how social inequalities become entrenched.

"Studying up" comes with a unique set of obstacles. In a study of the World Bank, sociologists Joseph Conti and Moira O'Neil faced challenges with access, self-presentation, and authority.[2] In response, they carefully presented and asserted themselves during interviews to earn participants' respect. Other researchers drew from existing personal or professional ties that provided the social and cultural capital necessary to secure access and build rapport.[3] The precedent has been to conduct an organizational ethnography, such as a school, agency, or corporation. By becoming embedded in an elite field, scholars can more easily establish trust and shared understanding.

From Insider to Outsider

Early on, I tried my best to follow the above model by making use of my previous industry experience. I reached out to my former colleagues to update them on my graduate school studies and the direction my research had taken. They were so encouraging that they offered to recruit participants, which is a big ask in an industry that values privacy and secrecy. I also created a LinkedIn profile (the industry's primary social media platform), so prospective participants could learn more about me.[4]

Initially, I sought to establish an organizational field site for a long-term immersion ethnography. I updated my résumé and cover letter and started applying for jobs. My goal was first to gain access, establish rapport at the firm, and then ask to conduct research. And, if denied, I would follow Karen Ho's model and only share my own experiences. But my approach fell through. I was either over- or underqualified based on my master's degree and niche specialization in my prior experience. One firm who interviewed me, in chapter 3, questioned whether I was either failing out of graduate school or only interested in the money.

As an alternative to an organizational ethnography, I went to industry events to track current goings-on, observe insiders interact, and recruit interviewees. At first, I led with the fact that I had worked in the industry, left to pursue graduate school, and then returned to study it. In keeping with the ethical standards for ethnographic research, I was always honest and up front about why I was there. I shared the purpose and nature of my study with the organizers and other people I met. But I also tried to blend in as much as possible to avoid calling attention to myself as an outsider.

I presented myself carefully, in part, because I feared they might think I was writing an exposé or had an ax to grind. People often asked questions about my motives. But, as I came to realize, it wasn't because they thought I had a personal or political agenda, as they often feared of journalists. Rather, the people I met assumed I wanted a job in the industry and wanted to help me find one. No matter how much I stressed that I would be writing scholarly articles, and, one day, a book for my academic career, I was met with questions about my job prospects at a hedge fund. What were my professional goals? What strategies did I specialize in? Would I like an introduction to so-and-so at such-and-such hedge fund? These questions echoed common beliefs that the industry is exciting and sought-after (no one wants to leave) and has a highly competitive labor market (everyone is trying to get an "in" or find a better job).

In fact, my insider status actually deterred people from participating in the study. This was largely because my previous employer was too well situated. People expressed hesitation because I represented an enormous institutional investor. Hedge funds tend to be wary of the news media but even more so of client investors. People who work at hedge funds do not want to open up and share personal details to clients who invest in their firms. Insiders were worried about what information I might share (even though I ensured privacy and confidentiality). In general, hedge funds finesse what is shared with clients to avoid disclosing proprietary secrets.

These obstacles yielded valuable insight into the industry's inner workings. First, failing to secure an organizational site shifted my focus to places where opportunities emerge in this labor market: conferences and social hours. I observed and participated in these events where people find jobs and investors, witnessing how these resources are guarded. I learned the import of reputation and how a scar can nearly ruin your future chances (refer to chapter 4). This was also revealing of the delicate nature of relationships and how they mediate who's allowed in and kept out. It became clear that advancement lay in relationships external to the firm. Even those gainfully employed always kept their options open and routinely searched for a better job. Thus, external labor markets are central to improving your status and pay, which helps to explain the high earnings and white men's dominance.

Second, the relationships I built shed light on social inequality and boundary-making. Being a white woman shaped how I interacted with the people I studied. However, being a woman didn't deny me access, as some research on elites suggests. In fact, it appeared that I was viewed as less threatening as a white woman in a field of mostly white men. And the three primary avenues through which I built relationships revealed the contours of the industry's racial, gendered, and classed boundaries.

Access: Race, Class, and Gender

As a younger, college-educated white woman, I generally gained access to three groups of people. First, men, especially white men, tended to either see me as a daughter figure or a sexual object. This made them more eager to talk to me at events, agree to participate, and introduce me to contacts. Second, I more easily established rapport with women's networks (who are mostly white), who identified gender as a barrier in the industry. Some wanted to share their experiences in the industry. Others obliged me because they valued helping and mentoring other women. Last, I often found myself among people who were marginalized by race and class and made efforts to include outsiders. Similarly, a number of women recalled how men of color more readily acknowledged the obstacles women faced and proactively supported their careers. These social dynamics reveal how gender, heterosexuality, race, and class funnel access to industry opportunities.

The first group exposed how sexual harassment upheld the industry's power dynamics. Yet, in my initial interviews, women rarely spoke about it. After encountering advances from men and watching them do so to other women, I became more creative in how I asked women about the topic (refer to chapter 5). At every event with men (as opposed to the women's events), men called me "beautiful" or "attractive." Men explicitly asked me on dates on five occasions. Several emailed me after networking events to invite me for a drink. In response, I thanked them for their interest in my research, provided my recruitment script, and never heard back. At one event, a debonair seventy-something white man offered to set me up with his son and his "handsome young business partner." He then introduced me to his partner at the event and then left us alone to mingle awkwardly.

Another time, at a weeknight event, I met an affable man who enthusiastically offered to do an interview and suggested that we do it over drinks afterward. I immediately thought of the advice to never turn down a research opportunity. But my initial perceptions of him, and that shaky line between gregarious and flirtatious behavior, led my gut to say no, much like the women I met. I suggested the next day instead.[5]

Throughout our interactions, the man called me "Doctor" or "Good Doctor." Since I was then a graduate student, I kept correcting him to explain that I was not yet a doctor. At our interview, he shared sexist and racist nicknames for his colleagues. One woman was "Scarlet Letter," because she complained about dating, and he called another, an Iranian man, the "Persian Rug." I realized then that the "Good Doctor" was my moniker. The next morning, I awoke at 6:30 a.m. to an unsettling text message: "The Tantalizing Tobias."

Lastly, at an industry happy hour, two men sipped on Macallan Scotch while making overtures to me on their friend's, a recent divorcé, behalf. He expressed embarrassment, apologized profusely, and volunteered to be interviewed. Unfortunately, recruiting this way did little to bolster my sense of authority as a junior scholar. It did, however, give me experience firsthand of the obstacles women face in building respectful relationships. Like many of the women I met, I had to repeatedly assert professional boundaries while doing my best to get the work done.

Clearly my experiences were not unique. I began using them as examples during interviews when I asked about harassment. And low and behold, women, in particular, disclosed more stories along these lines. The fact that women didn't label these types of uncomfortable interactions as sexual harassment revealed how deeply ingrained these heteronormative expressions of power are in the industry.

A Note on Gender and Access

Traditionally, the image of the ideal ethnographer has rested on the assumption that the researcher is a white man. As a result, how the scholar's embodied experience shapes knowledge production often has been ignored.[6] Feminist scholars have questioned this assumption, calling attention to how it has elided common experiences in the field. Rebecca Hanson and Patricia Richards identify how the tendency either to omit women's experiences of sexual harassment or characterize them as a "given" "show that the ethnographic fixations on solitary, dangerous, and intimate research not only put researchers at risk but also have negative implications for the construction of ethnographic knowledge."[7] Introducing the concept of an embodied ethnography, they identify how gendered bodies shape the interactions, experiences, and conversations used to construct theory.

How then can an embodied ethnography inform our understanding of the power dynamics of studying elites? One approach arises from deliberately using one's body as a tool to enter the power dynamics of the field of study. In her study of women executives in finance, Mary Blair-Loy presents a typology of women's strategies to cater to men clients: "emphasizing femininity, acting like one of the guys, and presenting oneself as a neutered expert."[8] A woman could adopt these same strategies to navigate the power dynamics of studying Wall Street (although these dispositions may be more readily available to white women). While helping to secure access and establish rapport, these strategies could reify the very unequal dimensions of social life that we seek to investigate and limit how we use these experiences to theorize gender.

For her book *Dealing in Desire,* Hoang recounted the necessity, rather than the strategy, of undergoing body transformations to work as a hostess. These arose from the aesthetic expectations for femininity and the physical toll of working twelve-hour shifts with little time to eat. Hoang centers the body in her research, what she calls carnal sociology, to show how she and her fellow hostesses subjected themselves to symbolic violence as part of the women's subordination to men. While men often emerge from the field as heroes, she concludes, "Feminine-centered ethnographers, on the other hand, subject themselves to a different set of *embodied costs,* objectifying gazes, and disciplining practices both in the field and in the broader academy."[9] For this reason, in her book, she centered her research subjects rather than her own embodied self.

For women and gender expansive scholars, do we write ourselves in or leave ourselves out of our work? And how do we navigate these spaces—in the field and academy—without reifying elite power, femininity, or symbolic violence?

Following Hoang's model, I initially shared my experiences only in the preface and methods to keep the focus on my research subjects. During presentations, however, audiences often asked about access and how my social position shaped the work. I found that people assumed that I had an elite upbringing or primarily relied on my prior work experience. Several—including a colleague who is gender expansive and a person of color—said they couldn't have studied this population. I disagree: I think others can and should, although their access likely would be different, leading to unique and important findings based on their own interactions in the field. Since positioning myself as a scholar-outsider elicited great trust, I want to encourage others to do the same and study all types of elites.

These types of questions compelled me to disclose details about how I composed myself in the field as well as how this shaped what I found. And, while Blair-Loy's typology provides rich insight into Wall Street, it made me worry that readers may misinterpret my explanation of how gender shaped my access as a "how to" for deploying femininity in qualitative research. In general, I found that my own ways of gaining access were more complex than any typology. This prompted me to reflect on how women navigate obstacles in the industry, how we contend with symbolic violence and white men's domination in our workplaces, and how we can generate knowledge from these experiences.

Judith Butler has theorized how gender is performative but not in the sense that we can easily turn it on or off. Femininity and masculinity are not cultural scripts but rather correspond to hegemonic ideologies that shape what we believe and expect of ourselves and others as we interact with one another. Gender is embedded deep into our psychological worlds and bodily dispositions in ways that we cannot always control, let alone use as a strategy. Because of this, gender—and enactments of femininity and masculinity—can't be understood as a tool kit, or set of strategies, for navigating the social world, whether as a researcher or a worker.[10]

This is not to say that I—or the women I met in my research—was without agency. At times, I felt the need to establish my own boundaries, reassert my authority, or question that of others. These feelings often arose through gendered interactions. And when they did, I made note of when, how, and why to help me empathize with women's own accounts of how they too navigated this tricky terrain.

A key to a feminist approach to qualitative research lies in theories of intersectionality and gender.[11] In the case of Black feminist thought, Patricia Hill Collins identifies how the outsider-within's unique perspective from holding unequal power reveals the power structures that be. This is because, as Cecilia Ridgeway theorizes, status characteristics provide a frame through which we interpret interactions and form unequal status hierarchies, which guides our own understanding of them. And, as Raewyn Connell shows, gender, as a system of inequality, is upheld by hegemonic beliefs about masculinity and femininity that serve to legitimize and uphold the practices that subordinate women and ensure the dominant position of certain men. As a gendered, racialized, and classed subject, I as the researcher navigated these status hierarchies and ideologies, which became more readily visible and salient through the relationships I established and my social interactions in the field. For instance, as I explained above, being a white woman opened some doors but not others. Experiencing this social world firsthand yielded a deeper understanding of the inequality-producing processes that insiders recounted.

A feminist approach to the theory of reflexivity helps to expose how my social position in the field reveals relations of power and authority within it.[12] In disclosing my own experiences, I don't want to reify the tendency to describe women's appearances and embodiments, while letting men's go unmarked. Rather, I want to highlight how my own position and interactions in the field were integral to theorizing my findings. Rather than merely disclosing that I am a middle-class white woman, my goal here has been to draw from that social position to develop theoretical insights into how and why elite white men dominate the field I study.

It is often assumed that, when studying elites, class foregrounds the power dynamics in the field. Yet, class intersects with gender, sexuality, race, nationality, and disability in how researchers gain access to—and develop theories about—elites. Rather than flipping or inverting the traditional conception of top-down or bottom-up power dynamics between researcher and those studied, power in these contexts should be conceived as multidimensional, varied, and contextual, an insight well-established in feminist and ethnographic research on other fields.

To conclude, how I gained access shaped how I understood the industry's power dynamics, but my access wasn't contingent on who I am. And while my previous industry experience eased understanding and familiarity, it alone did not grant access. Regardless of who they are and where they come from, scholars should study elite social worlds, because being an outsider will yield rich and distinct insights into the inner workings of elites. If only "insiders" study elites, we narrow what we can know about status, advantage, and power.

Methodological Details

Over a six-year period, I interviewed forty-eight hedge fund workers and observed thirty-five workplaces and industry events, ranging from 1.5 hours to three days. In 2013, I began preliminary research in New York. I then collected data from 2014 to 2016 in Texas and New York. Lastly, I conducted follow-up research from 2018 to 2019 in California. New York, Texas, and California are the states with the most hedge funds. Over one-third of global hedge fund assets are managed in New York, making it the world's hedge fund capital.[13]

One of my goals was to investigate patterns in people's professional trajectories that reveal inequalities. Interviews are well-suited for this aim, because while what we say doesn't always reflect what we actually do or did, it provides insight into the cultural meanings, ideals, and discourses we use to make sense of our experiences.[14] Our accounts of our lives, as Michèle Lamont and Ann Swidler explain, illustrate how social boundaries and status hierarchies organize our experiences, which are central to the study of inequality.[15] I asked each interviewee about their educational background, career paths, internal promotions, firm transitions, workplace culture and organization, professional relationships, current job responsibilities, work schedule, professional aspirations, and broader societal views.

I recruited via professional associations' mailing lists, conferences, and networking events; LinkedIn industry forums; and snowball sampling techniques. Snowball sampling relies on leads from other participants, which is helpful for reaching hard-to-access populations. It allowed me to reach people who were unresponsive to other recruiting techniques.[16] Finally, I attended industry events, where I made efforts to recruit a range of different people, from experts in the field, to members of the dominant networks, to those on the sidelines.

These recruitment techniques led to an interviewee sample more diverse than the population (refer to table 3 below). The sample has a fairly balanced number of men (n = 25) and women (n = 23). I oversampled women and racial minority men to solicit a wide range of experiences. The sample includes thirty-one white people, forty-one US-born people, and thirteen first- or second-generation immigrants (and two non-US nationals who live and work abroad). Twenty-five interviewees were over forty years old. Thirty-six had more than a decade of industry experience, of which fifteen have more than twenty-five-year tenures. To be included, I required a minimum of three years of industry experience, but made exceptions for two, who were amid launching funds based on professional experience in fields related to their investment strategies. A majority of the sample manages investments or works with investors in the "front office," while seven have support positions (operations, accounting, and administrative) in the "back office." The sample captures a range of firm types and sizes, from investment banks to single-employee firms.

To determine eligibility, I asked prospective participants whether they were currently or previously employed at a "hedge fund." Within the industry, what constitutes a "hedge fund" is open for debate. This is because a traditional hedging strategy refers to a type of investment that hedges risk, but hedge funds today employ a range of strategies. The SEC defines a hedge fund as a limited partnership that pools money from high-net-worth investors to invest in stocks, real estate, land, currencies, or virtually any other investment. Since this is a broad definition, I allowed people to self-identify, and then I conducted online research to verify their employment history and firm type. When necessary, I searched the SEC database to confirm. Because of these people's high visibility online, I was also able to catch gaps or omissions in their accounts, which provided some background information that helped me to ask effective follow-up questions and contextualize how they framed their experiences.

I conducted interviews in person or over the phone, a common mode for meetings in this industry. Most interviews were audio-recorded, except five for participants who felt more comfortable with handwritten notes. The interviews lasted between thirty minutes and three hours, with the average being one hour. The interviewee selected the location, which included cafés, homes, or offices. For interviews located outside of New York, California, and Texas, I conducted interviews over the phone.

Immediately following interviews, I wrote field notes on the person's appearance, mannerisms, demeanor, and tone. I also jotted down the context and our interactions before and after the interview. Finally, I reflected on my initial reflections to the interview, including details about how questions landed, the relevance of emerging themes, and any need for elaboration or follow-up in future interviews.[17]

Field observations provided a deeper understanding of the industry's informal norms and practices, allowing me to contextualize data from interviews. I participated in industry social events like conferences, investor panels, networking events, and an onsite job interview. At events, I made efforts to talk to a range of different people, both those on the sidelines of the social gatherings and those in the center of the action. To access leaders, experts, and other insiders, I introduced myself to the speakers after panels and inserted myself, albeit awkwardly at times, into the conversations of small, closed circles during receptions. As I stood on the fringes of these cliques of white men in suits, usually nodding my head as they pontificated on some arcane topic, I mused on Erving Goffman's dramaturgical model for how people go out of their way to help ensure social interaction go smoothly.[18] To my relief, people would eventually respond to my presence, even if it took minutes of me waiting patiently, and usually they were even gracious enough to express (or feign) interest in my work.

Opportunities to take field observations also arose during interviews. Ten interviewees allowed me to observe the social organization and physical environment at their workplaces. These interviewees often took me on tours of their office space and explained the division of labor, both in terms of physical layout and professional responsibilities.

For analysis, I merged an inductive approach and flexible approach to code and analyze interview transcripts and field notes.[19] First, I characterized and labeled fragmentary data to identify analytical themes according to my interview questionnaire organized around career trajectories, organizational structure, industry experiences, and broader worldviews. Then, I further investigated significant themes in a series of focused coding with attention to organizational and industry logics.[20] Primary themes initially emerged around professional goals, training, self-presentation, reputation, motivation, building relationships, compensation, career planning, and job transitions. From here, secondary themes concerned network closure, fraternal bonding, mentorship and apprenticeship, familial investor bases, and monetary flows among firms.

To ensure anonymity, I assigned each person a pseudonym (some like Sasha, Jerry, and Jamie selected their own), removed all firm identifiers, and altered minor details like school names and regions (when outside of New York, Texas, and California). For minor details, I swapped a school name or location with one comparable in connotation or status. Since many interviewees are visible online and in the news, I asked them to weigh in on any details that might make them identifiable. On the rare occasion that they did, it usually had to do with a career transition that could make them more recognizable, such as a cross-country move or an uncommon career path. These requests didn't pertain to my major findings, so omitting or anonymizing the detail didn't significantly affect my conclusions.

TABLE 3. Interviewees' Characteristics

Characteristic	Number
Age	
20–29	6
30–39	17
40–49	17
50–59	7
60–69	1
Education	
Doctorate	10
Masters	13
Bachelors	25
Gender	
Women	23
Men	25
Race/Ethnicity	
Other/Multiracial	1
Middle Eastern American	2
Black/African American	2
Hispanic/Latinx	4
Asian or Asian American	8
White	31
Role	
Investments	26
Sales	15
Operations/Support	7
Tenure	
Less than 10 years	12
11–20 years	21
More than 20 years	15

TABLE 4. List of Interviewees

Name	Age	Gender	Race or Ethnicity	Education	Job Function
Albert	40s	Man	White	PhD	Investment
Alyssa	20s	Woman	White	BS	Investment
Amanda	30s	Woman	White	BS	Client Services
Ana	40s	Woman	White	BA/BS	Client Services
Andrew	30s	Man	White	JD	Client Services
Bob	40s	Man	White	MBA	Investment
Bradley	20s	Man	White	BS	Investment
Brian	50s	Man	White	MBA	Investment
Craig	40s	Man	White	PhD	Investment
Cynthia	60s	Woman	White	BA	Client Services
Deborah	50s	Woman	White	PhD	Investment
Dennis	60s	Man	White	BA	Service Provider
Diane	50s	Woman	White	BA	Investment
Emily	40s	Woman	White	MIS	Client Services
Eric	30s	Man	White	MBA	Operations
Erica	30s	Woman	White	BS	Client Services
Farrah	40s	Woman	Middle Eastern American	BS	Client Services
Fernando	30s	Man	Latinx	MBA	Investment
Giovanni	40s	Man	White	MBA	Service Provider
Gita	30s	Woman	Asian	MBA	Investment
Jamie	30s	Man	Mixed Race	JD	Investment
Jay	30s	Man	Latinx	MS	Investment
Jeffrey	50s	Man	White	BA/BS	Investment
Jennifer	40s	Woman	White	MBA	Client Services
Jerry	20s	Man	Latinx	BS	Investment
Julie	30s	Woman	Asian American	BA	Investment
Justin	40s	Man	White	MBA	Investment
Sharon	40s	Woman	White	MBA	Investment
Ken	30s	Man	White	BA/BS	Investment
Kristen	30s	Woman	White	BA/BS	Client Services
Linda	30s	Woman	Asian American	BA	Operations
Lisa	30s	Woman	Asian	MBA	Investment
Manny	40s	Man	Latinx	BS	Investment
Margaret	20s	Woman	Asian American	BS	Investment
Matthew	40s	Man	Black	BS	Investment
Melissa	20s	Woman	White	BS	Client Services
Michelle	40s	Woman	White	BA/BS	Client Services

Natalya	30s	Woman	White	PhD	Client Services
Nicole	20s	Woman	White	BA/BS	Investment
Regina	30s	Woman	White	MBA	Service Provider
Sasha	30s	Woman	Black	BS	Client Services
Scott	40s	Man	White	JD	Client Services
Sebastian	30s	Man	Middle Eastern American	BA	Client Services
Sokhom	30s	Man	Asian American	BA	Investment
Steven	30s	Man	Asian American	BS	Investment
Vincent	50s	Man	White	JD	Investment
Wayne	40s	Man	Asian American	PhD	Investment
William	50s	Man	White	PhD	Contractor

Notes

Preface

1. All names are pseudonyms.
2. Bryan-Low, Mollenkamp, and Zuckerman, "Peloton Flew High, Fell Fast."
3. Short-selling is a type of investment in a security that is expected to decline in value. To do this, the investor takes out a loan in the form of the asset itself (a stock, for instance), rather than the monetary value of that asset, from a bank or other lender. The investor then sells the asset when it has reached a high price, waits for the asset to drop in value, then buys the asset at the lower price and pays the lender back in kind, pocketing the price difference.
4. Neely and Carmichael, "Profiting on Crisis."

Introduction

1. I anonymized all individual, school, and firm names to protect the participants' privacy.
2. Some race scholars, such as historian Nell Painter, have called for capitalizing white to explicitly racialize white people in keeping with other racial and ethnic groups. I recognize the value in this approach but decided to use a lowercase "w" to avoid the association with white supremacist organizations.
3. Piketty, Saez, and Zucman, "Distributional National Accounts."
4. Jimmy Carter signed the Depository Institutions Deregulation and Monetary Control Act in 1980. Financialization refers to the resulting growth and expansion of the financial sector: Krippner, *Capitalizing on Crisis*.

5. The average base salary was roughly $350,000. The remaining came in bonuses, commissions, and options. Refer to Harjani, "Hedge Fund Manager Pay Rises to $2.4 Million."

6. Institutional Investor, "All-America Buy-Side Compensation."

7. Yavorsky et al., "Women in the One Percent."

8. Although there is a dearth of industry research on race and ethnicity, industry data show that few people of color run hedge funds: Barclays Global, "Affirmative Investing"; Kruppa, "The 'David' Problem"; Preqin, "Women in Alternative Assets."

9. Manduca, "Income Inequality and the Persistence of Racial Economic Disparities"; Piketty, Saez, and Zucman, "Distributional National Accounts"; Yavorsky et al., "Women in the One Percent."

10. Blair-Loy, *Competing Devotions;* Charles and Grusky, *Occupational Ghettos;* Kellogg, *Challenging Operations;* Pierce, *Gender Trials;* Roth, *Selling Women Short;* Wingfield, *No More Invisible Man.*

11. Pew Research Center, "The American Middle Class Is Losing Ground."

12. Collins and Mayer, *Both Hands Tied;* Galbraith, *Created Unequal;* Kalleberg, *Good Jobs, Bad Jobs.*

13. Costa and Kahn, "Understanding the American Decline in Social Capital, 1952–1998"; Hacker and Pierson, "Winner-Take-All Politics"; Kang, "Inequality and Crime Revisited"; Mayer, "How Did the Increase in Economic Inequality between 1970 and 1990 Affect Children's Educational Attainment?"; Subramanian and Kawachi, "Whose Health Is Affected by Income Inequality?"

14. Delaney, *Money at Work;* Hardie and MacKenzie, "Assembling an Economic Actor"; MacKenzie, "Long-Term Capital Management and the Sociology of Arbitrage"; Riach and Cutcher, "Built to Last."

15. Preqin, "Global Hedge Fund Reports."

16. Industry insiders refer to these as quantitative, distressed debt, and event-driven strategies, respectively.

17. The highest rate for capital gains is 20 percent, compared to 37 percent for the highest income tax bracket. Capital gains refer to the sale of an asset, such as a share of a stock or an acre of land.

18. Hedge funds have incurred more detrimental costs than the profits generated for higher education: Eaton et al., "The Financialization of US Higher Education."

19. Gilbert and Hrdlicka, "A Hedge Fund That Has a University."

20. Derivatives are contracts among buyers and sellers in which the value is based on an underlying asset or collection of assets (e.g., stocks, commodities,

bonds, interest rates, currencies, and market indexes), which serve as a bench-mark. Derivatives include futures, swaps, and options, among others.

21. Brav, Jiang, and Kim, "The Real Effects of Hedge Fund Activism"; Elyasiani and Mansur, "Hedge Fund Return, Volatility Asymmetry, and Systemic Effects"; Lewis, *The Big Short*; Litterick, "Billionaire Who Broke the Bank of England"; Pitluck, "Watching Foreigners"; Strauss, "Why Hedge Funds Love Charter Schools"; Sullivan, "The 'Audacious Lie' behind a Hedge Fund's Promise to Sustain Local Journalism"; Zorn et al., "Managing Investors."

22. Preqin, "Global Hedge Fund Reports"; Preqin, "Private Capital Compensation and Employment Review."

23. Although stocks and bonds aren't included in gross domestic product (GDP), this example provides a frame of reference for the enormous scale. Percentage of GDP calculated using World Bank and Preqin data: World Bank, "United States." Profits and revenue reported in the Fortune 500 database. Employees and GDP percentage from Gross, "As Wal-Mart Goes . . ."; "G.M.'s 1955 Profit Exceeds a Billion, Setting U.S. Mark"; Welch, "GM Now Has Fewer UAW Employees Than FCA, Ford."

24. Cassidy, "Mastering the Machine"; Stevenson and Goldstein, "Bridgewater Manager Ray Dalio Defends His Firm's 'Radical Transparency.'" Employee incomes based on Institutional Investor, Glassdoor, Indeed, and LinkedIn self-reported data.

25. Hedge funds often have a dual fund structure, called a master/feeder fund, with one fund domiciled in an offshore tax haven, such as the Cayman or British Virgin Islands, and the other in the United States as a limited partnership, usually in Delaware where the regulatory and tax structures are most beneficial.

26. Harrington, *Capital without Borders*.

27. Piketty, *Capital in the Twenty-First Century*. On the central role of wages in rising inequality, refer also to Galbraith, *Created Unequal*.

28. Khan, *Privilege*; Lareau, *Unequal Childhoods*.

29. Friedman and Laurison, *Class Ceiling*.

30. Jack, *Privileged Poor*; Khan, *Privilege*; Naudet, *Stepping into the Elite*.

31. Sherman, *Uneasy Street*. Of course, in some circles, conspicuous consumption is still *en vogue:* Mears, *Pricing Beauty*; Mears, *Very Important People*.

32. On the myth of meritocracy in financial services, refer to Godechot, *Working Rich*; Roth, *Selling Women Short*.

33. Ho, *Liquidated*; Snyder, *Disrupted Workplace*.

34. Cooper, *Cut Adrift*; Hacker, *Great Risk Shift*; Pedulla, *Making the Cut*; Pugh, *Beyond the Cubicle*; Pugh, *Tumbleweed Society*; Rao, *Crunch Time*.

35. Freeland, *Plutocrats.*

36. Autor, Katz, and Kearney, "Polarization of the U.S. Labor Market."

37. Galbraith, *Created Unequal;* Lin, "Financial Premium in the US Labor Market"; Tomaskovic-Devey and Lin, "Income Dynamics, Economic Rents, and the Financialization of the U.S. Economy."

38. Krippner, "Financialization of the American Economy"; Lin and Neely, *Divested.*

39. Hacker and Pierson, "Winner-Take-All Politics"; Lin and Neely, *Divested;* Volscho and Kelly, "Rise of the Super-Rich."

40. Throughout the book, I will refer to various forms of capital. Financial capital refers to money, credit, and assets that allow you to generate profits and build wealth. Human capital captures the value of your experiences, skills, and knowledge. Social capital refers to the value of your social ties—familial, educational, and professional—while cultural capital refers to your soft skills, know-how, and dispositions that provide class advantage. Refer to Bourdieu, *Distinction;* Burt, "Structural Holes and Good Ideas"; Marx and Engels, *Marx-Engels Reader.*

41. Moyer, "Four Hedge Fund Managers Top $1 Billion in Pay."

42. Blau and Kahn, "Gender Wage Gap"; Lin and Neely, "Gender, Parental Status, and the Wage Premium in Finance"; Roth, *Selling Women Short.*

43. When executives slash wages or lay off employees, this stimulates an increase in the company's stock price and pays higher dividends. For more detail on the "shareholder value" movement in corporate governance and its effects on workers, refer to Davis, *Managed by the Markets;* Fligstein and Shin, "Shareholder Value and the Transformation of the U.S. Economy, 1984-2000"; Lazonick and O'Sullivan, "Maximizing Shareholder Value."

44. Goldstein, "Revenge of the Managers"; Lin and Tomaskovic-Devey, "Financialization and U.S. Income Inequality, 1970-2008"; Rosenfeld, *What Unions No Longer Do;* Shin, "Explaining Pay Disparities between Top Executives and Nonexecutive Employees."

45. Mills, *Power Elite.* For recent scholarship, refer to Mizruchi, *Fracturing of the American Corporate Elite.*

46. Weber, *Theory of Social and Economic Organization.*

47. Race and gender scholars who theorize this include: Alexander, *New Jim Crow;* Ferguson, *Aberrations in Black;* Fraser, "Feminism, Capitalism, and the Cunning of History"; Lipsitz, *Possessive Investment in Whiteness;* Robinson and Kelley, *Black Marxism.*

48. Adams, *Familial State.*

49. Neely, "Fit to Be King."

50. Altshuller, Peta, and Jordan, "Like Tiger, Like Cub."

51. Rosenfeld, *What Unions No Longer Do.*

52. Boltanski and Chiapello, *New Spirit of Capitalism;* Davis, *Managed by the Markets;* DiMaggio, *Twenty-First-Century Firm;* Kalleberg, *Good Jobs, Bad Jobs.*

53. Anderson and Brown, "Functions and Dysfunctions of Hierarchy"; Borgatti and Foster, "Network Paradigm in Organizational Research"; Hamel et al., "First, Let's Fire All the Managers."

54. Acker, "Hierarchies, Jobs, Bodies"; Ferguson, *Feminist Case against Bureaucracy;* Ferree and Martin, *Feminist Organizations;* Kanter, *Commitment and Community;* Kanter, *Men and Women of the Corporation;* Rothschild-Whitt, "Collectivist Organization; Sobering, "The Relational Production of Workplace Equality."

55. Cohen, Huffman, and Knauer, "Stalled Progress?"; England, "Gender Revolution Uneven and Stalled."

56. Kalev, "How You Downsize Is Who You Downsize."

57. Charrad and Adams, "Patrimonialism, Past and Present"; Collins, "Patrimonial Alliances and Failures of State Penetration."

58. Piketty, *Capital in the Twenty-First Century.*

59. Lachmann, "Coda."

60. Ogle, "Archipelago Capitalism."

61. Pistor, *Code of Capital.*

62. Erdmann and Engel, "Neopatrimonialism Reconsidered"; Glucksberg and Burrows, "Family Offices and the Contemporary Infrastructures of Dynastic Wealth."

63. Preqin, "Private Capital Compensation and Employment Review."

64. Godechot, *Working Rich;* MacKenzie, "Long-Term Capital Management and the Sociology of Arbitrage."

65. Ho, *Liquidated;* Roth, *Selling Women Short;* Turco, "Cultural Foundations of Tokenism."

66. Galbraith, *Inequality and Instability.*

67. On the topic of trust, instability, and exchange, refer to Cook, *Trust in Society;* Kollock, "Emergence of Exchange Structures"; Podolny, "Market Uncertainty and the Social Character of Economic Exchange"; Tilly, "Welcome to the Seventeenth Century."

68. Mueller and Philippon, "Family Firms and Labor Relations."

69. Luhmann, "Familiarity, Confidence, and Trust"; Rousseau et al., "Not So Different After All."

70. Correll et al., "It's the Conventional Thought That Counts"; Ridgeway, *Framed by Gender.*

71. Gambetta and Hamill, *Streetwise;* Rivera, *Pedigree;* Simpson, McGrimmon, and Irwin, "Are Blacks Really Less Trusting Than Whites?"; Smith, "Race and Trust."

72. Connell, *Gender and Power;* Feagin and Ducey, *Elite White Men Ruling;* Lipsitz, *Possessive Investment in Whiteness;* Martin, "Gender as Social Institution"; Ray, "Theory of Racialized Organizations"; Risman, "Gender as a Social Structure."

73. Bielby, "Minority Vulnerability in Privileged Occupations"; Lapavitsas, "Relations of Power and Trust in Contemporary Finance"; Lyons-Padilla et al., "Race Influences Professional Investors' Financial Judgments"; Rugh and Massey, "Racial Segregation and the American Foreclosure Crisis"; Schimank, "Against All Odds."

74. On the financial sector, lending disparities, and widening income and wealth inequality, refer to Adkins, *Time of Money;* Fligstein and Goldstein, "Emergence of a Finance Culture in American Households, 1989–2007"; Lin and Neely, *Divested.*

75. Ho, *Liquidated.*

76. Roth, *Selling Women Short.* Olivier Godechot similarly debunks the myth of meritocracy in financial services in France: Godechot, *Working Rich.*

77. Correll et al., "It's the Conventional Thought That Counts"; Ewens and Townsend, "Are Early Stage Investors Biased against Women?"; Lyons-Padilla et al., "Race Influences Professional Investors' Financial Judgments"; Tak, Correll, and Soule, "Gender Inequality in Product Markets."

78. Castilla, "Gender, Race, and Meritocracy in Organizational Careers"; Castilla and Benard, "Paradox of Meritocracy in Organizations."

79. With a background in Marxist organizing in Europe, Jones wrote his dissertation on labor and conflict in Akron, Ohio, then a site of labor strikes and a stark class divide. Jones later published a book, titled *Life, Liberty, and Property,* on the research.

80. Jaeger, *All About Hedge Funds;* Mallaby, *More Money Than God.*

81. When the market is in a downward spiral, as in a "bear" market, hedge funds must perform "hedges" and short-sell stock (bet that companies will fail) to profit. But when the market grows—that is, a "bull" market—hedge funds must take on more risk to outperform the market. This is also true when interest rates are low. For more detail, refer to Delevingne, "20 Percent Club"; Harper, "Hedge Funds."

82. Although hedge funds have averaged annual returns of 8 percent since 1994, they actually underperformed relative to the S&P 500 from 1994 to 2018

(7.5 percent versus 9.8 percent, respectively). Insiders defend these numbers as either a sign that too many hedge funds have flooded the industry (top firms report returns over 20 percent) or that the industry effectively minimizes risk. Refer to Harper, "Hedge Funds."

83. Elyasiani and Mansur, "Hedge Fund Return, Volatility Asymmetry, and Systemic Effects."

84. On elite solidarity, fragmentation, and boundary-making, refer to Bourdieu, *Distinction;* Cousin, Khan, and Mears, "Theoretical and Methodological Pathways for Research on Elites"; Lamont, *Money, Morals, and Manners;* Lamont and Molnár, "Study of Boundaries in the Social Sciences"; Rivera, *Pedigree.* On social closure and opportunity hoarding, refer to Tilly, *Durable Inequality;* Tomaskovic-Devey and Avent-Holt, *Relational Inequalities.*

85. Although in some cases this works to women's favor, as during the Great Recession. Refer to Fisher, *Wall Street Women.*

86. On the performance of women fund managers, refer to Aggarwal and Boyson, "Performance of Female Hedge Fund Managers"; Rothstein Kass, "Women in Alternative Investments." On gender and leadership, refer to Rudman et al., "Status Incongruity and Backlash Effects."

87. Nelson, *Gender and Risk-Taking.*

88. Carrington, *Race, Sport, and Politics;* Messner, *It's All for the Kids.*

89. Black et al., "On the Origins of Risk-Taking"; Fisk and Overton, "Who Wants to Lead?"; Levine and Rubinstein, "Smart and Illicit"; Nelson, *Gender and Risk-Taking;* Rosette and Livingston, "Failure Is Not an Option for Black Women."

90. Lapavitsas, "Relations of Power and Trust in Contemporary Finance."

91. DiPrete et al., "Segregation in Social Networks Based on Acquaintanceship and Trust"; Smith, "Race and Trust."

92. Crenshaw, "Mapping the Margins," 1244.

93. Crenshaw, "Mapping the Margins"; Hill Collins, *Black Feminist Thought.*

94. Cousin, Khan, and Mears, "Theoretical and Methodological Pathways for Research on Elites"; Nash, "On Difficulty"; Nash, "Re-Thinking Intersectionality."

95. Hill Collins, *Black Feminist Thought;* Smith, *Everyday World as Problematic.*

96. Ho, *Liquidated.*

97. Katz, "Ethnography's Warrants."

98. Ridgeway, *Framed by Gender.*

99. On intersectionality as a methodology and relational practice, refer to Choo and Ferree, "Practicing Intersectionality in Sociological Research"; McCall, "Complexity of Intersectionality."

100. For more on exceptional or negative cases, refer to Bettie, "Exceptions to the Rule"; Emigh, "Power of Negative Thinking."

Chapter 1: From Financial Steward to Flash Boy

1. Mallaby, *More Money Than God.*

2. This is also why women do well today as financial managers that manage a family's retirement and other investment accounts. The stereotype of women as risk-averse and nurturing makes them ideal workers for managing cautious, long-term investments for households.

3. Although Black cowboys and women played an important role in the American West, they have been systematically excluded from cultural and historical depictions. Refer to Campbell, "Black Cowboys in the American West."

4. For more on theories of masculinity, whiteness, and how ideology maintains the cultural hegemony of the white-men-dominant ruling class, refer to Connell, *Masculinities;* Feagin and Ducey, *Elite White Men Ruling;* Lipsitz, *Possessive Investment in Whiteness;* Omi and Winant, *Racial Formation in the United States.*

5. Gramsci, *Selections from the Prison Notebooks.* Refer also to Karl Marx's theory of hegemony: *Marx-Engels Reader.*

6. Connell, *Masculinities,* 77.

7. Refer also to Matlon, "Racial Capitalism and the Crisis of Black Masculinity."

8. Carrington, *Race, Sport, and Politics;* Connell, *Masculinities;* Ferguson, *Aberrations in Black;* Hoang, *Dealing in Desire;* Matlon, "Racial Capitalism and the Crisis of Black Masculinity"; Messner, *It's All for the Kids.*

9. Refer to the McFadden Act of 1927.

10. Mills, *Power Elite.*

11. Krippner, "Democracy of Credit."

12. Hyman, "Ending Discrimination, Legitimating Debt"; Krippner, "Democracy of Credit."

13. Sweeney, "How HR 5050 Changed Entrepreneurship for Women."

14. Connell, *Gender and Power,* 5.

15. Trumbull, "Credit Access and Social Welfare."

16. Hyman, "Ending Discrimination, Legitimating Debt"; Krippner, "Democracy of Credit"; Taylor, *Race for Profit;* Trumbull, "Credit Access and Social Welfare."

17. Quoted in Hyman, "Ending Discrimination, Legitimating Debt," 224–25.

18. Hyman, *Debtor Nation.*

19. Houle and Addo, "Racial Disparities in Student Debt and the Reproduction of the Fragile Black Middle Class"; Lin and Neely, *Divested;* Lipsitz, *Possessive Investment in Whiteness;* Seamster and Charron-Chénier, "Predatory Inclusion and Education Debt"; McMillan Cottom, *Lower Ed.*

20. Aponte et al., "Minority Veterans Report."

21. Hyman, *Debtor Nation;* Katznelson, *When Affirmative Action Was White.*

22. Dymski, Hernandez, and Mohanty, "Race, Gender, Power, and the US Subprime Mortgage and Foreclosure Crisis"; Rugh and Massey, "Racial Segregation and the American Foreclosure Crisis."

23. Krippner, *Capitalizing on Crisis.*

24. The Banking Act of 1933 separated commercial and investment banking activities to ensure the security of commercial banks that took deposits and issued loans in the event of a crisis involving investment securities, as in the Great Crash of 1929. Many of the restrictions imposed by the McFadden Act of 1927 on interstate banking were scaled back first by thirty-five state governments in the 1980s and then federally in the Riegle-Neal Interstate Banking and Branching Efficiency Act of 1994. Refer to McLaughlin, "Impact of Interstate Banking and Branching Reform."

25. Ho, *Liquidated.*

26. McDowell, *Capital Culture.*

27. Research on gender and race on Wall Street includes: Bielby, "Minority Vulnerability in Privileged Occupations"; Blair-Loy, *Competing Devotions;* Connell, "Inside the Glass Tower"; Fisher, *Wall Street Women;* Ho, *Liquidated;* Levin, "Gendering the Market"; Madden, "Performance-Support Bias and the Gender Pay Gap among Stockbrokers"; McDowell, *Capital Culture;* McGuire, "Gender, Race, and the Shadow Structure"; Roth, *Selling Women Short;* Turco, "Cultural Foundations of Tokenism"; Wingfield, *No More Invisible Man;* Zaloom, *Out of the Pits.*

28. On the "Boom-Boom Room" lawsuit, refer to Antilla, "Decades after 'Boom-Boom Room' Suit, Bias Persists for Women"; Antilla, *Tales from the Boom-Boom Room;* Downey Grimsley, "26 Women Sue Smith Barney, Allege Bias."

29. For research on workplace sexual violence, refer to McLaughlin, Uggen, and Blackstone, "Sexual Harassment, Workplace Authority, and the Paradox of Power"; Williams, Giuffre, and Dellinger, "Sexuality in the Workplace."

30. On the shareholder value movement's effects on workers, refer to the following: Davis, *Managed by the Markets;* Kalleberg, *Good Jobs, Bad Jobs.*

31. Kalev, "How You Downsize Is Who You Downsize"; Shin, "Explaining Pay Disparities between Top Executives and Nonexecutive Employees."

32. Lewis, *Big Short*, 33.

33. Bowley, "Lone Sale of $4.1 Billion in Contracts Led to 'Flash Crash' in May"; Lewis, *Flash Boys*.

34. Borch, *Social Avalanche;* Zaloom, *Out of the Pits.*

35. Kevin Roose found that young investment bankers reported higher use of performance drugs like Adderall than party drugs like cocaine. Similarly, Chrystia Freeland identifies how affluent millennials use Adderall in college. Freeland, *Plutocrats;* Roose, *Young Money.*

36. Investment manager Paul McCulley first introduced the term *shadow bank* in 2007 to describe investment vehicles that allowed banks to engage in risky activities kept off of their balance sheets. Today, regulators require investment banks to include these vehicles on their balance sheets; yet, the term *shadow bank* still refers to less-regulated entities. Refer to "How Shadow Banking Works"; Antill, Hou, and Sarkar, "Components of U.S. Financial-Sector Growth, 1950–2013"; International Monetary Fund, "Global Financial Stability Report."

37. Refer to Galbraith, *Inequality and Instability;* Lin and Neely, *Divested;* Wolff, "Household Wealth Inequality, Retirement Income Security, and Financial Market Swings 1983 through 2010."

38. Bonilla-Silva, *Racism without Racists;* Hill Collins, *Black Sexual Politics.*

39. DiTomaso, *American Non-Dilemma.*

40. Tilly, "Welcome to the Seventeenth Century."

41. Cook, "Networks, Norms, and Trust."

42. Harvey, *Enigma of Capital.*

43. Correll, "Reducing Gender Biases in Modern Workplaces"; Gorman, "Work Uncertainty and the Promotion of Professional Women"; Ridgeway, *Framed by Gender;* Thébaud and Sharkey, "Unequal Hard Times."

44. Carrigan, Connell, and Lee, "Toward a New Sociology of Masculinity"; Connell, *Masculinities;* Connell and Messerschmidt, "Hegemonic Masculinity: Rethinking the Concept"; Cooper, "Being the 'Go-To Guy'"; Hoang, *Dealing in Desire;* Messner, "Masculinity of the Governator."

45. Jaeger, *All About Hedge Funds;* Mallaby, *More Money Than God.*

46. I use the example of a barrel of oil to make the analogy more tangible. In practice, the investor would short a crude oil futures contract, which is a promise to buy a barrel of oil at some point in the future. Investors who trade futures don't actually buy a real barrel of oil, but just buy and sell the futures contract.

47. Leverage can be obtained through futures, options, margin, and other financial instruments. Futures are a contract between a buyer and seller to make a transaction at a future date and time. Options are a security on a futures contract.

An option gives the buyers the right to buy or sell the security, with no obligation. Finally, buying on margin means that an investor buys an asset using a loan from a bank or broker, which requires a down payment, that is, margin, on the loan.

48. The firm Long-Term Capital Management (LTCM) touted a mathematical model allowing for leverage on an unprecedented scale with theoretically zero risk. These promises proved to be false when the firm blew up on an astronomical scale in 1998 and nearly collapsed the global financial system. For more information, read MacKenzie, "Long-Term Capital Management and the Sociology of Arbitrage."

49. Jones's ideas echo the late economist Hyman Minsky who understood financial markets as fundamentally unstable and prone to crisis.

50. Asset-backed securities and collateralized debt obligations provide alternatives to investing in corporate and other forms of debt. Instead, an investor can purchase an asset-backed security that collateralizes a pool of assets such as mortgages or credit card debt. Similarly, a collateralized debt obligation is a product created by a bank that bundles securities into pools that are split up into tranches, that is, organized based on risk or other relevant characteristics. Lastly, a credit default swap is essentially an insurance policy that an investor buys for another security that would pay out if and when borrowers default on the underlying security.

51. Davis, *Managed by the Markets*.

52. "Financial Crisis Inquiry Commission"; Grusky, Western, and Wimer, *Great Recession*.

53. Marx and Engels, *Marx-Engels Reader*.

Chapter 2: Pathways to the Working Rich

1. Sherman, *Uneasy Street*.

2. Rap is often provided as an archetypal example of lowbrow music, along with country, heavy metal, and pop, and reflects how these cultural distinctions reflect racism and classism. Refer to Goldberg, "Mapping Shared Understandings Using Relational Class Analysis."

3. Khan, *Privilege*.

4. Ravenelle, *Hustle and Gig*; Schor, *After the Gig*.

5. Ho, *Liquidated*.

6. Rachel Sherman and Aliya Rao also find this among the affluent, even those unemployed: Rao, *Crunch Time*; Sherman, *Uneasy Street*.

7. In *Freedom from Work*, Daniel Fridman identifies how the financial self-help industry espouses a discourse of financial freedom that reflects a neoliberal ideology of individualism, entrepreneurialism, and responsibility.

8. Smith, "Race and Trust."

9. This gender-typing occurs in other high-paying industries such as high tech: Faulkner, "Nuts and Bolts and People."

10. Jaeger, *All About Hedge Funds;* Mallaby, *More Money Than God.*

11. One's habitus refers to the collection of habits and dispositions through which people respond to their social world: Bourdieu, *Distinction.*

12. Alegria, "Escalator or Step Stool?"

13. Jack, *Privileged Poor;* Khan, *Privilege.*

14. On race and networks in finance, refer to Bielby, "Minority Vulnerability in Privileged Occupations"; McGuire, "Gender, Race, Ethnicity, and Networks"; Turco, "Cultural Foundations of Tokenism"; Wingfield, "Crossing the Color Line."

15. In *You Don't Look Like a Lawyer,* Melaku identifies how Black women lawyers perform additional emotional and physical labor and struggle to network in elite professions.

16. Binder, Davis, and Bloom, "Career Funneling"; Ho, *Liquidated;* Roth, *Selling Women Short.*

17. Armstrong and Hamilton, *Paying for the Party;* Ho, *Liquidated;* Rivera, *Pedigree.*

18. Stone, *Opting Out?*

19. Bertrand, Goldin, and Katz, "Dynamics of the Gender Gap for Young Professionals in the Financial and Corporate Sectors"; Blair-Loy, "Career Patterns of Executive Women in Finance"; Roth, *Selling Women Short.*

20. See also Sterling, "Preentry Contacts and the Generation of Nascent Networks in Organizations."

21. On the transformation of work on the physical stock exchange floor to virtual trading, refer to Zaloom, *Out of the Pits.*

22. In *Automating Finance,* Juan Pablo Pardo-Guerra shows how a technology-driven community of exchange generates a form of kinship on the trading floor.

23. Extracurricular activities are commonly used to sort applicant in elite jobs, with a preference given for those whose activities are a cultural match for the firm. Refer to Rivera, "Hiring as Cultural Matching."

24. On trading floors, refer to Levin, "Gendering the Market"; Zaloom, *Out of the Pits.* On the class and racial intersections with masculinity, refer to Carrington, *Race, Sport, and Politics;* Messner, *It's All for the Kids.*

25. Current Population Survey, "Educational Attainment in the United States: 2018"; Funk and Parker, "Diversity in the STEM Workforce Varies Widely across Jobs"; Posselt and Grodsky, "Graduate Education and Social Stratification."

26. Black Scholes refers to a mathematical model of price variation over time.

Chapter 3: Getting the Job

1. I signed a nondisclosure agreement to not share the "confidential and proprietary information and trade secrets of the Company," so I do not provide specific details on the recruiting information. I changed the descriptors of the firm's culture to ensure anonymity. In keeping with "extreme openness," the firm is very open about this philosophy, so this isn't confidential or proprietary information.

2. Williams, *Still a Man's World*.

3. Social capital refers to a person's social ties generated through familial, educational, and professional connections. Meanwhile, cultural capital refers to a person's soft skills, dispositions, and knowledge that serve as markers of social class. Refer to Bourdieu, *Distinction*.

4. Rivera, *Pedigree*.

5. Smith, McPherson, and Smith-Lovin, "Social Distance in the United States."

6. Rivera, *Pedigree*. See also Chavez, "Getting a Job"; Friedman and Laurison, *Class Ceiling;* and Hartmann, *Sociology of Elites* on similar penalties to foreign-born applicants.

7. Cech, "The Self-Expressive Edge of Occupational Sex Segregation"; Correll, "Constraints into Preferences."

8. Hayes, "Why Ivy League Schools Are So Bad at Economic Diversity"; Karabel, *Chosen*.

9. Similarly, Emilio Castilla and Ben Rissing find that insider and alumni endorsements ease entrance for graduate school applicants at an elite school: "Best in Class."

10. Johnson, "Paul Tudor Jones."

11. Blair-Loy, *Competing Devotions*.

Chapter 4: Inside the Firm

1. Acker, "Hierarchies, Jobs, Bodies"; Acker, "Inequality Regimes"; Bonilla-Silva, *Racism without Racists;* Ray, "A Theory of Racialized Organizations."

2. Employee-reported data were less reliable for racial composition.

3. Hoang, *Dealing in Desire*.

4. Lee and Zhou, *Asian American Achievement Paradox*.

5. Refer to Chin, *Stuck*. On Asian Americans in finance and technology, refer to Alegria, "Escalator or Step Stool?"; Colby, "Asian American Executives Are Missing on Wall Street"; Gee and Peck, "Illusion of Asian Success."

6. Ahmed, *On Being Included;* Ahmed, "Phenomenology of Whiteness"; Mc-Dermott and Samson, "White Racial and Ethnic Identity in the United States."

7. Abad, "Race, Knowledge, and Tasks."

8. Abad, "Race, Knowledge, and Tasks"; Hill Collins, *Black Corporate Executives;* Ray, "A Theory of Racialized Organizations"; Wingfield and Alston, "Maintaining Hierarchies in Predominantly White Organizations."

9. Benschop and Doorewaard, "Covered by Equality."

10. Sociologists have documented that feminine-typed jobs do not actually accommodate childbearing and do not pose less of an economic or human capital penalty. Refer to England, *Comparable Worth;* Glass, "Impact of Occupational Segregation on Working Conditions."

11. Blair-Loy, *Competing Devotions.*

12. Hondagneu-Sotelo, *Domestica.*

13. Middle- and upper-class mothers carry an uneven burden for managing employment insecurity: Cooper, *Cut Adrift;* Rao, *Crunch Time.*

14. Blair-Loy, *Competing Devotions;* Roth, *Selling Women Short.*

15. In Scott's case, the chief executive officer is the head of business development and operations, which was the typical CEO role. The terminology, however, wasn't consistent across firms. Sometimes, the CEO also served as the chief investment officer, overseeing all investment decisions.

16. Preqin, "Global Hedge Fund Reports."

17. In *Enabling Creative Chaos,* Katherine Chen identifies how the Burning Man's collective had a flexible structure allowing for creativity.

18. Castilla and Benard, "Paradox of Meritocracy in Organizations"; Correll, "Reducing Gender Biases in Modern Workplaces"; McGuire and Bielby, "Variable Effects of Tie Strength and Social Resources"; Roth, *Selling Women Short.*

19. Management scholar Amy Edmonson calls this psychological safety, finding that it drives innovation and high performance: *Fearless Organization.*

20. Turco, *Conversational Firm.*

21. Foucault, *Discipline and Punishment.* On self-control and surveillance in investment banking, refer to Michel, "Transcending Socialization."

22. Barclays Global, "Affirmative Investing"; Kruppa, "The 'David' Problem."

23. Dobbin, Schrage, and Kalev, "Rage against the Iron Cage"; Edelman, *Working Law.*

24. Ray, "Theory of Racialized Organizations"; Ray and Purifoy, "Colorblind Organization." Refer also to Byron and Roscigno, "Bureaucracy, Discrimination, and the Racialized Character of Organizational Life."

25. Their understanding of value echoes that of other financial actors: Chong, *Best Practice;* Ho, *Liquidated;* Souleles, *Songs of Profit, Songs of Loss.*

26. Williams, Muller, and Kilanski, "Gendered Organizations in the New Economy."

27. On gender and racial tokenism, refer to Collins, *Black Corporate Executives;* Kanter, *Men and Women of the Corporation;* Puwar, *Space Invaders.* On negotiation, refer to Babcock and Laschever, *Women Don't Ask;* Hernandez et al., "Bargaining While Black"; Toosi et al., "Who Can Lean In?"

28. For example, Shelley Correll and colleagues find that, in performance evaluations, women are penalized for being too aggressive and men for being too soft-spoken: Correll et al., "Inside the Black Box of Organizational Life."

29. Hodges and Budig, "Who Gets the Daddy Bonus?"

30. Lin and Neely, "Gender, Parental Status, and the Wage Premium in Finance"; Roth, *Selling Women Short.*

31. Correll, "Reducing Gender Biases in Modern Workplaces."

32. Adkins, *Time of Money.*

33. On technology start-ups, refer to Mickey, "When Gendered Logics Collide"; Smith-Doerr, *Women's Work;* Turco, *Conversational Firm.*

Chapter 5: Moving Up the Ranks

1. Handy, Finding Sense in Uncertainty," 23; refer also to Arthur and Rousseau, *Boundaryless Career;* Hall, "Protean Careers of the 21st Century"; Handy, *Age of Unreason;* Inkson and Arthur, "How to Be a Successful Career Capitalist."

2. Neely, "Portfolio Ideal Worker."

3. Acker, "Hierarchies, Jobs, Bodies." On the ideal worker norm, also refer to Williams, *Unbending Gender.* Relatedly, Melaku identifies the existence of a white racial frame in the workplace to which people of color are judged and evaluated: *You Don't Look Like a Lawyer.*

4. For theories about how organizations are gendered, racialized, and classed, refer to Acker, "Hierarchies, Jobs, Bodies"; Acker, "Inequality Regimes"; Ray, "Theory of Racialized Organizations"; Wooten and Couloute, "Production of Racial Inequality within and among Organizations."

5. On the insecurity and long hours in financial services: Blair-Loy and Jacobs, "Globalization, Work Hours, and the Care Deficit among Stockbrokers"; Ho, *Liquidated;* Snyder, *Disrupted Workplace.*

6. Cooper, *Cut Adrift;* Williams, Muller, and Kilanski, "Gendered Organizations in the New Economy"; Wingfield, *Flatlining.*

7. Whyte, *Organization Man.*

8. In *The Working Rich,* Olivier Godechot theorizes the labor market in financial services in France as an asset transfer, trading in human and social capital.

9. Gershon, *Down and Out in the New Economy;* Vallas and Cummins, "Personal Branding and Identity Norms in the Popular Business Press.".

10. Schools and workplaces often encourage white men in ways that bolster their ambitions more so than women and minority men: Fisk and Overton, "Who Wants to Lead?"; Musto, "Brilliant or Bad."

11. Correll et al., "Inside the Black Box of Organizational Life"; Musto, "Brilliant or Bad."

12. Guillen, "Is the Confidence Gap between Men and Women a Myth?"

13. On *homo economicus,* refer to Foucault, *Birth of Biopolitics.* On the racial and gender dimensions of capital, refer to Hoang, *Dealing in Desire;* Matlon, "Racial Capitalism and the Crisis of Black Masculinity."

14. Eagly and Karau, "Role Congruity Theory of Prejudice toward Female Leaders"; Heilman, "Description and Prescription"; Rudman, "Self-Promotion as a Risk Factor for Women."

15. On the emotional nature of quantitative modeling: Delaney, *Money at Work.*

16. Chen, "Lives at the Center of the Periphery, Lives at the Periphery of the Center"; Wingfield, *No More Invisible Man.*

17. This is consistent with the research on expectations for devoted mothering and its impacts for women at work: Blair-Loy, *Competing Devotions;* Correll, Benard, and Paik, "Getting a Job."

18. On the emergence of passion as a cultural schema in white-collar work, refer to Cech, *The Trouble with Passion;* Gershon, *Down and Out in the New Economy;* Pugh, *Tumbleweed Society;* Rao and Neely, "What's Love Got to Do with It?"; Rivera, *Pedigree;* Wingfield, "Are Some Emotions Marked 'Whites Only'?"

19. Connell, *Masculinities.*

20. Rudman et al., "Status Incongruity and Backlash Effects." On the gendered discourses about risk-taking in finance, refer to Fisher, *Wall Street Women.*

21. Nelson, *Gender and Risk-Taking.*

22. Foschi, "Double Standards for Competence."

23. Riach and Cutcher, "Built to Last"; Zaloom, *Out of the Pits.*

24. Wingfield, *No More Invisible Man.*

25. Burt, "Structural Holes and Good Ideas."

26. Gendered networks affect job security in the oil and gas industry, too: Williams, "Gender of Layoffs in the Oil and Gas Industry."

27. Williams, Muller, and Kilanski, "Gendered Organizations in the New Economy."

28. Godechot, "Getting a Job in Finance: The Strength of Collaboration Ties"; McGuire, "Gender, Race, Ethnicity, and Networks"; McGuire, "Gender, Race, and the Shadow Structure"; Roth, *Selling Women Short*.

29. Ewens and Townsend, "Are Early Stage Investors Biased against Women?"; Lyons-Padilla et al., "Race Influences Professional Investors' Financial Judgments"; Tak, Correll, and Soule, "Gender Inequality in Product Markets."

30. Gorman, "Work Uncertainty and the Promotion of Professional Women."

31. Weber, *Theory of Social and Economic Organization*.

32. Adams, *Familial State*.

33. Weber, *Theory of Social and Economic Organization*.

34. Moore, *Reproducing Racism*.

35. Armstrong and Hamilton, *Paying for the Party*.

36. Quinn, "Paradox of Complaining."

37. Evans and Moore, "Impossible Burdens."

38. Pierce, "Racing for Innocence."

39. Kanter, *Men and Women of the Corporation*.

40. Levin, "Gendering the Market"; Roth, *Selling Women Short*.

41. On how epithets uphold masculinity, refer to Pascoe, *Dude, You're a Fag*.

42. Wilmers, "Job Turf or Variety."

43. This is consistent with Rebecca Hanson and Patricia Richards's findings on ethnographic fieldwork: *Harassed*.

44. Berdahl, "Sexual Harassment of Uppity Women"; Hanson and Richards, *Harassed*; McLaughlin, Uggen, and Blackstone, "Sexual Harassment, Workplace Authority, and the Paradox of Power."

45. Daniels, *Invisible Careers*; Kendall, *Power of Good Deeds*; Mears, *Very Important People*; Ostrander, *Women of the Upper Class*. Relatedly, on the gendered labor of elite women and the reproduction of inequality, refer to Glucksberg, "Gendered Ethnography of Elites."

46. This is consistent with Laurie Morgan and Karen Martin's research on women sales professionals: "Taking Women Professionals Out of the Office."

47. Hoang, *Dealing in Desire*; Mears, *Very Important People*.

48. Women in technology similarly report having to manage ambiguous sexual interactions: Hart, "Trajectory Guarding."

49. Louise Roth (*Selling Women Short*) also finds pervasive sexual harassment on Wall Street. She found that harassment from colleagues was harder to report and pursue recourse. I found hesitation to report client behavior as well, perhaps because of the close-knit networks and high monetary stakes.

50. Hart, "Penalties for Self-Reporting Sexual Harassment."

51. McLaughlin, Uggen, and Blackstone, "Economic and Career Effects of Sexual Harassment on Working Women."

52. Foucault, *Birth of Biopolitics*.

53. Cooper, "Being the 'Go-to Guy'"; Gershon, *Down and Out in the New Economy*; Lane, *Company of One*; Williams, Muller, and Kilanski, "Gendered Organizations in the New Economy."

54. Vallas and Prener, "Dualism, Job Polarization, and the Social Construction of Precarious Work," 344.

Chapter 6: Reaching the Top

1. "Making It Big"; Thornton, "Hedge Funds 101 for Emerging Managers."

2. Cheng, "Why Minority Women Now Control Nearly Half of All Women-Run Businesses"; Lange et al., "Global Entrepreneurship Monitor: United States Report 2017." On gender disparities in types of funding, refer to Ewens and Townsend, "Are Early Stage Investors Biased against Women?"; Kanze et al., "Male and Female Entrepreneurs Get Asked Different Questions by VCs—and It Affects How Much Funding They Get"; Settembre, "Venture Capitalists Still Give Most of Their Money to White Men, Study Finds"; Thébaud, "Status Beliefs and the Spirit of Capitalism."

3. Bielby, "Minority Vulnerability in Privileged Occupations"; Byrnes, Miller, and Schafer, "Gender Differences in Risk Taking"; Lyons-Padilla et al., "Race Influences Professional Investors' Financial Judgments"; Knight, "Production of the Female Entrepreneurial Subject"; Thébaud, "Business as Plan B"; Thébaud and Sharkey, "Unequal Hard Times"; Wingfield and Taylor, "Race, Gender, and Class in Entrepreneurship."

4. Thébaud, "Business as Plan B."

5. Bielby, "Minority Vulnerability in Privileged Occupations"; Lyons-Padilla et al., "Race Influences Professional Investors' Financial Judgments."

6. Levine and Rubinstein, "Smart and Illicit."

7. Bessière, *De génération en génération*; Byrne, Fattoum, and Thébaud, "A Suitable Boy?"; Lane, *A Company of One*; Rao, *Crunch Time*; Yang and Aldrich, "Who's the Boss?"

8. Nelson, *Gender and Risk-Taking;* Fisk and Overton, "Who Wants to Lead?"; Wingfield, *No More Invisible Man.*

9. Over the past twenty years, family offices have increasingly transferred their money to hedge funds: Preqin, "Global Hedge Fund Reports."

10. All funds with over $100 million in assets under advisement are required to register with the SEC (the average fund has around $235 million): "SEC Updates Accredited Investor Definition."

11. Whyte, "New Hedge Funds Are Asking for More Money from Investors."

12. Refer, for example, to the work of Sherman, *Uneasy Street.*

13. Activist investors take more proactive roles in the companies in which they invest.

14. Hoang, *Dealing in Desire;* Hoang, "Risky Investments."

15. "Asset and Wealth Management Revolution: Embracing Exponential Change"; "Asset Management 2020: A Brave New World"; Preqin, "Global Hedge Fund Reports."

16. Barclays Global, "Affirmative Investing."

17. Bielby, "Minority Vulnerability in Privileged Occupations."

18. Lyons-Padilla et al., "Race Influences Professional Investors' Financial Judgments."

19. Lane, *A Company of One.*

20. Soros also provided $2 billion in seed funding for a protégé, employee Scott Bessent, to launch his own hedge fund. Recently, Jonathan Soros established a separate family office to oversee his own wealth, and Robert Soros established a separate investment firm, Soros Capital, while remaining an owner of the Soros family office. Refer to Ablan and Goldstein, "Exclusive"; Burton, "Scott Bessent to Start His Own Hedge Fund with $2 Billion from Soros."

21. Copeland, "Financial Elite's Offspring Start Their Own Hedge Funds"; Prince, "From Hedge Fund to Family Office."

22. Kruppa, "The 'David' Problem."

23. The fifty-eight firms omitted from Novus's estimate aren't registered because they are either too small, inactive, or fund of funds (firms that invest in other hedge funds). Refer to Altshuller, Peta, and Jordan, "Like Tiger, Like Cub."

24. Abelson, "Hedge-Fund Billionaire Julian Robertson Shrugs as World Churns."

25. Cook and Glass, "Glass Cliffs and Organizational Saviors"; Ryan and Haslam, "Glass Cliff."

Chapter 7: View from the Top

1. Daniels, *Invisible Careers;* Giridharadas, *Winners Take All;* Lindsay, *View from the Top;* Sherman, *Uneasy Street.*

2. The financial self-help industry espouses the dream of "financial free-dom": Fridman, *Freedom from Work.*

3. Anderson, "Breadwinner Mothers by Race/Ethnicity and State."

4. Daniels, *Invisible Careers.*

5. The constraints posed by visa status is a problem researchers find among many Indian-born professionals in the United States: Banerjee, "Subversive Self-Employment."

6. England, "Emerging Theories of Care Work."

7. Sherman, *Uneasy Street.* Refer also to Daniels, *Invisible Careers.*

8. The general population, too, expects to retire later because they identify with their work and intend to end their careers with more fulfilling work: Moen, *Encore Adulthood;* Silver, *Retirement and Its Discontents.*

9. In *Cut Adrift,* Marianne Cooper shows how, in the Silicon Valley, the desire for an enormous financial safety net reflects a society in which institutions no longer protect people from employment risk, which is instead individualized.

10. Piketty, *Capital in the Twenty-First Century.*

11. Blair-Loy and Jacobs, "Globalization, Work Hours, and the Care Deficit among Stockbrokers"; Ho, *Liquidated.*

12. Ho, *Liquidated.*

13. In *Taking the Floor,* Daniel Beunza shows how financial modeling and the organizational practices that condition it causes traders to disassociate the implications for the bank's customers.

14. Adkins, *Time of Money.*

15. Lin and Neely, *Divested.*

16. The general population echoes this belief: Mijs, "The Paradox of Inequality."

17. Cassidy, "Great Hedge-Fund Mystery."

18. King, *Pink Ribbons, Inc.*

19. Mallaby, *More Money Than God.*

Conclusion

1. Catalyst, "Women in Financial Services"; McKinsey, "Racial Equity in Financial Services"; Preqin, "Women in Alternative Assets."

2. Vincent's hedge fund grew into a larger asset management firm with other investment units.

3. Chung, "Gender Difference in Suicide, Household Production, and Unemployment."

4. Cornwell and Dokshin, "Power of Integration"; DiPrete, Eirich, and Pittinsky, "Compensation Benchmarking, Leapfrogs, and the Surge in Executive Pay"; Harrington, *Capital without Borders;* Kim, Kogut, and Yang, "Executive Compensation, Fat Cats, and Best Athletes"; Mizruchi, *Fracturing of the American Corporate Elite.*

5. Hacker and Pierson, "Winner-Take-All Politics"; Lin and Neely, *Divested.*

6. Mayer, "The Reclusive Hedge-Fund Tycoon behind the Trump Presidency"; Meyer, Guida, and Toosi, "Mick Mulvaney's New Side Gig."

7. This carries over to international financial governance: Seabrooke and Tsingou, "Revolving Doors in International Financial Governance."

8. Pitluck, "Watching Foreigners."

9. Barron, "Curious Case of Aurelius Capital v. Puerto Rico"; Celarier, "How Hedge Funds Hurt Puerto Rico"; Cohan, "Puerto Rico's Human Catastrophe Is Hedge Funds' Inhuman Nightmare."

10. Baron et al., "In the Company of Women"; Merle, "How One Hedge Fund Made $2 Billion from Argentina's Economic Collapse."

11. Manduca, "Income Inequality and the Persistence of Racial Economic Disparities"; Yavorsky et al., "Women in the One Percent."

Methodological Appendix

1. Katz, "Ethnography's Warrants."

2. Conti and O'Neil, "Studying Power."

3. Harrington, "Immersion Ethnography of Elites"; Ho, *Liquidated;* Khan, *Privilege;* Mears, *Pricing Beauty;* Stephens, "Collecting Data from Elites and Ultra Elites."

4. Recruiting elite participants often requires online identity management: Marland and Esselment, "Negotiating with Gatekeepers to Get Interviews with Politicians."

5. Turning down these invitations made me worry that I was compromising my research, as is common among women ethnographers in Rebecca Hanson and Patricia Richards's book *Harassed.*

6. Hanson and Richards, *Harassed;* Hill Collins, *Black Feminist Thought;* Hoang, "Gendering Carnal Ethnography"; Morris, *Scholar Denied;* Smith, *Everyday World as Problematic.*

7. Hanson and Richards, *Harassed,* 4.

8. Blair-Loy, "It's Not Just What You Know, It's Who You Know," 68.

9. Hoang, "Gendering Carnal Ethnography," 243. Author's italics.

10. Butler, *Gender Trouble;* Chodorow, *Feminism and Psychoanalytic Theory;* Connell, *Gender and Power;* Connell, *Masculinities;* Williams, *Still a Man's World.*

11. Connell, *Masculinities;* Hill Collins, "Learning from the Outsider Within"; Ridgeway, *Framed by Gender.*

12. Bourdieu, *Invitation to Reflexive Sociology;* Foucault, *Order of Things;* Hill Collins, "Learning from the Outsider Within"; Smith, *Everyday World as Problematic.*

13. Preqin, "Hedge Funds in the U.S."

14. Jerolmack and Khan, "Talk Is Cheap"; Orbuch, "People's Accounts Count"; Pugh, "What Good Are Interviews for Thinking about Culture?"

15. Lamont and Swidler, "Methodological Pluralism and the Possibilities and Limits of Interviewing."

16. Lofland et al., *Analyzing Social Settings.*

17. Emerson, Fretz, and Shaw, *Writing Ethnographic Fieldnotes.*

18. Goffman, *Presentation of Self in Everyday Life.*

19. Charmaz, *Constructing Grounded Theory;* Deterding and Waters, "Flexible Coding of In-Depth Interviews."

20. Emerson, Fretz, and Shaw, *Writing Ethnographic Fieldnotes.*

Bibliography

Abad, Melissa V. "Race, Knowledge, and Tasks: Racialized Occupational Trajectories." In *Race, Organizations, and the Organizing Process,* edited by Melissa E. Wooten, 111–30. Vol. 60 of Research in the Sociology of Organizations. Bingley, UK: Emerald Publishing, 2019.

Abelson, Max. "Hedge-Fund Billionaire Julian Robertson Shrugs as World Churns." *Bloomberg,* June 29, 2015.

Ablan, Jennifer, and Matthew Goldstein. "Exclusive: Soros' Son Strikes Out on His Own." *Reuters,* April 1, 2012.

Acker, Joan. "Hierarchies, Jobs, Bodies: A Theory of Gendered Organizations." *Gender & Society* 4, no. 2 (June 1990): 139–58.

———. "Inequality Regimes: Gender, Class, and Race in Organizations." *Gender & Society* 20, no. 4 (August 2006): 441–64.

Adams, Julia. *The Familial State: Ruling Families and Merchant Capitalism in Early Modern Europe.* Ithaca, NY: Cornell University Press, 2007.

Adkins, Lisa. *The Time of Money.* Stanford, CA: Stanford University Press, 2018.

Aggarwal, Rajesh, and Nicole M. Boyson. "The Performance of Female Hedge Fund Managers." *Review of Financial Economics,* special issue, *Hedge Funds: Performance, Disclosure, and Regulation* 29 (April 2016): 23–36.

Ahmed, Sara. *On Being Included: Racism and Diversity in Institutional Life.* Durham, NC: Duke University Press, 2012.

———. "A Phenomenology of Whiteness." *Feminist Theory* 8, no. 2 (August 2007): 149–68.

Alegria, Sharla. "Escalator or Step Stool? Gendered Labor and Token Processes in Tech Work." *Gender & Society* 33, no. 5 (October 2019): 722–45.

Alexander, Michelle. *The New Jim Crow: Mass Incarceration in the Age of Colorblindness*. New York: New Press, 2012.

Altshuller, Stan, Joe Peta, and Christopher Jordan. "Like Tiger, Like Cub." Novus Research, 2014.

Anderson, Cameron, and Courtney Brown. "The Functions and Dysfunctions of Hierarchy." *Research in Organizational Behavior* 30 (January 2010): 55–89.

Anderson, Julie. "Breadwinner Mothers by Race/Ethnicity and State." Institute for Women's Policy Research, September 8, 2016.

Antill, Samuel, David Hou, and Asani Sarkar. "Components of U.S. Financial-Sector Growth, 1950–2013." *FRBNY Economic Policy Review*, 2014.

Antilla, Susan. "Decades after 'Boom-Boom Room' Suit, Bias Persists for Women." *New York Times*, December 21, 2017.

———. *Tales from the Boom-Boom Room: Women vs. Wall Street*. Princeton, NJ: Bloomberg Press, 2002.

Aponte, Maribel, Tom Garin, Dorothy Glasgow, Tamara Lee, Earl Newsome, Eddie Thomas, and Barbara Ward. "Minority Veterans Report: Military Service History and VA Benefit Utilization Statistics." Department of Veterans Affairs, March 2017.

Armstrong, Elizabeth A., and Laura T. Hamilton. *Paying for the Party: How College Maintains Inequality*. Cambridge, MA: Harvard University Press, 2013.

Arthur, Michael, and Denise M. Rousseau. *The Boundaryless Career: A New Employment Principle for a New Organizational Era*. Oxford: Oxford University Press, 1996.

"Asset and Wealth Management Revolution: Embracing Exponential Change." PWC, 2017.

"Asset Management 2020: A Brave New World." PWC, 2020.

Autor, David H., Lawrence F. Katz, and Melissa S. Kearney. "The Polarization of the U.S. Labor Market." *Measuring and Interpreting Trends in Economic Inequality* 96, no. 2 (May 2006): 189–94.

Babcock, Linda, and Sara Laschever. *Women Don't Ask: The High Cost of Avoiding Negotiation—and Positive Strategies for Change*. Princeton, NJ: Princeton University Press, 2003.

Banerjee, Pallavi. "Subversive Self-Employment: Intersectionality and Self-Employment among Dependent Visas Holders in the United States." *American Behavioral Scientist* 63, no. 2 (February 2019): 186–207.

Barclays Global. "Affirmative Investing: Women and Minority Owned Hedge Funds." Capital Solutions Group, June 2011.

Baron, James N., Michael T. Hannan, Greta Hsu, and Özgecan Koçak. "In the Company of Women: Gender Inequality and the Logic of Bureaucracy in Start-Up Firms." *Work and Occupations* 34, no. 1 (February 2007): 35–66.

Barron, Jesse. "The Curious Case of Aurelius Capital v. Puerto Rico." *New York Times,* November 26, 2019.

Benschop, Yvonne, and Hans Doorewaard. "Covered by Equality: The Gender Subtext of Organizations." *Organization Studies* 19, no. 5 (September 1998): 787–805.

Berdahl, Jennifer L. "The Sexual Harassment of Uppity Women." *Journal of Applied Psychology* 92, no. 2 (April 2007): 425.

Bertrand, Marianne, Claudia Goldin, and Lawrence F. Katz. "Dynamics of the Gender Gap for Young Professionals in the Financial and Corporate Sectors." *American Economic Journal: Applied Economics* 2, no. 3 (July 2010): 228–55.

Bessière, Céline. *De Génération en Génération: Arrangements de Famille dans les Entreprises Viticoles de Cognac.* Paris: Raisons d'agir, 2010.

Bettie, Julie. "Exceptions to the Rule: Upwardly Mobile White and Mexican American High School Girls." *Gender & Society* 16, no. 3 (June 2002): 403–22.

Beunza, Daniel. *Taking the Floor: Models, Morals, and Management in a Wall Street Trading Room.* Princeton, NJ: Princeton University Press, 2019.

Bielby, William. "Minority Vulnerability in Privileged Occupations." *ANNALS of the American Academy of Political and Social Science* 639, no. 1 (January 2012): 13–32.

Binder, Amy J., Daniel B. Davis, and Nick Bloom. "Career Funneling: How Elite Students Learn to Define and Desire 'Prestigious' Jobs." *Sociology of Education* 89, no. 1 (January 2016): 20–39.

BKD CPAs and Advisors. 2020. *SEC Updates Accredited Investor Definition.*

Black, Sandra E., Paul J Devereux, Petter Lundborg, and Kaveh Majlesi. "On the Origins of Risk-Taking." Working Paper. National Bureau of Economic Research, July 2015.

Blair-Loy, Mary. "Career Patterns of Executive Women in Finance: An Optimal Matching Analysis." *American Journal of Sociology* 104, no. 5 (March 1999): 1346–45.

———. *Competing Devotions: Career and Family among Women Executives.* Cambridge, MA: Harvard University Press, 2005.

———. "It's Not Just What You Know, It's Who You Know: Technical Knowledge, Rainmaking, and Gender among Finance Executives." *Research in the Sociology of Work* 10 (March 2001): 51–83.

Blair-Loy, Mary, and Jerry Jacobs. "Globalization, Work Hours, and the Care Deficit among Stockbrokers." *Gender & Society* 17, no. 2 (April 2003): 230–49.

Blau, Francine D., and Lawrence M. Kahn. "The Gender Wage Gap: Extent, Trends, and Explanations." *Journal of Economic Literature* 55, no. 3 (September 2017): 789–865.

Boltanski, Luc, and Eve Chiapello. *The New Spirit of Capitalism.* Translated by Gregory Elliott. London: Verso, 2007.

Bonilla-Silva, Eduardo. *Racism without Racists: Color-Blind Racism and the Persistence of Racial Inequality in America.* Lanham, MD: Rowman and Littlefield, 2003.

Borch, Christian. *Social Avalanche: Crowds, Cities, and Financial Markets.* Cambridge: Cambridge University Press, 2020.

Borgatti, Stephen, and Pacey Foster. "The Network Paradigm in Organizational Research: A Review and Typology." *Journal of Management* 29, no. 6 (December 2003): 991–1013.

Bourdieu, Pierre. *Distinction: A Social Critique of the Judgement of Taste.* New York: Routledge, 1979.

———. *An Invitation to Reflexive Sociology.* Chicago: University Of Chicago Press, 1992.

Bowley, Graham. "Lone Sale of $4.1 Billion in Contracts Led to 'Flash Crash' in May." *New York Times,* October 1, 2010.

Brav, Alon, Wei Jiang, and Hyunseob Kim. "The Real Effects of Hedge Fund Activism: Productivity, Asset Allocation, and Industry Concentration." *The Review of Financial Studies* 28, no. 10 (2015): 2723–2769.

Bryan-Low, Cassell, Carrick Mollenkamp, and Gregory Zuckerman. "Peloton Flew High, Fell Fast." *Wall Street Journal,* May 12, 2008.

Burnham, James. *The Managerial Revolution: What Is Happening in the World.* Westport, CT: Praeger, 1972.

Burt, Ronald S. "Structural Holes and Good Ideas." *American Journal of Sociology* 110, no. 2 (September 2004): 349–99.

Burton, Katherine. "Scott Bessent to Start His Own Hedge Fund with $2 Billion from Soros." *Bloomberg,* August 4, 2015.

Butler, Judith. *Gender Trouble: Feminism and the Subversion of Identity.* New York: Routledge, 2006.

Byrne, Janice, Salma Fattoum, and Sarah Thébaud. "A Suitable Boy? Gendered Roles and Hierarchies in Family Business Succession." *European Management Review* 16, no. 3 (November 2019): 579–96.

Byrnes, James P., David C. Miller, and William D. Schafer. "Gender Differences in Risk Taking: A Meta-Analysis." *Psychological Bulletin* 125, no. 3 (1999): 367–83.

Byron, Reginald A., and Vincent J. Roscigno. "Bureaucracy, Discrimination, and the Racialized Character of Organizational Life." In *Race, Organizations, and the Organizing Process*, edited by Melissa E. Wooten, 151–69. Vol. 60 of Research in the Sociology of Organizations. Bingley, UK: Emerald Publishing, 2019.

Campbell, Marne L. "Black Cowboys in the American West: On the Range, on the Stage, behind the Badge." *Journal of American History* 105, no. 1 (June 2018): 127.

Carrigan, Tim, Bob Connell, and John Lee. "Toward a New Sociology of Masculinity." *Theory and Society* 14, no. 5 (September 1985): 551–604.

Carrington, Ben. *Race, Sport, and Politics: The Sporting Black Diaspora*. Thousand Oaks, CA: Sage Publications, 2010.

Cassidy, John. "The Great Hedge-Fund Mystery: Why Do They Make So Much?" *New Yorker*, May 12, 2014.

———. "Mastering the Machine." *New Yorker*, July 25, 2011.

Castilla, Emilio J. "Gender, Race, and Meritocracy in Organizational Careers." *American Journal of Sociology* 113, no. 6 (May 2008): 1479–526.

Castilla, Emilio J., and Stephen Benard. "The Paradox of Meritocracy in Organizations." *Administrative Science Quarterly* 55, no. 4 (December 2010): 543–76.

Castilla, Emilio J., and Ben J. Rissing. "Best in Class: The Returns on Application Endorsements in Higher Education." *Administrative Science Quarterly* 64, no. 1 (March 2019): 230–70.

Catalyst. "Women in Financial Services." Catalyst, June 29, 2020.

Cech, Erin A. *The Trouble with Passion: How Searching for Fulfillment at Work Fosters Inequality*. Berkeley: University of California Press, 2021.

Cech, Erin A. "The Self-Expressive Edge of Occupational Sex Segregation." *American Journal of Sociology* 119, no. 3 (November 2013): 747–89.

Celarier, Michelle. "How Hedge Funds Hurt Puerto Rico." *Institutional Investor*, November 30, 2017.

Chandler, Alfred D. *The Visible Hand: The Managerial Revolution in American Business*. Cambridge, MA: Belknap Press of Harvard University Press, 1977.

Charles, Maria, and David Grusky. *Occupational Ghettos: The Worldwide Segregation of Women and Men*. Stanford, CA: Stanford University Press, 2005.

Charmaz, Kathy. *Constructing Grounded Theory: A Practical Guide through Qualitative Analysis*. Thousand Oaks, CA: Sage Publications, 2006.

Charrad, Mounira M., and Julia Adams. "Patrimonialism, Past and Present." *ANNALS of the American Academy of Political and Social Science* 636, no. 1 (July 2011): 6–15.

Chavez, Koji. "Getting a Job: Cultural Norms, Emotional Energy, and the Foreign-Educated Immigrant Hiring Penalty." *Academy of Management Proceedings* 2017, no. 1 (August 2017): 17652.

Chen, Anthony S. "Lives at the Center of the Periphery, Lives at the Periphery of the Center: Chinese American Masculinities and Bargaining with Hegemony." *Gender & Society* 13, no. 5 (October 1999): 584–607.

Chen, Katherine K. *Enabling Creative Chaos: The Organization behind the Burning Man Event*. Chicago: University of Chicago Press, 2009.

Cheng, Michelle. "Why Minority Women Now Control Nearly Half of All Women-Run Businesses." *Inc.*, November 6, 2018.

Chin, Margaret M. *Stuck: Why Asian Americans Don't Reach the Top of the Corporate Ladder*. New York: New York University Press, 2020.

Chodorow, Nancy J. *Feminism and Psychoanalytic Theory*. New Haven, CT: Yale University Press, 1978.

Chong, Kimberly. *Best Practice: Management Consulting and the Ethics of Financialization in China*. Durham, NC: Duke University Press, 2018.

Choo, Hae Yeon, and Myra Marx Ferree. "Practicing Intersectionality in Sociological Research: A Critical Analysis of Inclusions, Interactions, and Institutions in the Study of Inequalities." *Sociological Theory* 28, no. 2 (June 2010): 129–49.

Chung, Andy. "Gender Difference in Suicide, Household Production, and Unemployment." *Applied Economics* 41, no. 19 (August 2009): 2495–504.

Cohan, William. "Puerto Rico's Human Catastrophe Is Hedge Funds' Inhuman Nightmare." *Vanity Fair*, October 2, 2017.

Cohen, Philip N., Matt L. Huffman, and Stefanie Knauer. "Stalled Progress? Gender Segregation and Wage Inequality among Managers, 1980–2000." *Work and Occupations* 36, no. 4 (November 2009): 318–42.

Colby, Laura. "Asian American Executives Are Missing on Wall Street." *Bloomberg*, November 22, 2017.

Collins, Jane Lou, and Victoria Mayer. *Both Hands Tied: Welfare Reform and the Race to the Bottom in the Low-Wage Labor Market*. Chicago: University of Chicago Press, 2010.

Collins, Randall. "Patrimonial Alliances and Failures of State Penetration: A Historical Dynamic of Crime, Corruption, Gangs, and Mafias." *ANNALS of the American Academy of Political and Social Science* 636, no. 1 (July 2011): 16–31.

Collins, Sharon. *Black Corporate Executives.* Philadelphia: Temple University Press, 1997.

Connell, Raewyn. *Gender and Power: Society, the Person, and Sexual Politics.* Stanford, CA: Stanford University Press, 1987.

———. "Inside the Glass Tower: The Construction of Masculinities in Finance Capital." In *Men, Wage Work, and Family,* edited by Paula McDonald and Emma Jeanes, 65–79. New York: Routledge, 2012.

———. *Masculinities.* 2nd ed. Berkeley: University of California Press, 2005.

Connell, Raewyn W., and James W. Messerschmidt. "Hegemonic Masculinity: Rethinking the Concept." *Gender & Society* 19, no. 6 (December 2005): 829–59.

Conti, Joseph, and Moira O'Neil. "Studying Power: Qualitative Methods and the Global Elite." *Qualitative Research* 7, no. 1 (February 2007): 63–82.

Cook, Alison, and Christy Glass. "Glass Cliffs and Organizational Saviors: Barriers to Minority Leadership in Work Organizations?" *Social Problems* 60, no. 2 (May 2013): 168–87.

Cook, Karen S. "Networks, Norms, and Trust: The Social Psychology of Social Capital." *Social Psychology Quarterly* 68, no. 1 (March 2005): 4–14.

———. *Trust in Society.* New York: Russell Sage Foundation, 2001.

Cooper, Marianne. "Being the 'Go-to Guy': Fatherhood, Masculinity, and the Organization of Work in Silicon Valley." *Qualitative Sociology* 23, no. 4 (December 2000): 379–405.

———. *Cut Adrift: Families in Insecure Times.* Berkeley: University of California Press, 2014.

Copeland, Rob. "Financial Elite's Offspring Start Their Own Hedge Funds." *Wall Street Journal,* September 22, 2014.

Cornwell, Benjamin, and Fedor A. Dokshin. "The Power of Integration: Affiliation and Cohesion in a Diverse Elite Network." *Social Forces* 93, no. 2 (December 2014): 803–31.

Correll, Shelley J. "Constraints into Preferences: Gender, Status, and Emerging Career Aspirations." *American Sociological Review* 69, no. 1 (February 2004): 93–113.

———. "Reducing Gender Biases in Modern Workplaces: A Small Wins Approach to Organizational Change." *Gender & Society* 31, no. 6 (December 2017): 725–50.

Correll, Shelley J., Stephen Benard, and In Paik. "Getting a Job: Is There a Motherhood Penalty?" *American Journal of Sociology* 112, no. 5 (March 2007): 1297–339.

Correll, Shelley J., Cecilia L. Ridgeway, Ezra W. Zuckerman, Sharon Jank, Sara Jordan-Bloch, and Sandra Nakagawa. "It's the Conventional Thought That Counts: How Third-Order Inference Produces Status Advantage." *American Sociological Review* 82, no. 2 (April 2017): 297–327.

Correll, Shelley J., Katherine R. Weisshaar, Alison T. Wynn, and JoAnne Delfino Wehner. "Inside the Black Box of Organizational Life: The Gendered Language of Performance Assessment." *American Sociological Review* 85, no. 6 (December 2020): 1022–50.

Costa, Dora L., and Matthew E. Kahn. "Understanding the American Decline in Social Capital, 1952–1998." *Kyklos* 56, no. 1 (February 2003): 17–46.

Cousin, Bruno, Shamus Khan, and Ashley Mears. "Theoretical and Methodological Pathways for Research on Elites." *Socio-Economic Review* 16, no. 2 (April 2018): 225–49.

Crenshaw, Kimberlé. "Mapping the Margins: Intersectionality, Identity Politics, and Violence against Women of Color." *Stanford Law Review* 43, no. 6 (July 1991): 1241–99.

Current Population Survey. "Educational Attainment in the United States: 2018." Washington, DC: US Census Bureau, 2018.

Daniels, Arlene. *Invisible Careers: Women Civic Leaders from the Volunteer World.* Chicago: University of Chicago Press, 1988.

Davis, Gerald. *Managed by the Markets: How Finance Re-Shaped America.* Oxford: Oxford University Press, 2009.

Delaney, Kevin J. *Money at Work: On the Job with Priests, Poker Players, and Hedge Fund Traders.* New York: New York University Press, 2012.

Delevingne, Lawrence. "The 20 Percent Club: Hedge Fund Stars of an Industry Rebound." *Reuters,* November 10, 2017.

Deterding, Nicole M., and Mary C. Waters. "Flexible Coding of In-Depth Interviews: A Twenty-First-Century Approach." *Sociological Methods & Research* 50, no. 2 (May 2021): 708–39.

DiMaggio, Paul. *The Twenty-First-Century Firm: Changing Economic Organization in International Perspective.* Princeton, NJ: Princeton University Press, 2001.

DiPrete, Thomas A., Gregory M. Eirich, and Matthew Pittinsky. "Compensation Benchmarking, Leapfrogs, and the Surge in Executive Pay." *American Journal of Sociology* 115, no. 6 (May 2010): 1671–712.

DiPrete, Thomas A., Andrew Gelman, Tyler McCormick, Julien Teitler, and Tian Zheng. "Segregation in Social Networks Based on Acquaintanceship and Trust." *American Journal of Sociology* 116, no. 4 (January 2011): 1234-83.

DiTomaso, Nancy. *The American Non-Dilemma: Racial Inequality without Racism.* New York: Russell Sage Foundation, 2013.

Dobbin, Frank, Daniel Schrage, and Alexandra Kalev. "Rage against the Iron Cage: The Varied Effects of Bureaucratic Personnel Reforms on Diversity." *American Sociological Review* 80, no. 5 (September 2015): 1014-44.

Downey Grimsley, Kristin. "26 Women Sue Smith Barney, Allege Bias." *Washington Post,* November 6, 1996.

Dymski, Gary, Jesus Hernandez, and Lisa Mohanty. "Race, Gender, Power, and the US Subprime Mortgage and Foreclosure Crisis: A Meso Analysis." *Feminist Economics* 19, no. 3 (July 2013): 124-51.

Eagly, Alice H., and Steven J. Karau. "Role Congruity Theory of Prejudice toward Female Leaders." *Psychological Review* 109, no. 3 (August 2002): 573-98.

Eaton, Charlie, Jacob Habinek, Adam Goldstein, Cyrus Dioun, Santibáñez Godoy, Daniela García, and Robert Osley-Thomas. "The Financialization of US Higher Education." *Socio-Economic Review* 14, no. 3 (July 2016): 507-35.

Edelman, Lauren B. *Working Law: Courts, Corporations, and Symbolic Civil Rights.* Chicago: University of Chicago Press, 2016.

Edmondson, Amy C. *The Fearless Organization: Creating Psychological Safety in the Workplace for Learning, Innovation, and Growth.* Hoboken, NJ: Wiley, 2018.

Elyasiani, Elyas, and Iqbal Mansur. "Hedge Fund Return, Volatility Asymmetry, and Systemic Effects: A Higher-Moment Factor-EGARCH Model." *Journal of Financial Stability* 28 (February 2017): 49-65.

Emerson, Robert, Rachel Fretz, and Linda Shaw. *Writing Ethnographic Fieldnotes.* Chicago: University of Chicago Press, 2011.

Emigh, Rebecca Jean. "The Power of Negative Thinking: The Use of Negative Case Methodology in the Development of Sociological Theory." *Theory and Society* 26, no. 5 (October 1997): 649-84.

England, Paula. *Comparable Worth: Theories and Evidence.* New Brunswick, NJ: Aldine Transaction, 1992.

———. "Emerging Theories of Care Work." *Annual Review of Sociology* 31, no. 1 (August 2005): 381-99.

———. "The Gender Revolution Uneven and Stalled." *Gender & Society* 24, no. 2 (April 2010): 149-66.

Erdmann, Gero, and Ulf Engel. "Neopatrimonialism Reconsidered: Critical Review and Elaboration of an Elusive Concept." *Commonwealth and Comparative Politics* 45, no. 1 (February 2007): 95–119.

Evans, Louwanda, and Wendy Leo Moore. "Impossible Burdens: White Institutions, Emotional Labor, and Micro-Resistance." *Social Problems* 62, no. 3 (August 2015): 439–54.

Ewens, Michael, and Richard R. Townsend. "Are Early Stage Investors Biased against Women?" *Journal of Financial Economics* 135, no. 3 (March 2020): 653–77.

Faulkner, Wendy. "'Nuts and Bolts and People': Gender-Troubled Engineering Identities." *Social Studies of Science* 37, no. 3 (June 2007): 331–56.

Feagin, Joe R., and Kimberley Ducey. *Elite White Men Ruling: Who, What, When, Where, and How.* New York: Routledge, 2017.

Ferguson, Kathy. *Feminist Case against Bureaucracy.* Philadelphia: Temple University Press, 1984.

Ferguson, Roderick A. *Aberrations in Black: Toward a Queer of Color Critique.* Minneapolis: University of Minnesota Press, 2004.

Ferree, Myra Marx, and Patricia Yancey Martin. *Feminist Organizations: Harvest of the New Women's Movement.* Philadelphia: Temple University Press, 1995.

"The Financial Crisis Inquiry Commission: Final Report of the National Commission on the Causes of the Financial and Economic Crisis in the United States." Washington, DC: Financial Crisis Inquiry Commission, 2011.

Fisher, Melissa S. *Wall Street Women.* Durham, NC: Duke University Press, 2012.

Fisk, Susan R., and Jon Overton. "Who Wants to Lead? Anticipated Gender Discrimination Reduces Women's Leadership Ambitions." *Social Psychology Quarterly* 82, no. 3 (August 2019): 319–332.

Fligstein, Neil, and Adam Goldstein. "The Emergence of a Finance Culture in American Households, 1989–2007." *Socio-Economic Review* 13, no. 3 (July 2015): 575–601.

Fligstein, Neil, and Taekjin Shin. "Shareholder Value and the Transformation of the U.S. Economy, 1984–2000." *Sociological Forum* 22, no. 4 (December 2007): 399–424.

Foschi, Martha. "Double Standards for Competence: Theory and Research." *Annual Review of Sociology* 26, no. 1 (August 2000): 21–42.

Foucault, Michel. *The Birth of Biopolitics: Lectures at the Collège de France, 1978–1979.* New York: Picador, 2010.

———. *Discipline and Punish: The Birth of the Prison.* Translated by Alan Sheridan. New York: Vintage, 1995.

———. *The Order of Things: An Archaeology of the Human Sciences*. New York: Vintage, 1994.

Fraser, Nancy. "Feminism, Capitalism, and the Cunning of History." *New Left Review*, 2, no. 56 (April 2009): 97–117.

Freeland, Chrystia. *Plutocrats: The Rise of the New Global Super-Rich and the Fall of Everyone Else*. New York: Penguin, 2012.

Friedan, Betty. *The Feminine Mystique*. New York: W.W. Norton, 1963.

Fridman, Daniel. *Freedom from Work: Embracing Financial Self-Help in the United States and Argentina*. Stanford, CA: Stanford University Press, 2017.

Friedman, Sam, and Daniel Laurison. *The Class Ceiling: Why It Pays to Be Privileged*. Bristol, UK: Policy Press, 2019.

Funk, Cary, and Kim Parker. "Diversity in the STEM Workforce Varies Widely across Jobs." Washington, DC: Pew Research Center, January 9, 2018.

Galbraith, James K. *Created Unequal: The Crisis in American Pay*. Chicago: University of Chicago Press, 2000.

———. *Inequality and Instability: A Study of the World Economy Just Before the Great Crisis*. New York: Oxford University Press, 2012.

Gambetta, Diego, and Heather Hamill. *Streetwise: How Taxi Drivers Establish Customer's Trustworthiness*. New York: Russell Sage, 2005.

Gee, Buck, and Denise Peck. "The Illusion of Asian Success: Scant Progress for Minorities in Cracking the Glass Ceiling from 2007–2015." Ascend Pan Asian Leaders, 2017.

Gershon, Ilana. *Down and Out in the New Economy: How People Find (or Don't Find) Work Today*. Chicago: University of Chicago Press, 2017.

Gilbert, Thomas, and Christopher Hrdlicka. "A Hedge Fund That Has a University." *Wall Street Journal*, November 13, 2017.

Giridharadas, Anand. *Winners Take All: The Elite Charade of Changing the World*. New York: Vintage, 2018.

Glass, Jennifer. "The Impact of Occupational Segregation on Working Conditions." *Social Forces* 68, no. 3 (March 1990): 779–96.

Glucksberg, Luna. "A Gendered Ethnography of Elites: Women, Inequality, and Social Reproduction." *Focaal* 2018, no. 81 (June 2018): 16–28.

Glucksberg, Luna, and Roger Burrows. "Family Offices and the Contemporary Infrastructures of Dynastic Wealth." *Sociologica* 2 (May 2016).

"G.M.'s 1955 Profit Exceeds a Billion, Setting U.S. Mark." *New York Times*, February 3, 1956.

Godechot, Olivier. "Getting a Job in Finance: The Strength of Collaboration Ties." *European Journal of Sociology* 55, no. 01 (April 2014): 25–56.

———. *The Working Rich: Wages, Bonuses, and Appropriation of Profit in the Financial Industry.* London: Routledge, 2016.

Goffman, Erving. *The Presentation of Self in Everyday Life.* New York: Anchor, 1959.

Goldberg, Amir. "Mapping Shared Understandings Using Relational Class Analysis: The Case of the Cultural Omnivore Reexamined." *American Journal of Sociology* 116, no. 5 (March 2011): 1397–436.

Goldstein, Adam. "Revenge of the Managers: Labor Cost-Cutting and the Paradoxical Resurgence of Managerialism in the Shareholder Value Era, 1984 to 2001." *American Sociological Review* 77, no. 2 (April 2012): 268–94.

Gorman, Elizabeth H. "Work Uncertainty and the Promotion of Professional Women: The Case of Law Firm Partnership." *Social Forces* 85, no. 2 (December 2006): 865–90.

Gramsci, Antonio. *Selections from the Prison Notebooks.* Edited by Quintin Hoare and Geoffrey Nowell Smith. New York: International Publishers, 1947.

Gross, Daniel. "As Wal-Mart Goes . . . ." *Slate,* June 10, 2003.

Grusky, David, Bruce Western, and Christopher Wimer. *The Great Recession.* New York: Russell Sage Foundation, 2011.

Guillen, Laura. "Is the Confidence Gap between Men and Women a Myth?" *Harvard Business Review,* March 26, 2018.

Hacker, Jacob S. *The Great Risk Shift: The Assault on American Jobs, Families, Health Care, and Retirement and How You Can Fight Back.* Oxford: Oxford University Press, 2006.

Hacker, Jacob S., and Paul Pierson. "Winner-Take-All Politics: Public Policy, Political Organization, and the Precipitous Rise of Top Incomes in the United States." *Politics and Society* 38, no. 2 (June 2010): 152–204.

Hall, Douglas T. "Protean Careers of the 21st Century." *Academy of Management Executive* 10, no. 4 (November 1996): 8–16.

Hamel, Gary, David Chard, Roy Luebke, Stephen Booth, Uriel Cantarero, Bhavesh Parikh, and Faly Ranaivoson. "First, Let's Fire All the Managers." *Harvard Business Review* 90, no. 3 (March 2012): 20–21.

Handy, Charles. *The Age of Unreason.* Boston: Harvard Business Review Press, 1989.

Handy, Charles. "Finding Sense in Uncertainty." In *Rethinking the Future: Rethinking Business Principles, Competition, Control and Complexity, Leadership, Markets and the World,* edited by R. Gibson, 16–33. London: John Murray Press, 1999.

Hanson, Rebecca, and Patricia Richards. *Harassed: Gender, Bodies, and Ethnographic Research.* Berkeley: University of California Press, 2019.

Hardie, Iain, and Donald MacKenzie. "Assembling an Economic Actor: The Agencement of a Hedge Fund." *Sociological Review* 55, no. 1 (February 2007): 57–80.

Harjani, Ansuya. "Hedge Fund Manager Pay Rises to $2.4 Million." *CNBC,* November 6, 2014.

Harper, David R. "Hedge Funds: Higher Returns or Just High Fees?" *Investopedia,* October 16, 2018.

Harrington, Brooke. *Capital without Borders: Wealth Managers and the One Percent.* Cambridge, MA: Harvard University Press, 2016.

———. "Immersion Ethnography of Elites." In *Handbook of Qualitative Organizational Research,* edited by Kimberly D. Elsbach, 134–42. New York: Routledge, 2015.

Hart, Chloe Grace. "Trajectory Guarding: Managing Unwanted, Ambiguously Sexual Interactions at Work." *American Sociological Review* 86, no. 2 (March 2021): 256–278.

———. "The Penalties for Self-Reporting Sexual Harassment." *Gender & Society* 33, no. 4 (August 2019): 534–59.

Hartmann, Michael. *The Sociology of Elites.* New York: Routledge, 2006.

Harvey, David. *The Enigma of Capital: And the Crises of Capitalism.* Oxford: Oxford University Press, 2011.

Hayes, Robin J. "Why Ivy League Schools Are So Bad at Economic Diversity." *The Atlantic,* February 27, 2014.

Heilman, Madeline E. "Description and Prescription: How Gender Stereotypes Prevent Women's Ascent Up the Organizational Ladder." *Journal of Social Issues* 57, no. 4 (December 2001): 657–74.

Hernandez, Morela, Derek R. Avery, Sabrina D. Volpone, and Cheryl R. Kaiser. "Bargaining While Black: The Role of Race in Salary Negotiations." *Journal of Applied Psychology* 104, no. 4 (April 2019): 581–92.

Hill Collins, Patricia. *Black Feminist Thought: Knowledge, Consciousness, and the Politics of Empowerment.* New York: Routledge, 2000.

———. *Black Sexual Politics: African Americans, Gender, and the New Racism.* New York: Routledge, 2005.

———. "Learning from the Outsider Within: The Sociological Significance of Black Feminist Thought." *Social Problems* 33, no. 6 (December 1986): 20.

Ho, Karen. *Liquidated: An Ethnography of Wall Street.* Durham, NC: Duke University Press, 2009.

Hoang, Kimberly Kay. *Dealing in Desire: Asian Ascendancy, Western Decline, and the Hidden Currencies of Global Sex Work*. Berkeley: University of California Press, 2015.

———. "Gendering Carnal Ethnography: A Queer Reception." In *Other, Please Specify*. Berkeley: University of California Press, 2019.

———. "Risky Investments: How Local and Foreign Investors Finesse Corruption-Rife Emerging Markets." *American Sociological Review* 83, no. 4 (August 2018): 657–85.

Hodges, Melissa J., and Michelle J. Budig. "Who Gets the Daddy Bonus? Organizational Hegemonic Masculinity and the Impact of Fatherhood on Earnings." *Gender & Society* 24, no. 6 (December 2010): 717–45.

Hondagneu-Sotelo, Pierrette. *Domestica: Immigrant Workers Cleaning and Caring in the Shadows of Affluence*. Berkeley: University of California Press, 2007.

Houle, Jason N., and Fenaba R. Addo. "Racial Disparities in Student Debt and the Reproduction of the Fragile Black Middle Class." *Sociology of Race and Ethnicity* 5, no. 4 (October 2019): 1–16.

"How Shadow Banking Works." *The Economist*, February 2, 2016.

Hyman, Louis. *Debtor Nation: The History of America in Red Ink*. Princeton, NJ: Princeton University Press, 2012.

———. "Ending Discrimination, Legitimating Debt: The Political Economy of Race, Gender, and Credit Access in the 1960s and 1970s." *Enterprise and Society* 12, no. 1 (March 2011): 200–232.

Inkson, Kerr, and Michael B Arthur. "How to Be a Successful Career Capitalist." *Organizational Dynamics* 30, no. 1 (June 2001): 48–61.

Institutional Investor. "All-America Buy-Side Compensation." Institutional Investor LLC., 2019.

International Monetary Fund. "Global Financial Stability Report: Risk Taking, Liquidity, and Shadow Banking Curbing Excess While Promoting Growth." World Economic and Financial Surveys, 2014.

Jack, Anthony Abraham. *The Privileged Poor: How Elite Colleges Are Failing Disadvantaged Students*. Cambridge, MA: Harvard University Press, 2019.

Jaeger, Robert. *All About Hedge Funds: The Easy Way to Get Started*. New York: McGraw-Hill, 2002.

Jerolmack, Colin, and Shamus Khan. "Talk Is Cheap: Ethnography and the Attitudinal Fallacy." *Sociological Methods & Research* 43, no. 2 (May 2014): 178–209.

Johnson, Jenna. "Paul Tudor Jones: In Macro Trading, Babies Are a 'Killer' to a Woman's Focus." *Washington Post*, May 23, 2013.

Jones, Alfred Winslow. *Life, Liberty, and Property: A Story of Conflict and a Measurement of Conflicting Rights.* Akron, OH: University of Akron Press, 1941.

Kalev, Alexandra. "How You Downsize Is Who You Downsize: Biased Formalization, Accountability, and Managerial Diversity." *American Sociological Review* 79, no. 1 (February 2014): 109–35.

Kalleberg, Arne. *Good Jobs, Bad Jobs: The Rise of Polarized and Precarious Employment Systems in the United States, 1970s to 2000s.* New York: Russell Sage, 2011.

Kang, Songman. "Inequality and Crime Revisited: Effects of Local Inequality and Economic Segregation on Crime." *Journal of Population Economics* 29, no. 2 (December 2015): 593–626.

Kanter, Rosabeth Moss. *Commitment and Community: Communes and Utopias in Sociological Perspective.* Cambridge, MA: Harvard University Press, 1972.

——. *Men and Women of the Corporation.* New York: Basic Books, 1977.

Kanze, Dana, Laura Huang, Mark A. Conley, and E. Tory Higgins. "Male and Female Entrepreneurs Get Asked Different Questions by VCs—and It Affects How Much Funding They Get." *Harvard Business Review,* June 27, 2017.

Karabel, Jerome. *The Chosen: The Hidden History of Admission and Exclusion at Harvard, Yale, and Princeton.* Boston: Mariner Books, 2006.

Katz, Jack. "Ethnography's Warrants." *Sociological Methods & Research* 25, no. 4 (May 1997): 391–423.

Katznelson, Ira. *When Affirmative Action Was White: An Untold History of Racial Inequality in Twentieth-Century America.* New York: W. W. Norton, 2005.

Kellogg, Katherine. *Challenging Operations.* Chicago: University of Chicago Press, 2011.

Kendall, Diana. *The Power of Good Deeds: Privileged Women and the Social Reproduction of the Upper Class.* Lanham, MD: Rowman and Littlefield, 2002.

Khan, Shamus. *Privilege: The Making of an Adolescent Elite at St. Paul's School.* Princeton, NJ: Princeton University Press, 2011.

Kim, Jerry W., Bruce Kogut, and Jae-Suk Yang. "Executive Compensation, Fat Cats, and Best Athletes." *American Sociological Review* 80, no. 2 (April 2015): 299–328.

King, Samantha. *Pink Ribbons, Inc.* Minneapolis,: University of Minnesota Press, 2006.

Knight, Mélanie. "The Production of the Female Entrepreneurial Subject: A Space of Exclusion for Women of Color?" *Journal of Women, Politics, & Policy* 27, no. 3–4 (January 2006): 151–59.

Kollock, Peter. "The Emergence of Exchange Structures: An Experimental Study of Uncertainty, Commitment, and Trust." *American Journal of Sociology* 100, no. 2 (September 1994): 313–45.

Krippner, Greta R. *Capitalizing on Crisis: The Political Origins of the Rise of Finance.* Cambridge, MA: Harvard University Press, 2011.

———. "Democracy of Credit: Ownership and the Politics of Credit Access in Late Twentieth-Century America." *American Journal of Sociology* 123, no. 1 (July 2017): 1–47.

———. "The Financialization of the American Economy." *Socio-Economic Review* 3, no. 2 (May 2005): 173–208.

Kruppa, Miles. "The 'David' Problem." *Absolute Return,* September 7, 2018.

Lachmann, Richard. "Coda: American Patrimonialism The Return of the Repressed." *ANNALS of the American Academy of Political and Social Science* 636, no. 1 (July 2011): 204–30.

Lamont, Michèle. *Money, Morals, and Manners: The Culture of the French and the American Upper-Middle Class.* Chicago: University Of Chicago Press, 1992.

Lamont, Michèle, and Virág Molnár. "The Study of Boundaries in the Social Sciences." *Annual Review of Sociology* 28, no. 1 (August 2002): 167–95.

Lamont, Michèle, and Ann Swidler. "Methodological Pluralism and the Possibilities and Limits of Interviewing." *Qualitative Sociology* 37, no. 2 (June 2014): 153–71.

Lane, Carrie M. *A Company of One: Insecurity, Independence, and the New World of White-Collar Unemployment.* Ithaca, NY: Cornell University Press, 2011.

Lange, Julian E., Abdul Ali, Candida G. Brush, Andrew C. Corbett, Donna J. Kelley, Phillip H. Kim, and Mahdi Majbouri. "Global Entrepreneurship Monitor: United States Report 2017." Babson Park, MA: Babson College, 2017.

Lapavitsas, Costas. "Relations of Power and Trust in Contemporary Finance." *Historical Materialism* 14, no. 1 (March 2006): 129–54.

Lareau, Annette. *Unequal Childhoods: Class, Race, and Family Life,* 2nd ed. Berkeley: University of California Press, 2011.

Lazonick, William, and Mary O'Sullivan. "Maximizing Shareholder Value: A New Ideology for Corporate Governance." *Economy and Society* 29, no. 1 (January 2000): 13–35.

Lee, Jennifer, and Min Zhou. *The Asian American Achievement Paradox.* New York: Russell Sage Foundation, 2015.

Levin, Peter. "Gendering the Market: Temporality, Work, and Gender on a National Futures Exchange." *Work and Occupations* 28, no. 1 (February 2001): 112–30.

Levine, Ross, and Yona Rubinstein. "Smart and Illicit: Who Becomes an Entrepreneur and Do They Earn More?" *Quarterly Journal of Economics* 132, no. 2 (May 2017): 963–1018.

Lewis, Michael. *The Big Short: Inside the Doomsday Machine.* New York: W.W. Norton, 2011.

———. *Flash Boys.* New York: W.W. Norton, 2014.

Lin, Ken-Hou. "The Financial Premium in the U.S. Labor Market: A Distributional Analysis." *Social Forces* 94, no. 1 (September 2015): 1–30.

Lin, Ken-Hou, and Megan Tobias Neely. *Divested: Inequality in the Age of Finance.* Oxford: Oxford University Press, 2020.

———. "Gender, Parental Status, and the Wage Premium in Finance." *Social Currents* 4, no. 6 (January 2017): 535–55.

Lin, Ken-Hou, and Donald Tomaskovic-Devey. "Financialization and U.S. Income Inequality, 1970–2008." *American Journal of Sociology* 118, no. 5 (March 2013): 1284–329.

Lindsay, D. Michael. *View from the Top: An Inside Look at How People in Power See and Shape the World.* Hoboken, NJ: Wiley, 2014.

Lipsitz, George. *The Possessive Investment in Whiteness: How White People Profit from Identity Politics.* Revised and expanded ed. Philadelphia: Temple University Press, 1998.

Litterick, David. "Billionaire Who Broke the Bank of England." *The Telegraph,* September 13, 2002.

Lofland, John, David Snow, Leon Anderson, and Lyn Lofland. *Analyzing Social Settings: A Guide to Qualitative Observation and Analysis.* Belmont, CA: Wadsworth Publishing, 2005.

Luhmann, Niklas. "Familiarity, Confidence, and Trust: Problems and Alternatives." In *Trust: Making and Breaking Cooperative Relations,* edited by Diego Gambetta, 95–107. New York: Blackwell, 1990.

Lyons-Padilla, Sarah, Hazel Rose Markus, Ashby Monk, Sid Radhakrishna, Radhika Shah, Norris A. "Daryn" Dodson, and Jennifer L. Eberhardt. "Race Influences Professional Investors' Financial Judgments." *Proceedings of the National Academy of Sciences* 116, no. 35 (August 2019): 17225–30.

MacKenzie, Donald. "Long-Term Capital Management and the Sociology of Arbitrage." *Economy and Society* 32, no. 3 (January 2003): 349–80.

Madden, Janice Fanning. "Performance-Support Bias and the Gender Pay Gap among Stockbrokers." *Gender & Society* 26, no. 3 (June 2012): 488–518.

"Making It Big." Hedge Fund Manager Survey 2018. London: AIMA, 2018.

Mallaby, Sebastian. *More Money Than God: Hedge Funds and the Making of a New Elite*. New York: Penguin Books, 2011.

Manduca, Robert. "Income Inequality and the Persistence of Racial Economic Disparities." *Sociological Science* 5 (March 2018): 182–205.

Marland, Alex, and Anna Lennox Esselment. "Negotiating with Gatekeepers to Get Interviews with Politicians: Qualitative Research Recruitment in a Digital Media Environment." *Qualitative Research* 19, no. 6 (December 2019): 685–702.

Martin, Patricia Yancey. "Gender as Social Institution." *Social Forces* 82, no. 4 (June 2004): 1249–73.

Marx, Karl, and Friedrich Engels. *The Marx-Engels Reader*. New York: W. W. Norton, 1978.

Matlon, Jordanna. "Racial Capitalism and the Crisis of Black Masculinity." *American Sociological Review* 81, no. 5 (October 2016): 1014–38.

Mayer, Jane. "The Reclusive Hedge-Fund Tycoon behind the Trump Presidency." *New Yorker*, March 27, 2017.

Mayer, Susan E. "How Did the Increase in Economic Inequality between 1970 and 1990 Affect Children's Educational Attainment?" *American Journal of Sociology* 107, no. 1 (July 2001): 1–32.

McCall, Leslie. "The Complexity of Intersectionality." *Signs* 30, no. 3 (March 2005): 1771–800.

McDermott, Monica, and Frank Samson. "White Racial and Ethnic Identity in the United States." *Annual Review of Sociology* 31, no. 1 (August 2005): 245–61.

McDowell, Linda. *Capital Culture: Gender at Work in the City*. Oxford: Wiley-Blackwell, 1997.

McGuire, Gail M. "Gender, Race, and the Shadow Structure: A Study of Informal Networks and Inequality in a Work Organization." *Gender & Society* 16, no. 3 (June 2002): 303–22.

———. "Gender, Race, Ethnicity, and Networks: The Factors Affecting the Status of Employees' Network Members." *Work and Occupations* 27, no. 4 (November 2000): 501–24.

McGuire, Gail M., and William T. Bielby. "The Variable Effects of Tie Strength and Social Resources: How Type of Support Matters." *Work and Occupations* 43, no. 1 (February 2016): 38–74.

McKinsey. "Racial Equity in Financial Services." McKinsey and Company, September 10, 2020.

McLaughlin, Heather, Christopher Uggen, and Amy Blackstone. "The Economic and Career Effects of Sexual Harassment on Working Women." *Gender & Society* 31, no. 3 (June 2017): 333–58.

——. "Sexual Harassment, Workplace Authority, and the Paradox of Power." *American Sociological Review* 77, no. 4 (August 2012): 625–47.

McLaughlin, Susan. "The Impact of Interstate Banking and Branching Reform: Evidence from the States." *Federal Reserve Bank of New York* 1, no. 2 (May 1995): 1–6.

McMillan Cottom, Tressie. *Lower Ed: The Troubling Rise of For-Profit Colleges in the New Economy*. New York: New Press, 2017.

Mears, Ashley. *Pricing Beauty: The Making of a Fashion Model*. Berkeley: University of California Press, 2011.

——. *Very Important People: Status and Beauty in the Global Party Circuit*. Princeton, NJ: Princeton University Press, 2020.

Melaku, Tsedale M. *You Don't Look Like a Lawyer: Black Women and Systemic Gendered Racism*. Lanham, MD: Rowman and Littlefield, 2019.

Merle, Renae. "How One Hedge Fund Made $2 Billion from Argentina's Economic Collapse." *Washington Post*, March 29, 2016.

Messner, Michael A. *It's All for the Kids*. Berkeley: University of California Press, 1986.

——. "The Masculinity of the Governator: Muscle and Compassion in American Politics." *Gender & Society* 21, no. 4 (August 2007): 461–80.

Meyer, Theodoric, Victoria Guida, and Nahal Toosi. "Mick Mulvaney's New Side Gig: A Hedge Fund Betting on D.C." *Politico*, August 28, 2020.

Michel, Alexandra. "Transcending Socialization A Nine-Year Ethnography of the Body's Role in Organizational Control and Knowledge Workers' Transformation." *Administrative Science Quarterly* 56 no. 3 (September 2011): 325–68.

Mickey, Ethel L. "When Gendered Logics Collide: Going Public and Restructuring in a High-Tech Organization." *Gender & Society* 33, no. 4 (August 2019).

Mijs, Jonathan J. B. "The Paradox of Inequality: Income Inequality and Belief in Meritocracy Go Hand in Hand." *Socio-Economic Review* 19, no. 1 (January 2019): 7–35.

Mills, C. Wright. *The Power Elite*. Oxford: Oxford University Press, 1956.

Mizruchi, Mark S. *The Fracturing of the American Corporate Elite*. Cambridge, MA: Harvard University Press, 2013.

Moen, Phyllis. *Encore Adulthood: Boomers on the Edge of Risk, Renewal, and Purpose.* Oxford: Oxford University Press, 2016.

Moore, Wendy Leo. *Reproducing Racism: White Space, Elite Law Schools, and Racial Inequality.* Lanham, MD: Rowman and Littlefield, 2008.

Morgan, Laurie A., and Karin A. Martin. "Taking Women Professionals Out of the Office: The Case of Women in Sales." *Gender & Society* 20, no. 1 (February 2006): 108–28.

Morris, Aldon. *The Scholar Denied: W. E. B. Du Bois and the Birth of Modern Sociology.* Oakland: University of California Press, 2015.

Moyer, Liz. "Four Hedge Fund Managers Top $1 Billion in Pay." *CNBC*, May 30, 2018.

Mueller, Holger M., and Thomas Philippon. "Family Firms and Labor Relations." *American Economic Journal: Macroeconomics* 3, no. 2 (April 2011): 218–45.

Musto, Michela. "Brilliant or Bad: The Gendered Social Construction of Exceptionalism in Early Adolescence." *American Sociological Review* 84, no. 3 (April 2019): 369–393.

Nash, Jennifer C. "On Difficulty: Intersectionality as Feminist Labor." *Scholar and Feminist Online* 8, no. 3 (Summer 2010).

———. "Re-Thinking Intersectionality." *Feminist Review* 89, no. 1 (June 2008): 1–15.

Naudet, Jules. *Stepping into the Elite: Trajectories of Social Achievement in India, France, and the United States.* Oxford: Oxford University Press, 2018.

Neely, Megan Tobias. "Fit to Be King: How Patrimonialism on Wall Street Leads to Inequality." *Socio-Economic Review* 16, no. 2 (April 2018): 365–85.

———. "The Portfolio Ideal Worker: Insecurity and Inequality in the New Economy." *Qualitative Sociology* 43, no. 2 (June 2020): 271–96.

Neely, Megan Tobias, and Donna Carmichael. "Profiting on Crisis: How Predatory Financial Investors Have Worsened Inequality in the Coronavirus Crisis." *American Behavioral Scientist* (March 2021): 1–22.

Nelson, Julie A. *Gender and Risk-Taking.* New York: Routledge, 2017.

Ogle, Vanessa. "Archipelago Capitalism: Tax Havens, Offshore Money, and the State, 1950s–1970s." *American Historical Review* 122, no. 5 (December 2017): 1431–58.

Omi, Michael, and Howard Winant. *Racial Formation in the United States.* New York: Routledge, 1986.

Orbuch, Terri L. "People's Accounts Count: The Sociology of Accounts." *Annual Review of Sociology* 23, no. 1 (August 1997): 455–78.

Ostrander, Susan. *Women of the Upper Class.* Philadelphia: Temple University Press, 1984.

Pardo-Guerra, Juan Pablo. *Automating Finance: Infrastructures, Engineers, and the Making of Electronic Markets.* Cambridge: Cambridge University Press, 2019.

Pascoe, C. J. *Dude, You're a Fag: Masculinity and Sexuality in High School.* Berkeley: University of California Press, 2007.

Pedulla, David S. *Making the Cut.* Princeton, NJ: Princeton University Press, 2020.

Pew Research Center. "The American Middle Class Is Losing Ground." *Pew Research Center's Social and Demographic Trends Project,* December 9, 2015.

Pierce, Jennifer L. *Gender Trials: Emotional Lives in Contemporary Law Firms.* Berkeley: University of California Press, 1996.

———. "'Racing for Innocence': Whiteness, Corporate Culture, and the Backlash against Affirmative Action." *Qualitative Sociology* 26, no. 1 (March 2003): 53–70.

Piketty, Thomas. *Capital in the Twenty-First Century.* Cambridge, MA: Belknap Press of Harvard University Press, 2014.

Piketty, Thomas, Emmanuel Saez, and Gabriel Zucman. "Distributional National Accounts: Methods and Estimates for the United States." *Quarterly Journal of Economics* 133, no. 2 (May 2018): 553–609.

Pistor, Katharina. *The Code of Capital: How the Law Creates Wealth and Inequality.* Princeton, NJ: Princeton University Press, 2019.

Pitluck, Aaron Z. "Watching Foreigners: How Counterparties Enable Herds, Crowds, and Generate Liquidity in Financial Markets." *Socio-Economic Review* 12, no. 1 (January 2014): 5–31.

Podolny, Joel M. "Market Uncertainty and the Social Character of Economic Exchange." *Administrative Science Quarterly* 39, no. 3 (September 1994): 458–83.

Posselt, Julie R., and Eric Grodsky. "Graduate Education and Social Stratification." *Annual Review of Sociology* 43 (August 2017): 353–78.

Preqin. "Global Hedge Fund Reports: 2015–2020." New York: Preqin, 2020.

———. "Hedge Funds in the U.S." New York: Preqin, 2018.

———. "Private Capital Compensation and Employment Review." New York: Preqin, 2017.

———. "Women in Alternative Assets." New York: Preqin, October 2017.

Prince, Russ Alan. "From Hedge Fund to Family Office." *Forbes,* November 20, 2013.

Pugh, Allison J. *The Tumbleweed Society: Working and Caring in an Age of Insecurity.* New York: Oxford University Press, 2015.

———. "What Good Are Interviews for Thinking about Culture? Demystifying Interpretive Analysis." *American Journal of Cultural Sociology* 1, no. 1 (February 2013): 42–68.

Pugh, Allison J., ed. *Beyond the Cubicle*. New York: Oxford University Press, 2016.

Puwar, Nirmal. *Space Invaders: Race, Gender, and Bodies Out of Place*. New York: Bloomsbury Academic, 2004.

Quinn, Beth A. "The Paradox of Complaining: Law, Humor, and Harassment in the Everyday Work World." *Law and Social Inquiry* 25, no. 4 (Autumn 2000): 1151–85.

Rao, Aliya Hamid. *Crunch Time: How Married Couples Confront Unemployment*. Berkeley: University of California Press, 2020.

Rao, Aliya Hamid, and Megan Tobias Neely. "What's Love Got to Do with It? Passion and Inequality in White-Collar Work." *Sociology Compass* 13, no. 12 (December 2019): 1–14.

Ravenelle, Alexandrea J. *Hustle and Gig: Struggling and Surviving in the Sharing Economy*. Berkeley: University of California Press, 2019.

Ray, Victor. "A Theory of Racialized Organizations." *American Sociological Review* 84, no. 1 (January 2019): 26–53.

Ray, Victor, and Danielle Purifoy. "The Colorblind Organization." In *Race, Organizations, and the Organizing Process*, edited by Melissa E. Wooten, 131–50. Vol. 60 of Research in the Sociology of Organizations. Bingley, UK: Emerald Publishing, 2019.

Riach, Kathleen, and Leanne Cutcher. "Built to Last: Ageing, Class, and the Masculine Body in a UK Hedge Fund." *Work, Employment, and Society* 28, no. 5 (October 2014): 771–87.

Ridgeway, Cecilia L. *Framed by Gender: How Gender Inequality Persists in the Modern World*. Oxford: Oxford University Press, 2011.

Risman, Barbara J. "Gender as a Social Structure: Theory Wrestling with Activism." *Gender & Society* 18, no. 4 (August 2004): 429–50.

Rivera, Lauren. "Hiring as Cultural Matching: The Case of Elite Professional Service Firms." *American Sociological Review* 77, no. 6 (December 2012): 999–1022.

———. *Pedigree: How Elite Students Get Elite Jobs*. Princeton, NJ: Princeton University Press, 2015.

Robinson, Cedric J., and Robin D. G. Kelley. *Black Marxism: The Making of the Black Radical Tradition*. Chapel Hill: University of North Carolina Press, 1983.

Roose, Kevin. *Young Money: Inside the Hidden World of Wall Street's Post-Crash Recruits*. New York: Grand Central Publishing, 2014.

Rosenfeld, Jake. *What Unions No Longer Do*. Cambridge, MA: Harvard University Press, 2014.

Rosette, Ashleigh, and Robert W. Livingston. "Failure Is Not an Option for Black Women: Effects of Organizational Performance on Leaders with Single versus Dual-Subordinate Identities." *Journal of Experimental Social Psychology* 48, no. 5 (September 2012): 1162–67.

Roth, Louise Marie. *Selling Women Short: Gender and Money on Wall Street*. Princeton, NJ: Princeton University Press, 2006.

Rothschild-Whitt, Joyce. "The Collectivist Organization: An Alternative to Rational-Bureaucratic Models." *American Sociological Review* 44, no. 4 (August 1979): 509–27.

Rothstein Kass. "Women in Alternative Investments: A Marathon, Not a Sprint." Rothstein Kass Institute, December 2013.

Rousseau, Denise M., Sim B. Sitkin, Ronald S. Burt, and Colin Camerer. "Not So Different after All: A Cross-Discipline View of Trust." *Academy of Management Review* 23, no. 3 (July 1998): 393–404.

Rudman, Laurie A. "Self-Promotion as a Risk Factor for Women: The Costs and Benefits of Counterstereotypical Impression Management." *Journal of Personality and Social Psychology* 74, no. 3 (March 1998): 629–45.

Rudman, Laurie A., Corinne A. Moss-Racusin, Julie E. Phelan, and Sanne Nauts. "Status Incongruity and Backlash Effects: Defending the Gender Hierarchy Motivates Prejudice against Female Leaders." *Journal of Experimental Social Psychology* 48, no. 1 (January 2012): 165–79.

Rugh, Jacob S., and Douglas S. Massey. "Racial Segregation and the American Foreclosure Crisis." *American Sociological Review* 75, no. 5 (October 2010): 629–51.

Ryan, Michelle K., and S. Alexander Haslam. "The Glass Cliff: Evidence That Women Are Over-Represented in Precarious Leadership Positions." *British Journal of Management* 16, no. 2 (March 2007): 81–90.

Schimank, Uwe. "Against All Odds: The 'Loyalty' of Small Investors." *Socio-Economic Review* 9, no. 1 (January 2011): 107–35.

Schor, Juliet B. *After the Gig: How the Sharing Economy Got Hijacked and How to Win It Back*. Berkeley: University of California Press, 2020.

Seabrooke, Leonard, and Eleni Tsingou. "Revolving Doors in International Financial Governance." *Global Networks*, 2020.

Seamster, Louise, and Raphaël Charron-Chénier. "Predatory Inclusion and Education Debt: Rethinking the Racial Wealth Gap." *Social Currents* 4, no. 3 (June 2017): 199–207.

Settembre, Jeanette. "Venture Capitalists Still Give Most of Their Money to White Men, Study Finds." *MarketWatch,* February 13, 2019.

Sherman, Rachel. *Uneasy Street: The Anxieties of Affluence.* Princeton, NJ: Princeton University Press, 2017.

Shin, Taekjin. "Explaining Pay Disparities between Top Executives and Nonexecutive Employees: A Relative Bargaining Power Approach." *Social Forces* 92, no. 4 (June 2014): 1339–72.

Silver, Michelle P. *Retirement and Its Discontents: Why We Won't Stop Working, Even If We Can.* New York: Columbia University Press, 2018.

Simpson, Brent, Tucker McGrimmon, and Kyle Irwin. "Are Blacks Really Less Trusting Than Whites? Revisiting the Race and Trust Question." *Social Forces* 86, no. 2 (December 2007): 525–52.

Smith, Dorothy E. *The Everyday World as Problematic: A Feminist Sociology.* Boston: Northeastern University Press, 1989.

Smith, Jeffrey A., Miller McPherson, and Lynn Smith-Lovin. "Social Distance in the United States: Sex, Race, Religion, Age, and Education Homophily among Confidants, 1985 to 2004." *American Sociological Review* 79, no. 3 (June 2014): 432–56.

Smith, Sandra. "Race and Trust." *Annual Review of Sociology* 36, no. 1 (August 2010): 453–75.

Smith-Doerr, Laurel. *Women's Work: Gender Equality Vs. Hierarchy in the Life Sciences.* Boulder, CO: Lynne Rienner Publishers, 2004.

Snyder, Benjamin H. *The Disrupted Workplace: Time and the Moral Order of Flexible Capitalism.* Oxford: Oxford University Press, 2016.

Sobering, Katherine. "The Relational Production of Workplace Equality: The Case of Worker-Recuperated Businesses in Argentina." *Qualitative Sociology* 42, no. 4 (December 2019): 543–65.

Souleles, Daniel Scott. *Songs of Profit, Songs of Loss: Private Equity, Wealth, and Inequality.* Lincoln: University of Nebraska Press, 2019.

Stephens, Neil. "Collecting Data from Elites and Ultra Elites: Telephone and Face-to-Face Interviews with Macroeconomists." *Qualitative Research* 7, no. 2 (May 2007): 203–16.

Sterling, Adina D. "Preentry Contacts and the Generation of Nascent Networks in Organizations." *Organization Science* 26, no. 3 (June 2014): 650–67.

Stevenson, Alexandra, and Matthew Goldstein. "Bridgewater Manager Ray Dalio Defends His Firm's 'Radical Transparency.'" *New York Times,* September 13, 2016.

Stone, Pamela. *Opting Out?: Why Women Really Quit Careers and Head Home.* Berkeley: University of California Press, 2007.

Strauss, Valerie. "Why Hedge Funds Love Charter Schools." *Washington Post,* June 4, 2014.

Subramanian, S. V., and Ichiro Kawachi. "Whose Health Is Affected by Income Inequality?" *Health and Place* 12, no. 2 (June 2006): 141–56.

Sullivan, Margaret. "The 'Audacious Lie' behind a Hedge Fund's Promise to Sustain Local Journalism." *Washington Post,* February 17, 2021.

Sweeney, Deborah. "How HR 5050 Changed Entrepreneurship for Women." *Forbes,* August 21, 2018.

Tak, Elise, Shelley J. Correll, and Sarah A. Soule. "Gender Inequality in Product Markets: When and How Status Beliefs Transfer to Products." *Social Forces* 98, no. 2 (December 2019): 548–77.

Taylor, Keeanga-Yamahtta. *Race for Profit: How Banks and the Real Estate Industry Undermined Black Homeownership.* Chapel Hill: University of North Carolina Press, 2019.

Thébaud, Sarah. "Business as Plan B: Institutional Foundations of Gender Inequality in Entrepreneurship across 24 Industrialized Countries." *Administrative Science Quarterly* 60, no. 4 (December 2015): 671–711.

———. "Status Beliefs and the Spirit of Capitalism: Accounting for Gender Biases in Entrepreneurship and Innovation." *Social Forces* 94, no. 1 (September 2015): 61–86.

Thébaud, Sarah, and Amanda J. Sharkey. "Unequal Hard Times: The Influence of the Great Recession on Gender Bias in Entrepreneurial Financing." *Sociological Science* 3 (January 2016): 1–31.

Tilly, Charles. *Durable Inequality.* Berkeley: University of California Press, 1999.

———. "Welcome to the Seventeenth Century." In *The Twenty-First-Century Firm Changing Economic Organization in International Perspective,* 200–209. Princeton, NJ: Princeton University Press, 2001.

Tomaskovic-Devey, Donald, and Dustin Avent-Holt. *Relational Inequalities: An Organizational Approach.* New York: Oxford University Press, 2019.

Tomaskovic-Devey, Donald, and Ken-Hou Lin. "Income Dynamics, Economic Rents, and the Financialization of the U.S. Economy." *American Sociological Review* 76, no. 4 (August 2011): 538–59.

Toosi, Negin R., Shira Mor, Zhaleh Semnani-Azad, Katherine W. Phillips, and Emily T. Amanatullah. "Who Can Lean In? The Intersecting Role of Race and Gender in Negotiations." *Psychology of Women Quarterly* 43, no. 1 (March 2019): 7–21.

Trumbull, Gunnar. "Credit Access and Social Welfare: The Rise of Consumer Lending in the United States and France." *Politics & Society* 40, no. 1 (March 2012): 9–34.

Turco, Catherine. *The Conversational Firm: Rethinking Bureaucracy in the Age of Social Media.* New York: Columbia University Press, 2016.

———. "Cultural Foundations of Tokenism: Evidence from the Leveraged Buyout Industry." *American Sociological Review* 75, no. 6 (December 2010): 894–913.

Vallas, Steven, and Emily R. Cummins. "Personal Branding and Identity Norms in the Popular Business Press: Enterprise Culture in an Age of Precarity." *Organization Studies* 36, no. 3 (March 2015): 293–319.

Vallas, Steven, and Christopher Prener. "Dualism, Job Polarization, and the Social Construction of Precarious Work." *Work and Occupations* 39, no. 4 (November 2012): 331–53.

Veblen, Thorstein. *The Theory of the Leisure Class: An Economic Study of Institutions.* Washington, DC: Prometheus, 1899.

Volscho, Thomas W., and Nathan J. Kelly. "The Rise of the Super-Rich: Power Resources, Taxes, Financial Markets, and the Dynamics of the Top 1 Percent, 1949 to 2008." *American Sociological Review* 77, no. 5 (October 2012): 679–99.

Weber, Max. *The Theory of Social and Economic Organization.* Edited by Talcott Parsons. Mansfield Center, CT: Martino Fine Books, 1922.

Welch, David. "GM Now Has Fewer UAW Employees Than FCA, Ford." *Automotive News,* August 29, 2019.

Whyte, Amy. "New Hedge Funds Are Asking for More Money from Investors." *Institutional Investor,* April 3, 2019.

Whyte, William H. *The Organization Man.* Philadelphia: University of Pennsylvania Press, 1956.

Williams, Christine L. "The Gender of Layoffs in the Oil and Gas Industry." In *Precarious Work,* edited by Arne L. Kalleberg and Steven P. Vallas, 31: 215–41. Research in the Sociology of Work 31. Bingley, UK: Emerald Publishing, 2017.

———. *Still a Man's World: Men Who Do Women's Work.* Berkeley: University of California Press, 1995.

Williams, Christine L., Patti A. Giuffre, and Kirsten Dellinger. "Sexuality in the Workplace: Organizational Control, Sexual Harassment, and the Pursuit of Pleasure." *Annual Review of Sociology* 25, no. 1 (August 1999): 73–93.

Williams, Christine L., Chandra Muller, and Kristine Kilanski. "Gendered Organizations in the New Economy." *Gender & Society* 26, no. 4 (August 2012): 549–73.

Williams, Joan C. *Unbending Gender: Why Family and Work Conflict and What to Do about It.* Oxford: Oxford University Press, 2001.

Wilmers, Nathan. "Job Turf or Variety: Task Structure as a Source of Organizational Inequality." *Administrative Science Quarterly* 65, no. 4 (December 2020): 1018–57.

Wingfield, Adia Harvey. "Are Some Emotions Marked 'Whites Only'? Racialized Feeling Rules in Professional Workplaces." *Social Problems* 57, no. 2 (May 2010): 251–68.

———. "Crossing the Color Line: Black Professional Men's Development of Interracial Social Networks." *Societies* 4 (December 2014): 240–55.

———. *Flatlining: Race, Work, and Health Care in the New Economy.* Oakland: University of California Press, 2019.

———. *No More Invisible Man: Race and Gender in Men's Work.* Philadelphia: Temple University Press, 2013.

Wingfield, Adia Harvey, and Renée Skeete Alston. "Maintaining Hierarchies in Predominantly White Organizations: A Theory of Racial Tasks." *American Behavioral Scientist* 58, no. 2 (February 2014): 274–87.

Wingfield, Adia Harvey, and Taura Taylor. "Race, Gender, and Class in Entrepreneurship: Intersectional Counterframes and Black Business Owners." *Ethnic and Racial Studies* 39, no. 9 (July 2016): 1676–96.

Wolfe, Tom. 1987. *The Bonfire of the Vanities.* New York: Picador.

Wolff, Edward N. "Household Wealth Inequality, Retirement Income Security, and Financial Market Swings 1983 through 2010." In *Inequality, Uncertainty, and Opportunity: The Varied and Growing Role of Finance in Labor Relations,* edited by Christian E. Weller. LERA Research Volumes. Ithaca, NY: Cornell University Press, 2015.

Wooten, Melissa E., and Lucius Couloute. "The Production of Racial Inequality within and among Organizations." *Sociology Compass* 11, no. 1 (January 2017).

World Bank. "United States." Country Profile. World Development Indicators Database, 2016.

Yang, Tiantian, and Howard E. Aldrich. "Who's the Boss? Explaining Gender Inequality in Entrepreneurial Teams." *American Sociological Review* 79, no. 2 (April 2014): 303–27.

Yavorsky, Jill, Lisa Keister, Yue Qian, and Michael Nau. "Women in the One Percent: Gender Dynamics in Top Income Positions." *American Sociological Review* 84, no. 1 (February 2019): 54–81.

Zaloom, Caitlin. *Out of the Pits: Traders and Technology from Chicago to London.* Chicago: University of Chicago Press, 2006.

Zorn, Dirk, Frank Dobbin, Julian Dierkes, and Man-shan Kwok. "Managing Investors: How Financial Markets Reshaped the American Firm." In *The Sociology of Financial Markets,* edited by K. Knorr-Cetina and A. Preda, 269–89. Oxford: Oxford University Press, 2006.

Index

divorce, 152
Dodd-Frank Wall Street Reform and
    Consumer Protection Act of 2010,
    46
downsizing, 11, 13–15, 43–44, 143, 163

Edmonson, Amy, 268n19
elite, white masculinity, xv, 26–27, 31,
    51–52, 56, 82, 224–225; access to
    networks and, 189, 201; in
    community banking era, 36, 40;
    compensation and, 3; hedge fund
    founding and, xvi; historical eras
    of, 33–35; in investment banking
    era, 41–42, 44; "natural" leadership
    and, 177; patronage and, 12, 16, 239;
    privilege and, 21–22, 67, 201, 226;
    risk management and, xv, 18, 20,
    22, 31, 210; in shadow banking ear,
    46. See also elites; masculinity;
    hedgemonic masculinity
elites, 26, 54, 225–226, 239–240;
    consumption and, 7, 202; as cultural
    omnivores, 55; economic inequality
    and, 6–7, 239; ethnographic study
    of, 22–23, 241, 243, 245–247; global
    impact of, 238–239; government
    policy and, 14–15; hegemonic
    masculinity and, 31–34; meritoc-
    racy and, 8, 17, 239; patrimonialism
    and, 16, 65, 236; race and, 67, 189,
    226; solidarity among, 11, 65,
    235–236; working rich and, 8. See
    also elite, white masculinity
Elliott Management, 238
employee turnover, 120, 142, 163
entrepreneurial chaos, 116
entrepreneurialism, 57, 61, 137, 140,
    178, 198–199; 265n7
entrepreneurship, 57, 61, 111, 178–180,
    201, 207, 229; risk and, 27, 58, 188,

191, 200, 227, 229, 234; wives and,
    191
Epstein, Jeffrey, 31
Equal Credit Opportunity Act, 40
ethnographic participant-observation,
    xiii–xiv, 22–24, 241–250; gender and,
    245–247; lists of interviewees,
    251–253; methodological details,
    247–250
executive office, 114–115. See also
    C-suite

"fake it till you make it" mentality,
    53–54
family offices, 14, 29, 65, 180, 183, 187,
    195, 210, 273n9, 273n20
fatherhood. See parenting
Federal Housing Authority (FHA),
    38–39
femininity, 33, 42, 161, 170, 245–247;
    hedgemonic masculinity and, 32,
    154, 156; upper class, 161, 171, 206,
    268n13
Ferguson, Kathy, 14
Fernández de Kirchner, Cristina, 238
financial crisis of 2008, xvi–xvii, 47,
    198, 213, 230; discriminatory
    lending and, 39; founding of hedge
    funds and, 198–199; government
    regulations and, 46, 214; layoffs
    and, 163, 230; risk-taking and, 19, 51
financial freedom discourse, 59–61,
    205, 208–210, 228, 265n7, 274n2
financialization, 239, 255n4
"Flash Boys," 35, 45–46, 48, 54
"flat" hedge fund structure, 27,
    101–105, 117–118, 137–138, 227,
    230–232; anti-bureaucratic
    sentiment and, 235; gendered work
    and, 14, 114–115, 137, 178, 196–197,
    224, 227, 230–231; hedgemonic

168–169, 171–176, 244, 272n49;
social exclusion and, 21, 91–92,
167–168; social status and, 25, 16–17,
137, 246; social ties and, 68–69, 72,
91; terminology of, 103–104, 137. *See
also* femininity; masculinity
gender-typing, 106–110, 266n9
General Motors, 5
Gephardt, Dick, 236
"Glass Cliff" phenomenon, 200
Glass-Steagall Act, 212–213
Global South, 14, 108, 110
Glucksberg, Luna, 14–15, 271n45
Golden Dutch Age, 12
Goldman Sachs, 236
government regulation of hedge
funds, 6–7, 9–10, 14, 203–204,
212–217; taxation and, 4–6, 219–221,
223, 257n25
Gramsci, Antonio, 31
Grand Cub firms, 12, 194
Great Recession, 47, 51, 160, 179, 222,
261n85
Greenspan, Alan, 236
gross domestic product (GDP), 257n23

Handy, Charles, 139–140
Hanson, Rebecca, 245, 271n43, 275n5
Harrington, Brooke, 6
hedged out, 17, 19–21, 25, 37, 48, 52, 56,
76–77, 225, 227, 232, 235; hiring
practices and, 88, 94; patrimonialism and, 141
hedge funds, 4–7, 48–49, 101–102,
180–182; caricatures of, 1; closing
of, 228–236; currency collapse and,
237; defined, 249; effect of on
wages, 11; fees charged by, 4–5, 18,
128, 134, 211, 218–219; financial
crisis of 2008 and, xviii; firm as
"tribe," 163–164, 169; "flat" nature

of (*See* "flat" hedge fund structure);
founding of (*See* founding of hedge
funds); government regulation of,
6–7, 9–10, 14, 203–204, 212–217;
implications for democracy, 6,
236–239; industry origins of, 65;
investment strategies of, 4, 11,
18–19, 49–51, 260n81; investors in,
4–5, 180–182; neoliberalism and,
9–10; organizational chart of, 106;
origin of, 18; outsourcing of labor
and, 84; patronage at, 12; philanthropy and, 203, 222–223; physical
organization of, 120–121; political
connections of, 236–237; profitabil-
ity of, 10, 256n18, 260n82;
risk-taking and, 18–19, 136; shadow
banks and, 47; social value of, xvii–
xviii, 211, 218; startup costs of,
178–179; taxation of, 4–6, 219–221,
223, 257n25; workers at (*See* hedge
fund workers)
hedge fund workers, 6; academic
track to employment, 78–82;
attitudes towards government
regulation, 212–217; as capitalizable
person, 176; class privilege and,
8–9, 63, 67–68, 78, 82, 98; compensation for, 126–137; diversity
initiatives and, 71; financial
freedom and, 59–61, 205–206,
208–210; "flatness" and, 27,
101–105, 114–115, 117–120, 122, 125,
127, 130, 137–138, 197, 227, 230–232,
239; following closing of hedge
fund, 228–236; founders as, 182–201;
heteronormativity and, 64;
hierarchies among, 101–103; ideal
workers and, 140–143; incomes of,
2, 3, 6, 10, 17, 35, 126–138, 202–210,
235, 256n5; infatuation with work

hedge fund workers *(continued)*
and, 7, 9, 35, 90, 142, 150, 153, 170, 176, 207, 210, 234, 238; in international affairs, 237–238; interview process and, xiii–xiv, 53–54, 82, 83–92, 98–100; investment banking tack to employment, 68–72; manager-employee relations and, 118; mentor-protégé relations and, 165–166, 192–195, 197; meritocracy and, 8, 24, 55, 57, 67, 76, 82, 116, 118–120, 130–132, 212, 227, 239–240; motivations for applying, 55–61; parents as, 110–114; passion expectation and, 56, 58, 60, 85, 89–91, 94–95, 143, 149–153, 158–159, 165–166, 176–177, 205, 207, 227, 234; patrimonialism and, 81; personal brands and, 143–149, 159–160, 176–177, 224; philanthropy and, 203–204, 206, 211, 221–223; portability of, 176, 215, 224; precarious nature of employment, 15, 55, 76–77, 142; retirement and, 61, 206, 208–209, 208–210, 228–229; risk-taking and, 17–22, 129, 136–137, 139, 153–159, 177; as scapegoats for inequality, 202–203, 206–207; self-promotion and, 146–148; social bonds among, 164; social circle track to employment, 62–68, 82; social value of, 211, 221; taxes paid by, 219–221; top-level employees, 10, 114–119, 137, 163–164, 227; trading track to employment, 72–78; transparency and, 119–122; "tribal" identification and, 163–164, 169; turnover and, 120, 142, 163
hedgemonic masculinity, 31–32, 51–52, 210, 227–228; closing of hedge fund and, 233–235; contrasted with femininity/marginalized masculinity, 154, 156; financial freedom and, 209–210; hedge fund founders and, 186; hiring processes and, 94; portfolio ideal and, 140, 176–177; racial privilege and, 77; risk-taking and, 31, 61, 77, 153–154, 239; in shadow-banking era, 48; vouchers for, 88, 94, 98
hiring processes, 53–54, 82, 83–100; author's experience of, xiii–xiv, 83–86, 98–100; compensation and, 126–127; cultural capital and, 88–89, 94, 98; "culture" interviews, 84–85; "fit" and, 88–89, 91–92; gender discrimination and, 88, 90–98
Ho, Karen, 17, 58–59, 69, 242
Hoang, Kimberly, 32, 172, 189, 245–246, 270n13
Home Mortgage Disclosure Act, 40
homo economicus, 148, 176, 224
homophily, 16, 88–89, 94, 97–98, 166–167, 226; race and, 16, 63, 88–89, 166–167, 226; trust and, 63, 89, 97, 226

ideal workers, 140–143, 262n2, 269n3; portfolio ideal, 140–143, 170, 176–177, 205, 227; white collar *vs.* portfolio ideals, 143
income inequality, xv, 2–3, 7–8, 16, 219, 224–225, 235–236, 239–240; debt and, 47; financial sector and, 27, 34–35; hedge funds and, 5–6, 26, 202, 211, 225, 239; history of, 7–8; lending and, 16, 39; new economy and, 13; patrimonialism and, 14, 16; risk-taking and, 19
individualism, 101–102, 148, 177, 186, 265n7

individualized profit compensation system, 128–129

informality, 117–119

insecurity, xix, 16, 27, 56, 129, 240; employment, 9, 13, 44, 55, 77, 98, 142–143, 163, 174, 178, 212, 268n13, 269n5; "flat" firms and, 138, 143, 159, 239; hedgemonic masculinity and, xv, 18, 31; inequality and, 16, 239–240; portfolio ideal and, 141–143, 176. *See also* instability; uncertainty

instability, xvi–xvii, xix, 16, 47, 200; employment and, 11, 76, 208; stock market, 15, 142, 213. *See also* insecurity; uncertainty

intersectionality, 21, 32, 179, 246–247, 261n99

investment banking era, 33–35, 40–44

investment banking track to employment, 62, 68–72

investment thesis, 144

It's a Wonderful Life (movie, 1946), 33–36, 37–38

Jones, Alfred W., 18, 48–51, 260n79

Juárez, 188

Kanter, Rosabeth Moss, 14

"key man" clauses, 103–104

key personnel, 103

Khan, Shamus, 8

"kings," 163–164, 178, 227

labor market, 37, 44, 77, 87, 122, 124–125; external labor markets, 143, 159

Lamont, Michèle, 19, 248

Lasry, Marc, 221

Laurison, Daniel, 8

Lehman Brothers, xvii

leverage, 49–50, 264n47, 265n48; networks and, 160–161, 163, 177, 229

Levitt, Arthur, 236

Lewis, Michael, 44

lifestyle inflation, 206

Lipsitz, George 39

Long-Term Capital Management (LTCM), 265n48

loyalty, 21, 52, 96, 141, 191, 209; discrimination and, 16; mentor-protégé relations and, 165; patrimonialism and, 11, 65, 96, 141, 175, 186, 191, 230, 239; social capital and, 143

management fees, 104

markets: electronic markets, 73, 75, 143; financial markets, 14, 18, 27, 47, 50, 52, 61, 130, 142, 176–177, 203–205, 211–214, 239, 265n49; global, 41, 49, 56, 58–59, 108, 112, 141–142, 188; labor market, 37, 44, 55, 77, 87, 122, 124–125, 132–133, 141, 143, 148, 159, 232, 242–243, 279n8; market-maker, 75; moving of, 59; stock markets, xiii, xv–xvii, 2, 4, 9, 15, 17–20, 35, 40, 42, 44–45, 48–50, 58, 62, 78, 102, 124, 131, 141, 146–147, 150, 152, 155–157, 161, 182, 216, 218, 220, 229, 260n81

Marks, Andrew, 193

Marks, Howard, 193

Martens, Pamela, 43

Marx, Karl, 13, 51

masculinity, 22, 27, 31, 51–52, 77, 82, 227; boundary-making and, 19, 227; closing of hedge fund and, 233–235; in community banking era, 33–40; contexts of uncertainty and, 48, 52; contextuality of, 32–33, 206, 208,

masculinity *(continued)*
240, 246; contrasted with bureaucracy, 15; elite (*See* elite, white masculinity); fragility of, 233–234; hedge fund employment and, 55–56, 61, 64–65, 82, 92; hedgemonic (*See* hedgemonic masculinity); historical eras of, 33–48, 51; ideology of, 31–35, 51–52, 227; intersectionality and, 21; in investment banking era, 33–35, 40–44; managerial roles and, 102; marginalized, 148, 154, 156, 158, 170, 238; market language and, 177; masculine stereotypes, 30–31, 73; passion expectation and, 150, 152, 158–159; patrimonialism and, 170, 186, 227–228; personal branding and, 176–177, 224; portfolio ideal and, 148, 176–177; racial minority men and, 31–32, 42, 74, 77, 123, 148, 158; relative nature of, 208; retirement and, 209; risk-taking and, 18, 30, 48, 61, 77, 148, 154, 156, 227; sexual harassment and, 238; in shadow banking era, 33–35, 44–48; vouchers for, 88, 94, 98. *See also* hedgemonic masculinity
master/feeder funds, 257n25
"Masters of the Universe," 35, 42, 44–45
Mays, Lisa, 43
McCulley, Paul, 264n36
McFadden Act of 1927, 263n24
M-C-M circuit, 51
Mears, Ashley, 172, 257n31
Melvin Capital, xvi
mentor-protégé relations, 165–166, 192, 194; founding of hedge funds and, 192–195, 197, 201, 273n20
Mercer, Robert, 236

meritocracy, 8, 24, 55, 57, 67, 76, 82, 116, 118–120, 130–132, 212, 227, 239–240, 257n32; bias and, 17
Mills, C. Wright, 1, 11, 13, 36
Minsky, Hyman, 265n49
Mizruchi, Mark, 235, 258n45
"mommy track," 110–112, 136, 151
Morgan, J. P., 1
motherhood. *See* parenting
Mulvaney, Mark, 237

National Association for the Advancement of Colored People (NAACP), 39
National Organization for Women (NOW), 39
National Welfare Rights Organization, 39–40
Nelson, Julie, 20
neoliberalism, 15, 102, 124, 141, 163, 205, 220; compensation and, 130; financial freedom and, 61, 209, 265n7; "flat" firms and, 102, 104; personal branding and, 144, 148, 158; policy, 9; redistribution and, 222
netting risk, 128–129
network building, 159–163; women employees and, 161–162; leveraging of networks, 160–161; social inequality and, 163; trust networks, 16, 47–48, 181, 191
new economy, 13, 149, 159, 163
New York Stock Exchange (NYSE), 72–75
no netting compensation systems, 128–129

Oaktree Capital Management, 193
Occupy Wall Street movement, xviii
O'Neil, Moira, 241

race *(continued)*
  masculinity and, 31–33, 42, 74, 77,
  123, 148, 158, 238; mentor-protégé
  relations and, 165–166; meritocracy
  and, 17, 24, 132–133, 239–240;
  negotiation and, 133; network building and, 170, 177; passion expectation and, 16, 158–159, 177; patrimonialism and, 11–12, 17, 164, 178, 182;
  personal brands and, 144; "pipeline
  problem" and, 190, 226, 239–240;
  portfolio ideal and, 141, 148,
  176–177; racial discrimination
  lawsuits and, 122–123; racial
  inequality, 21, 37, 39, 47–48, 137, 227,
  235; racial segregation, 67, 84;
  racial stereotypes, 16, 20, 109, 148,
  152, 169; racism, 67, 90, 96, 122–125,
  148, 169–170, 174, 244; risk-taking
  and, 20, 31, 153, 158–159, 177, 180;
  self-promotion and, 147–148;
  sexual harassment and, 43, 174;
  social capital and, 15, 67–68, 166;
  social inequality and, 140–141, 166;
  transparency and, 121–122; unions
  and, 13; work assignments and,
  106–110, 114, 128, 151, 224. *See also*
  Asian Americans; diversity;
  whiteness
rags-to-riches myth, 8, 53, 55, 59–60,
  76, 87
Rao, Aliya Hamid, 265n6
redistribution, 222
redlining, 39
reflexivity, theory of, 144
reflexivity, research methodology of
  241–247
Renaissance Technologies, 10, 236
research methodology, 22–26, 241,
  247–250, 262n100

retirement, 61, 206, 208–210, 218–219,
  228–229, 274n8
Richards, Patricia, 245, 271n43,
  275n5
Ridgeway, Cecilia, 16, 25, 246–247
Riegle-Neal Interstate Banking and
  Branching Efficiency Act of 1994,
  263n24
risk: compensation and 17–18, 22, 25,
  126, 128, 134, 137–138, 224–225, 239;
  culture of 9, 239; employment, 148,
  162–163, 177, 274n9; entrepreneurial, 27, 58, 188, 191, 200, 227, 229,
  234; financial, 19, 126, 130, 181–182,
  220; hedge funds and, 4–7, 18–19,
  27, 46–51, 218, 249, 260n81, 261n82;
  hiring, 88, 98, 127; investment, xvii,
  2, 4–5, 19–20, 39, 48–51, 108–110,
  129, 134, 153–159, 160, 176, 199, 216,
  264n36, 265n48, 265n50; management and elite, white masculinity,
  xv, 18, 20, 22, 31, 210; patrimonialism and, 141, 239; personal, 129;
  professional, 27, 76–77, 80, 114, 119,
  138, 139, 143–144, 147, 153, 160, 176,
  180, 228–229; stock market, xv,
  17–19, 48–51, 215, 239; trust and 21,
  47, 52, 63, 179, 259n67. *See also*
  risk-taking
risk-taking, 17–22, 41–42, 77, 129,
  136–137, 139, 141, 153–159, 177, 227,
  238; elite, white masculinity and,
  xv, 18, 22, 31, 61; gender stereotypes
  and, 20, 148, 154–156, 158–159,
  261n85, 262n2; inequality and, 19;
  masculinity and, 18, 48, 61, 148,
  154, 156, 227
Rivera, Lauren, 16, 89, 98, 266n23
Robertson, Julian, 12, 194–195
Roker, Al, 66